THE EVERYTHING® EXECUTOR AND TRUSTEE BOOK

Dear Reader,

This is my second book on the subject of settling estates and managing trusts, and I am just as impassioned about providing help to executors and trustees this time around as I was the first. I have a lot of sympathy for those who take on this responsibility. Having dealt with estates and trusts for over forty years, I understand how bewildering it can be. People who find themselves in these roles are usually overwhelmed by the process and don't have a clue what to do. The job can be huge; it can require a large time commitment, or it can be short and fairly straightforward. Whatever the case, the process will be completely new for most people, and the language used will be foreign. My objective in writing this guide is to provide a framework so that any individual executor or trustee will have enough of an understanding to handle the job by him-or herself, or, at the very least, be able to converse intelligently with advisors while overseeing the process. I hope this book will help relieve some of your anxiety.

Douglas D. Wilson, CFP, CTFA

Welcome to the EVERYTHING® Series!

These handy, accessible books give you all you need to tackle a difficult project, gain a new hobby, comprehend a fascinating topic, prepare for an exam, or even brush up on something you learned back in school but have since forgotten.

You can choose to read an Everything® book from cover to cover or just pick out the information you want from our four useful boxes: e-questions, e-facts, e-alerts, and e-ssentials.

We give you everything you need to know on the subject, but throw in a lot of fun stuff along the way, too.

We now have more than 400 Everything® books in print, spanning such wide-ranging categories as weddings, pregnancy, cooking, music instruction, foreign language, crafts, pets, New Age, and so much more. When you're done reading them all, you can finally say you know Everything®!

QUESTION
Answers to common questions

FACT
Important snippets of information

ALERT
Urgent warnings

ESSENTIAL
Quick handy tips

PUBLISHER Karen Cooper

MANAGING EDITOR, EVERYTHING® SERIES Lisa Laing

COPY CHIEF Casey Ebert

ASSISTANT PRODUCTION EDITOR Alex Guarco

ACQUISITIONS EDITOR Pam Wissman

DEVELOPMENT EDITOR Brett Palana-Shanahan

EVERYTHING® SERIES COVER DESIGNER Erin Alexander

Visit the entire Everything® series at *www.everything.com*

THE
EVERYTHING®
EXECUTOR AND TRUSTEE
BOOK

A step-by-step guide to estate
and trust administration

Douglas D. Wilson, CFP, CTFA

Adams Media
New York London Toronto Sydney New Delhi

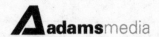

Adams Media
An Imprint of Simon & Schuster, Inc.
100 Technology Center Drive
Stoughton, MA 02072

An Everything® Series Book.
Everything® and everything.com® are registered trademarks of Simon & Schuster, Inc.

For information about special discounts for bulk purchases, please contact Simon & Schuster Special Sales at 1-866-506-1949 or business@simonandschuster.com.

The Simon & Schuster Speakers Bureau can bring authors to your live event. For more information or to book an event contact the Simon & Schuster Speakers Bureau at 1-866-248-3049 or visit our website at www.simonspeakers.com.

Manufactured in the United States of America

11 2024

Library of Congress Cataloging-in-Publication Data has been applied for.

ISBN 978-1-4405-7087-2
ISBN 978-1-4405-7132-9 (ebook)

Contents

Phase One of Administering the Estate / 77

Administering the Estate: Taxes and More / 95

From Maintaining Records to Closing the Estate / 115

Definition of a Trust and the Responsibilities of a Trustee / 129

Contents

Acknowledgments

I want to thank my wife, Linda Quarberg, for her tireless efforts in assisting me with writing this book. She put in untold hours in helping me review and edit the initial manuscript and provided a "reader's look" to my formatting of the text. I also want to thank the folks at Adams Media, a division of F+W Media, Inc., for their patience and support throughout this process.

Top 10 Things Every Executor and Trustee Should Know

1. Read the document, read the document, read the document!

2. You are not required to accept the job of executor or trustee even if you are named under a will or trust.

3. You, and no one else, are in charge of and responsible for how the estate or trust is handled.

4. Understanding the basics of the process and what your responsibilities are will help you administer the estate or trust correctly.

5. You don't have to, and in most cases should not, do it alone. Don't hesitate to hire professionals when needed.

6. Keeping open and frequent communications with beneficiaries is the best way to avoid criticism.

7. You must treat all beneficiaries the same, especially if you are one of them.

8. Your job is to carry out the decedent's specific directives and protect the interests of all beneficiaries.

9. You are entitled to get paid for the job you do.

10. Read the document, read the document, read the document!

Introduction

This guide is intended to give individuals a working knowledge of what is involved in settling an estate and managing a trust. Its purpose is to assist executors and trustees who find themselves in these roles and those who simply want to oversee the process. The chapters in this book will take you through the entire estate settlement process and describe in some detail what your responsibilities will be when managing a trust. Both the estate settlement and trust administration processes follow a logical order and that is how this guide has been formatted. You should not skip any of the chapters or sections as you go through the text. To do so might cause you to leave out an important step or responsibility that relates to another part of the process.

The first two chapters deal with basic definitions and the standards of care that apply to all executors and trustees. These are important topics and you should cover them thoroughly before proceeding to the other chapters. Most of the chapters have checklists, which can be used as a quick review of the material covered in the chapter and to assist you with your administration. As you go through this guide it might also be helpful to refer to the Estate Administration Checklist and/or the Trust Administration Checklist located in Appendix A & B respectively to make sure you have covered all of the items that come into play when you administer an estate or trust.

CHAPTER 1

Serving as an Executor and/or Trustee

Most of us are familiar with the two certainties of life: death and taxes. Once we pass on, most of us will leave things behind that need to be attended to, whether we plan properly during our lifetimes or not. A legal representative must be put in charge to handle these matters. That's where an executor or trustee steps in. An executor (personal representative) is appointed to manage the decedent's estate and a trustee is named to handle the trust, if the decedent had one. To clarify, executors are nominated under a will and appointed by the probate court. A trustee is named in the decedent's trust.

Someone Must Be in Charge of a Decedent's Affairs after Death

Before the settlement process begins, there is usually a lot of anxiety among the decedent's heirs. As the grieving process is running its course, family members often perceive a financial crisis. How are we going to pay the bills? How much will the taxes be? When will they have to be paid? Will there be anything left? Who will be in charge? Concerns such as these commonly surround someone's death, and usually with a great deal of emotion. A decedent's legal representative (executor or trustee) will be responsible for addressing these concerns and managing the decedent's estate.

Family members are typically confused about the settlement process. They will usually want matters settled in an unrealistically short time. The representative (this might be you!) should understand that settling the estate or managing the trust must be done methodically, with great care given to managing the process and avoiding mistakes that could be detrimental to the estate and the decedent's heirs.

FACT

An executor or trustee is the one in charge of a decedent's affairs after death. The term *executor* is the same as the term *personal representative*. This book will use *executor* to describe the person in charge of a decedent's estate.

Executors and trustees generally feel honored to have been chosen but seldom ask themselves if they are up to the task. Settling an estate has many time-sensitive steps; missing a deadline can be costly. It can also require a significant time commitment. Managing a trust can require an even greater time commitment that can extend over a very long period. Before deciding whether to accept the assignment, you should understand the unique characteristics of the estate or trust and what responsibilities are involved.

Serving as an executor or trustee can be a perplexing and often daunting responsibility, but it does not have to be. If you take the time to understand the basics of the process and seek professional assistance when needed, the responsibility is manageable for most people. And, by the way, just because you have been named (nominated) in a will or trust doesn't mean you have to accept the responsibility. This is why a properly drafted document includes a provision for alternates and successors.

ALERT

Every estate and trust is unique. No two are alike.

The Job of Being an Executor (Personal Representative)

When someone dies, a legal representative takes charge of the property that was titled in the decedent's own (individual) name and oversees the legal transfer of that property to the decedent's legal heirs. This process is called *probate*. The representative is also responsible for paying the decedent's obligations and distributing what is left to the heirs. This person (or institution, such as a bank or trust company) is commonly called an *executor* (or *executrix* if a female) and is usually named by an individual in his or her will. If no reference is made in the will, or if the individual dies without a will, a court that has jurisdiction over the decedent's estate appoints an executor (in some states the court appoints an administrator). Under the Unified Probate Code, which most states have adopted, executors are now referred to as *personal representatives*.

Frankly, it can be a pain in the neck to be an executor. The job carries many responsibilities and can require a sizable time commitment. It might be akin to taking over a business without knowing much about the enterprise. The executor must determine what assets the decedent accumulated over an entire lifetime, what he owed, and manage the assets and liabilities on behalf of the decedent's creditors and heirs until the estate has been closed. You need to be organized and have the ability to deal with an assortment of financial information.

To Serve or Not to Serve

The job of an executor can be straightforward; it might involve no more than collecting a few items belonging to the decedent, paying a bill or two, and distributing what remains to their heirs. On the other hand, an estate can be very complex. The executor might have to deal with legal issues left behind by the decedent and make decisions involving tax elections under the Internal Revenue Code that may have a material affect on the interests of the beneficiaries. The executor might have to run a business, negotiate leases, buy and sell assets, and complete other involved and time-consuming tasks.

What are your options if Uncle Harry names you as his executor? Well, for one thing, you have no legal obligation to serve. That is, no one can hold you legally accountable if you choose not to be Uncle Harry's executor. What about a moral obligation? That depends on the situation. You may feel morally obligated if Uncle Harry had asked you to handle his affairs prior to his death. Or you may even feel that you owe it to him because he has left you something in his will. Some feel that the decedent has honored them because only a trusted family member or friend would be named to such an important position. Whatever the situation, you must decide soon after the decedent's death whether or not you will accept the responsibility. The settlement of the estate must be completed as expeditiously as possible, and the sooner the executor accepts the appointment and gets started, the better.

ESSENTIAL

While you don't have to serve as executor or trustee even if you are named, it would be wise to take time to understand the basic responsibilities of an executor, the complexity of the particular estate, your relationship with the beneficiaries, the requirements of local law, and the need for professional advisors. You don't want to get in over your head.

What should you consider before accepting the nomination as executor? First you should look at the complexity of the estate. No two are alike. Some are relatively simple, requiring little time and minimal expertise. Others can require as much time and effort as a full-time job and involve a period of administration that may extend over several years. To properly manage a complex estate, you may also require the assistance of accountants, attorneys, and other professionals. Because the executor is ultimately responsible for proper administration of the estate, you must monitor the activities of these professionals continuously until the estate is closed.

Time commitment is obviously another principal consideration. For several reasons, the duties of settling an estate cannot be performed at the convenience of the executor. For one thing, the heirs expect their inheritance the day after Uncle Harry dies. Your explanation of the technical reasons delaying it is not what they want to hear. They do have a right, however, to expect that the estate will be settled efficiently and that distribution of their inheritance will be made in a timely manner. Even if the heirs are not pressuring the executor, state laws require distribution of the estate's assets within a reasonable period. The executor will be faced with many deadlines, including court filings and appearances, publishing a public notice to creditors, filing tax returns, and other requirements promulgated by state and federal laws.

An executor should consult with a qualified estate attorney to get an estimate of the time required to settle the estate. Accountants familiar with settling estates, or a trust company or bank, are good sources of information as well. The clerk of the probate court with jurisdiction over the estate can tell you any specific requirements of the court and how long the average estate takes to make its way through the system. This will give you an indication of the time it takes to settle an estate in your area. If the time commitment is more than you can devote, you should consider declining the nomination. To do otherwise would be unfair to the beneficiaries and might also expose you to unnecessary liability. Also consider that it will be disruptive to the efficient settlement of the estate if you were to accept and later decide to resign.

Can You Handle the Job?

In most situations, the answer is clearly yes. Almost anyone can manage an estate if they simply hire a professional, such as a bank or trust company, to handle the day-to-day administration. Of course, this may not be what you have in mind. You might feel obligated to minimize the costs of settling Uncle Harry's estate by doing everything yourself. Minimizing estate settlement costs is the right thing to do; it is also a basic responsibility of the executor. However, executors (as well as other fiduciaries) are permitted to, and should, incur reasonable expenses for administration. An executor is allowed to hire professionals to assist with estate administration. If you do not have the time or expertise, you should hire professionals. By law, any administration costs that executors incur for these services are properly chargeable to the estate.

Whether you handle the estate through professionals or manage it yourself, ultimately you are responsible for protection of the interests of the decedent's creditors and heirs. If you pay attention to the job, get things done when they need to be, and hire professional expertise when you need it, you should not have any problems carrying out these responsibilities. The role of an executor is time sensitive, usually from eighteen months to two years. However, settling some estates may take longer than that.

What Is a Trust?

Most people are not familiar with trusts. The typical trust is set up for the purpose of minimizing estate taxes, avoiding probate, and in some cases, providing protection for family members. In the case of a protection trust, many beneficiaries do not understand why someone else (the trustee) decides what they can have and are convinced that "this is not what my wife, husband, father, mother, grandfather, aunt, Uncle Joe, had in mind." The reality is that the trustee has been given explicit instructions, under the terms of the trust, to make those decisions. Nevertheless, beneficiaries often are not convinced.

The Definition of a Trust

A trust is created when an individual transfers property into an entity (trust) and then appoints someone called a *trustee* to manage the property for the benefit of someone else (called the *beneficiary*) in accordance with a trust document or instrument. A trust is used to deal with a variety of estate planning, tax, incapacity, and asset management issues. A trust can address the full spectrum of estate planning, including estate tax savings, avoiding probate, protecting family members, and handling how and when to distribute assets to named beneficiaries.

There are two general types of trusts: the *revocable* trust and the *irrevocable* trust. The revocable trust can be altered or terminated by its creator, who is called the *settlor.* The irrevocable trust cannot be altered or terminated except by court order. Normally, the court will not order a trust revoked or altered unless there is fraud, proof that there was undue influence when the trust was established, or a technical change that needs to be made that does not adversely affect the interests of the beneficiaries or the purposes and intent of the trust.

The Revocable Living Trust

One of the most popular and widely used estate planning tools is the revocable living trust. This arrangement is designed to address several estate planning concerns:

Avoiding Probate

Property held in a revocable living trust avoids having to go through the court-supervised probate process at the death of the settlor of the trust. The title to the property is registered in the name of the trust, not in the name of the individual who created it. Only property that is owned individually by a decedent is subject to probate.

Minimizing or Avoiding Federal Estate Tax

Federal estate tax is by far the largest expense associated with death. A revocable living trust can reduce, or even eliminate altogether in some cases, the federal estate tax. A properly drafted living trust assures that the personal exemption available to both husband and wife is fully utilized to maximize the amount of property that can pass free of estate tax to children, grandchildren, and other beneficiaries. How this works is explained later in this book.

Protection upon Incapacity

When someone becomes physically or mentally incapacitated and cannot handle his or her financial affairs, someone else must manage them. This can be handled with a durable power of attorney, guardianship, or a trust. If the incapacitated person has not given power of attorney to anyone or does not have a trust, the court appoints a guardian. In some states this person is called a *conservator*. This is expensive and inflexible. In addition, because the court supervises this arrangement, the incapacitated person's affairs are a matter of public record. The court's permission may be required for certain payments to be made on behalf of the incapacitated person. Even a durable power of attorney has limitations. Some financial institutions will accept them only under certain conditions. Others may not accept them at all. All of these issues can be avoided through a living trust. The trust simply gives the trustee the authority to handle the affairs of the incapacitated settlor. This authority lapses upon the settlor's recovery.

Bequests to Heirs

Most people think of their will as the primary means of passing property to their heirs. A trust can do anything a will can do and more. Since the living trust usually has the title to most, if not all, of an individual's property, in a properly established estate plan, it becomes the principal means for distributing the decedent's property. Beneficiaries are named in the trust document to receive the trust's property. A trust, in addition to passing property at death, can delay distribution until a beneficiary reaches a certain age or can continue for the lifetime of a beneficiary. A will typically transfers property at death and ends when the transfer has been completed.

Protection of Minors and Other Heirs

No one knows when he or she is going to die, and whether or not he or she will leave minor children. If a minor survives a decedent, and provisions have not been made, a guardianship proceeding may be required to manage the minor's property until he or she attains legal age. As mentioned, this is an expensive and inflexible arrangement. A trust can provide for the needs of a minor and avoid interference by the court. A trust can also be used to protect a beneficiary who has disabilities. A properly drafted trust can also protect a beneficiary from creditors and divorce.

Types of Revocable Living Trusts

The settlor (creator) of the revocable living trust can also be the trustee of the trust. This type of arrangement is known as a *self-trusteed trust* or *self-administered trust*. The settlor signs checks, stock powers, deeds, and other legal documents as trustee instead of signing in his or her individual name. Other than this technical difference, the self-trusteed trust, as a practical matter, is no different than owning property in one's individual name.

Someone other than the settlor can also be the trustee. A spouse, child, friend, relative, attorney, CPA, trust company, bank, or any combination of these can be appointed the trustee while the settlor is alive or after death. Anyone of legal age who is competent can serve as a trustee. The difference between the self-trusteed trust and this arrangement is that the trustee must conduct the affairs of the trust at the direction of the settlor, if competent, who is also the beneficiary of the trust and, in the absence of any direction, solely for his or her benefit. A settlor will appoint a trustee other than herself because she does not want to be bothered with the nuances of managing her own affairs, wants to take advantage of the expertise of a particular trustee, or wants the assurance of continuity in the management of her affairs in the event of incapacity or death.

The settlor can also appoint himself and someone else as co-trustee. In this case, the responsibility for managing the trust property is shared, although as long as the settlor is competent the co-trustee must act in accordance with the settlor's instructions. If two or more trustees, other than the settlor, are appointed they must act in concert in dealing with the trust property. Co-trustees are often used in situations that require the special knowledge or expertise of more than one person.

Revocable Living Trusts That Terminate at Death

Many people establish a revocable living trust simply to avoid probate and to protect against guardianship in the event of incapacity. These types of trusts typically terminate at death. In terms of disposition of estate assets, they serve a similar purpose as a will. That is, once all of the decedent's expenses and taxes have been paid, the property in the trust is distributed to the beneficiaries named in the trust. The responsibilities of the trustee under a revocable living trust that terminates at death are similar to that of an executor under a will. The trust property must be collected, final expenses paid, tax returns filed, and the remaining property distributed to the trust beneficiaries.

Don't worry. Handling a trust that terminates at death is very similar to the job of settling an estate, except that it's easier!

The major advantage of handling someone's estate this way is the fact that probate is avoided and the trustee does not have to deal with the court. No hearings or court filings are necessary, and the decedent's estate can often be settled quickly. However, the time to settle an estate depends on whether or not estate taxes are payable, how long it takes to appraise assets, whether there are matters being litigated, and how long it takes to liquidate assets to pay expenses and satisfy bequests.

Like the executor under a will, the trustee distributes the remaining property to the beneficiaries and closes the trust once the expenses, taxes, and other obligations of the trust have been satisfied. Unlike the executor, the trustee does not usually need to seek a discharge and release of responsibility from the court. Instead, the trustee's duties terminate at the final distribution of the assets and closing of the trust.

Trusts That Continue after Death

A trust that continues after death can either be a revocable living trust, created during one's lifetime, or a testamentary trust, created under a decedent's will. Continuing trusts fall into two general categories.

One is designed to manage property and protect a beneficiary from himself and his creditors. These trusts are typically set up for a beneficiary until he reaches a certain age or until the beneficiary's death. They are designed to have a trustee pick up where the decedent left off in terms of protecting and providing for the beneficiary. For example, a minor child or a child with a lifelong disability may have survived a decedent.

The other category of continuing trust is the more common in estate planning. In addition to providing financial protection and management for family members, its primary purpose is to minimize estate taxes. The key feature under this type is the *credit shelter trust*, commonly referred to as the *family trust, bypass trust, residuary trust,* or *"B" trust*. The credit shelter trust is a separate trust created at death under the terms of a revocable living trust.

It is funded with an amount equal to the decedent's personal exemption from the federal estate tax (i.e., Unified Credit Exemption Equivalent) determined at the decedent's death. The assets not transferred to the credit shelter trust are either distributed outright to the surviving spouse or retained in another trust called the *marital trust.*

FACT

A trustee's responsibilities in a continuing trust are considerably more complex, and require a commitment over a longer period of time.

Continuing trusts can extend for a fixed period after death, for the life of a surviving spouse, or beyond an entire generation. The trustee is responsible for managing the trust until it finally terminates. The trustee is responsible for managing all administration during the term of the trust, including funding of the marital and credit shelter trusts, making tax elections, maintaining fiduciary accounting records, exercising discretion with regard to payments to beneficiaries, and investing trust assets.

The Nature of Irrevocable Trusts

Irrevocable trusts can be used for a wide range of purposes but are usually designed to minimize estate and income taxes. They have one thing in common: the individual who transferred the property no longer owns property transferred to an irrevocable trust. The property is owned by the trust and controlled by the trustee, the terms of the trust, and applicable state and federal laws. As the name implies, the trust cannot be revoked and usually cannot be altered. Once property has been transferred into an irrevocable trust the transferor has, in effect, given the property away.

As a general rule, the settlor of an irrevocable trust is not the trustee. (There could be adverse tax consequences.) Unlike a revocable living trust, the trustee under an irrevocable trust must act independently and is precluded from taking direction from the settlor in managing the trust. Each type of irrevocable trust has its own unique characteristics. Although the basic fiduciary responsibilities of the trustee are the same, the trustee's administrative duties will differ from one trust to another, depending on the terms of the trust and the laws that apply to the particular type of trust. The different common uses for irrevocable trusts are covered later in this book in much greater detail.

What Is a Fiduciary?

For those who have never been an executor or trustee, the term *fiduciary* is probably mysterious. Most people associate it with something legal. Defined in its simplest terms, a fiduciary relationship is a relationship of trust. It is the act of managing property for, and representing the interests of, others. Examples of fiduciary relationships include the relationship between members of the board of directors of a company and its stockholders, an attorney and her client, a guardian and a protected person, an executor and the estate's beneficiaries and creditors, and a trustee and the beneficiaries of the trust.

ESSENTIAL

A fiduciary relationship is one of trust. As fiduciaries, executors and trustees have a duty to be honest and faithful and to act solely in the interests of the beneficiaries they serve and no one else.

In a trust, the fiduciary relationship requires the trustee to hold property, or an interest in property, and use that property for the benefit of the beneficiaries. At the same time, the personal representative must protect the interests of the creditors of a decedent's estate as well as the beneficiaries of the estate. Personal representatives and trustees are usually given full authority to manage assets and distribute those assets to the decedent's beneficiaries. Under common law, the duty of loyalty is an important part of this relationship. Fiduciaries are expected to act solely in the interest of creditors and beneficiaries and, by law, are held to a high standard of ethical and moral conduct.

FACT

In basic terms, a fiduciary is someone (an agent, a director of a corporation, a partner, a guardian, an executor, trustee, etc.) who has a responsibility to someone else. A trustee is a fiduciary because he/she has a duty to represent the interests of someone else (a beneficiary).

This standard of conduct is different than the ethics associated with ordinary business relationships, where a transaction between parties at "arm's length" may be acceptable behavior. The fact that a personal representative or trustee has total control over the management and disposition of assets in an estate or trust requires that the fiduciary show extraordinary candor in dealing with beneficiaries and their interests in the estate or trust. The standards of conduct that apply to personal representatives and trustees are intended to assure that a decedent's wishes with regard to the disposition and management of his estate are carried out as he intended.

CHAPTER 2

The Fiduciary Standards That Apply to Executors and Trustees

It is important for executors and trustees (fiduciaries) to understand exactly where their authority and power to act comes from. They should also understand that, as fiduciaries, they will be held to standards of conduct while carrying out their responsibilities. Most people select an executor or trustee based on whom they feel they can trust to settle their affairs. The key word is "trust."

Where Does Your Power and Authority Come From?

The power and authority that a fiduciary needs in order to carry out the administration of an estate or trust are normally written in the will or trust instrument. These powers are fairly standard, and most wills and trust documents contain "boilerplate" provisions to give the fiduciary sufficient power to conduct the business of the estate or trust.

ESSENTIAL

The laws that govern estate and trust administration are designed to assure that this responsibility of trust is not breached. Much of what the law addresses has to do with how to carry out the responsibilities associated with settling an estate or managing a trust. A fundamental understanding of what these laws and standards of conduct mean should substantially reduce the risk of making a mistake. At the very least, it should relieve some of the anxiety.

The common boilerplate provisions found in most wills and trusts are the power to:

- Retain assets.
- Receive assets.
- Sell or exchange property.
- Invest and reinvest assets (trusts).
- Lease, manage, repair, improve, subdivide, and develop real estate, or dedicate it for public use.
- Employ attorneys, accountants, and other agents.
- Borrow funds with or without security.
- Allocate items of income and expense between the income and principal accounts.
- Satisfy and settle claims.
- Negotiate, prosecute, or defend claims.
- Pay taxes, assessments, and other administration expenses.
- Make distributions to beneficiaries in cash or kind.
- Continue any business or venture.

- Vote stocks and other securities in person or by proxy.
- Insure assets against damage, loss, or liability.

Some wills and trust documents may limit or broaden the fiduciary's authority. For example, the creator of the will or trust may prohibit the sale of a particular stock, though that stock may be a logical security to liquidate because of current market conditions. He or she could also direct that the personal representative or trustee liquidate a business in a prescribed manner even though it would be logical, from a business point of view, to carry on the enterprise.

FACT

As executor or trustee, you will be given the power and authority to do the job under the terms of the will or trust, state statutes, and the probate court.

All estates and estate plans are unique. It is imperative that a fiduciary thoroughly examine the will or trust to determine what powers have been specifically authorized and whether any restrictions have been imposed. Beyond the powers provided by the governing document, a fiduciary can exercise those powers provided by law to carry out the administration of the estate or trust—as long as they are not prohibited by the terms of the will or trust.

Statutory Laws

The most commonly referred to state and local statutes in the administration of estates and trusts include the following:

- **The Uniform Probate Code**
  The rules and regulations governing the administration of probate estates are covered under the Uniform Probate Code, which has been adopted in one form or another by most states. In addition to defining the requirements for probating a decedent's estate, the code also provides the necessary powers, such as the authority to sue, to the personal representative so that he may carry out his responsibilities. The code may also contain provisions that affect some aspects of trust administration.

- **The Revised Uniform Principal and Income Act**

One of the most difficult tasks of estate and trust administration is preparing and maintaining accounting records. Fiduciary accounting is unique; it involves keeping separate records for income and principal transactions. The Revised Uniform Principal and Income Act describes how fiduciaries account for receipts and expenditures during the administration of an estate or trust. A will or trust document may not always give sufficient guidance.

- **Other Uniform Laws**

Many states have adopted uniform laws that give guidance to executors and trustees, such as the Uniform Prudent Investor Act and the Uniform Trustees' Powers Act. These laws are all designed to assist executors and trustees in their administration, especially if the will or trust does not specifically address these matters.

Case Law

Many of the general rules that govern fiduciaries have evolved from case law. That is, a legal action or suit is looked to or cited as a precedent for handling a particular administration matter. The laws that govern the administration of estates and trusts are largely statutory. However, decisions in new court cases continue to clarify how fiduciaries should deal with particular estate and trust issues. If a fiduciary finds that a transaction is not covered by the terms of a will or trust or by statutory law, an attorney should be consulted to see if any case law exists to give guidance on the subject.

Court Authority

The express powers articulated in a will or trust or under statutory law are what the executor or trustee should rely on. There may be circumstances, though, where the language in the document is ambiguous or where a deviation from the terms of the trust would be in the best interest of the beneficiaries. In these instances, a fiduciary can and should seek court clarification or authority to modify the terms of the will or trust. This should be done sparingly and only in those situations where doing nothing would bring harm to the beneficiaries.

Standards of Conduct

If you think settling an estate or managing a trust is a simple and straightforward responsibility, try obtaining liability insurance. Insurance companies often will not underwrite personal fiduciary liability coverage for an individual personal executor or trustee. Why? Simple. It is too risky. Considerable liability can be associated with being an executor or a trustee, because it is easy to make a mistake. In addition to understanding the specific tasks associated with estate and trust administration, personal executors and trustees must also know how the law expects them to conduct themselves in carrying out the duties of the job. The law, again, focuses on protecting the interests of beneficiaries and following the instructions of the decedent with respect to the disposition of his or her property.

ESSENTIAL

The standards of conduct that apply to executors and trustees are, to a large extent, common sense. Their intent is to make sure that the fiduciary "does the right thing" for and on behalf of the beneficiaries.

Now you may be ready to resign and let someone else put her life's fortunes at risk. Hang in there. It is not as bad as it sounds if you follow the rules (basic standards of conduct that all fiduciaries are expected to follow). Established by common law, case law, tradition, and common sense, these principles of conduct are used to determine whether or not a fiduciary is doing the right thing. These are the rules that fiduciaries are expected to live by. Those who understand and adhere to these tenets will avoid any difficulties while carrying out their responsibilities under the law.

Duty of Loyalty

A trustee shall administer the trust solely in the interest of the beneficiaries, and in the case of an executor, for the benefit of the creditors first and then the beneficiaries. The duty of loyalty is perhaps the most important rule for executor and trustees. It mandates that the fiduciary cannot be in a position where self-interest will influence the performance of his or her duties. In other words, a fiduciary may not profit at the expense of a beneficiary or creditor.

For example, a fiduciary with the power to sell trust property may not buy it, or otherwise acquire any interest in the asset, though it might be purchased at a fair price and at "arm's length." Even if the fiduciary does not conduct the transaction himself, he violates the duty of loyalty in spite of purchasing the property at a foreclosure sale. To permit a fiduciary to purchase the property in this way would be in conflict with his duty to sell the property at the highest possible price. In other words, he should be exclusively on the selling side of the transaction—seeking a buyer who will pay the best price. Obviously, if the fiduciary were permitted to be the only bidder, it would be to his advantage to limit the number of bidders as well as the bid price. The point is that it is next to impossible for someone to act impartially in a situation in which he can benefit.

The duty of loyalty also applies to transactions involving the sale of property by the fiduciary to the estate or trust. For example, the sale of an investment owned by a fiduciary to an estate or trust she manages is improper even if the investment is a proper one for the estate or trust and she acted in good faith. It is also a violation of the duty of loyalty for the fiduciary to enter into any transaction with an entity (i.e., a corporation, partnership, or proprietorship) in which she has a substantial ownership interest. Any activities that may give the fiduciary an advantage she otherwise would not have will almost invariably be in violation of the duty of loyalty.

Duty of Impartiality

The fiduciary shall deal impartially with all beneficiaries. An executor or trustee may not favor one beneficiary over another. In the case of a trust, the trustee must balance the competing interests between the current and future beneficiaries. Income beneficiaries are concerned with one thing and one thing only: how much income they can get. The future beneficiaries (referred to as *remaindermen*) are interested in how much the assets will grow and what the value of their future inheritance will be. The trustee cannot bend to the pressure from the income beneficiaries to maximize the current yield from the portfolio. By weighting the portfolio toward high-income-producing assets, the trustee is violating his or her duty of impartiality by favoring the income takers. The trustee must balance the portfolio to meet the needs of the income beneficiaries and protect the value of the assets for the remaindermen.

Keep in mind, a fiduciary must treat all beneficiaries the same way. No special favors.

The duty of impartiality also applies with regard to the charging of expenses. Expenses charged against income obviously affect the current income beneficiaries. Charges against principal affect the amount that will be inherited by the remaindermen upon the termination of the trust.

Distributions of income and/or principal among current beneficiaries must be made with impartiality. One beneficiary cannot receive favored treatment over another with regard to discretionary payments from the trust. However, the trust document may alter the trustee's duties by directing the trustee to favor one beneficiary over another under certain circumstances. If, as a trustee, you use reasonable care in carrying out these provisions, you are usually protected from liability.

Duty to Make Property Productive

A trustee shall use reasonable care and skill to make trust property productive. A trustee is duty-bound to manage trust property so that it produces income to meet the needs of the income beneficiaries and increases principal for the remainder beneficiaries who will receive the trust assets upon termination. This entails balancing the interests of two sets of beneficiaries.

FACT

A trustee cannot leave monies uninvested if those assets can earn a return. This also applies to an executor with respect to cash and real estate assets held during the period of administration.

Making trust assets productive means different things to different people. The duty of impartiality does not allow the trustee to invest all of the trust property into assets with a high current yield. Neither can the trustee invest exclusively in property that will appreciate in value, but produce no income. Making the trust productive means that the trust assets must produce reasonable income and growth of principal. Assets cannot be void of both income and capital growth. A trustee who leaves money uninvested for a long period of time may be liable for the return that the funds would have earned if properly invested. In the case of an executor, in addition to protecting the assets of the estate, property such as real estate must be rented if at all possible, and cash that is not being used should earn interest.

Duty of Care

A fiduciary shall exercise the same skill and care as an individual would exercise in dealing with his or her own property. The prudent investor rule requires a fiduciary to invest trust assets with a high degree of care. One obvious example of exercising proper care is being thoroughly familiar with the provisions of the will or trust and what specifically is required. As a fiduciary you must exercise caution. Care and skill must be used in every aspect of managing a trust or probate estate. When a beneficiary questions a transaction involving his or her interest, the test will be whether or not the fiduciary exercised reasonable care to protect those interests.

ESSENTIAL

General care must be exercised in all aspects of administration. Be sure you know exactly what you are doing at all times.

Duty to Preserve and Protect Property

A fiduciary shall ensure that all assets are protected and not lost or destroyed. In addition to safekeeping cash and securities, a fiduciary has the duty to protect assets by making repairs to buildings; seeing that property tax and mortgage payments are made; storing valuables, such as jewelry and artifacts, in a secure place; and maintaining adequate insurance coverage. The duty to preserve and protect property requires that the fiduciary ensure that assets will not be subject to any loss of value. All property that can be insured against loss must be covered by an appropriate amount of insurance. Should a loss occur, a fiduciary could be held personally liable for inadequate insurance coverage.

FACT

You must protect the assets of the estate or trust the same way you protect your own property, and then some.

Protecting property is most critical in the early stages of a probate estate. One of the first things a personal representative must do is gather all of the decedent's property, including tangible personal property such as jewelry, silverware, paintings, artifacts, etc. When someone dies, these things sometimes have a way of disappearing. Family members will distribute these items to themselves and others because "that is what Uncle Harry wanted." Uncle Harry may have instructed otherwise in his will, and the personal representative could be held responsible if these items end up in the wrong hands. The personal representative must protect the items until they are distributed to the heirs who are legally entitled to them.

Protection and preservation of property also includes depositing securities in a safe place and monitoring the portfolio. This includes not letting stock options and warrants expire if they can be exercised to the advantage of the beneficiaries. For securities held in a brokerage account, proper legal documentation must be provided to the broker to give the fiduciary control over the account.

Duty to Segregate Assets

The fiduciary shall keep all trust and estate property separate from his own property. It is improper for a personal representative or trustee to deposit trust or estate assets in his personal account, whether it is a bank or brokerage account. Trying to separate what is owned by the estate or trust from what is individually owned by the fiduciary in a personal account can be difficult. In addition, there is always the possibility that the fiduciary could inadvertently access the funds for his own use. The practical reason for not commingling funds is because it causes an accounting nightmare. Take for example the interest earned on a savings or checking account. The portion of the account that belongs to the estate or trust must receive its share of the interest. The amount of interest to be allocated to the estate or trust will change every time a payment is made and every time funds are deposited. If transactions are put through the account daily or even weekly, accounting for the interest alone could be costly in terms of the time spent. It may be very expensive to hire an accountant to unscramble the mess.

Earmarking assets and accounts that belong to an estate or trust is obviously very important. Assets, such as checking accounts, brokerage accounts, etc., should be registered in the name of the estate or trust, or in the name of the fiduciary as personal representative or trustee.

ALERT

Unless funds have been distributed to you as a beneficiary, they do not belong in your account.

Duty to Keep Accounts

The fiduciary shall keep up-to-date and accurate records of the activities of the estate or trust. Accountings of the financial activities of the estate or trust must be maintained for the courts and beneficiaries. This requires the fiduciary to maintain current records of all transactions in the estate or trust. Keeping good records is not as easy as it sounds. The fiduciary can personally maintain accounting records and other documentation or can hire an accountant. In either case, the records must be current. A fiduciary needs to update these records frequently, because the volume of transactions makes it difficult to catch up should one fall behind.

In some states, accountings for both estates and trusts must be filed with the probate court. In other states, the fiduciary is only obligated to provide accountings to the beneficiaries. However, a beneficiary can ask the court to compel the fiduciary to render an accounting if the beneficiary suspects that the fiduciary is not managing the estate or trust properly. Take the case of a trustee who decides that it is none of the beneficiary's business to know how the trust is being managed. The fiduciary might feel he or she is in charge and "knows what is in their best interest." After unsuccessful attempts to get an accounting and other information from the trustee, the beneficiary is likely to seek the services of an attorney. A petition is usually filed in court to order the trustee to provide an accounting to the beneficiary. The court will so order and may also order the removal of the trustee.

You must keep complete and accurate records of everything you do. It might be helpful to buy a file cabinet or storage bin to keep all of the paperwork you will accumulate.

Duty Not to Delegate

A fiduciary shall not delegate to others those duties that he or she can reasonably perform. A fiduciary is obligated to perform the duties of a trustee or personal representative and cannot transfer these responsibilities to another person or institution unless authorized to do so under the terms of the trust document, will, or court order. However, the fiduciary can delegate those acts that might be unreasonable for him or her to perform. Factors that are important to consider in determining whether a proposed delegation is reasonable or not include:

- The amount of discretion involved in performing the delegated act.
- The value and character of the asset affected by the delegated act.
- Will the performance of the delegated act directly or indirectly affect the assets of the estate or trust or its beneficiaries?
- Will the delegated act affect the principal or income of the estate or trust to the detriment of the beneficiaries?
- Does the delegated act call for certain skills that the trustee or executor does not possess and cannot reasonably be expected to acquire?

It is important to distinguish between the delegation of a duty and the hiring of an agent to assist the fiduciary in discharging his or her responsibilities. For example, a trustee may hire an independent investment manager or investment management firm to handle the trust's portfolio, even with complete discretion. The ultimate responsibility still rests with the trustee; though the investment manager performs the actual management of the investments, the fiduciary must closely supervise any agent that is retained.

ALERT

Hiring someone to assist you with the administration is not a delegation of your duties.

A fiduciary may be permitted to delegate certain administrative duties to agents, co-trustees, or other individuals under the terms of the will or trust document. However, the fiduciary still has an obligation to the beneficiaries to oversee the activities of the person to whom the duty has been delegated.

Duty to Pay or Apply Income

The trustee has a duty to pay the net income of the property at reasonable intervals to any current income beneficiaries in the manner prescribed by the terms of the trust. If the trust does not specify the frequency of income distributions, they can be made annually, semiannually, or quarterly, depending on local law. A reasonable amount of income can be withheld to meet current and future expenses that are properly chargeable against income. If a beneficiary is a minor or under a legal disability, the trustee also has a duty to apply the income for the benefit of that beneficiary, if the trust document so authorizes. The duty to pay income can be modified by the terms of the trust document in the following ways:

- If the trust document directs the trustee to accumulate income, then the trustee is under no obligation to distribute income to the beneficiary.
- If the trust document gives the trustee the discretion to distribute income, he or she has no obligation to pay out income unless, in the trustee's judgment, a distribution is necessary and appropriate.
- If the trustee is directed to pay the income for a beneficiary's support, he or she is not required to distribute the income directly to that beneficiary.

The terms of the trust document may allow accumulation of income that is not needed currently for the beneficiary's support. The trust document may also allow the accumulated amount to be transferred to and become a part of the principal of the trust. However, the trustee must always look to the trust document for guidance before making decisions concerning the payment, or nonpayment, of income from the trust.

A trustee must use the trust's income for the beneficiary and cannot withhold it without good reason.

Duty to Defend Actions and Enforce Claims

Fiduciaries will defend claims of third parties against the estate or trust and enforce claims held by the estate or trust. The estate or trust must be defended against any claims that would result in a loss if they were successful. In this regard, the executor or trustee has a duty to the beneficiaries to act reasonably in preventing the dilution or destruction of estate or trust assets.

An executor or trustee must take whatever legal action is necessary to protect the interests of the beneficiaries.

The executor or trustee must also take all reasonable steps in enforcing claims. If someone fails to pay a debt owed to the estate or trust, the personal representative or trustee has a duty to bring an action to enforce payment. If a claim is not enforced, the personal representative or trustee could be surcharged for any uncollected sums. The personal representative or trustee must act reasonably, however, in enforcing a claim. If there is a high probability that the expenses of litigating a claim might exceed the amount that could ultimately be collected, the claim should not be pursued.

How to Deal with Conflicts of Interest

Whatever your rationale, dealing directly with an estate or trust where there is a possibility of personal gains or advantage is a conflict of interest. Even if the deal is fair and equitable, the mere appearance of a conflict of interest may raise questions about the integrity of the executor or trustee. If others might think that a conflict exists, the fiduciary should consider finding another way of handling the transaction or situation.

Avoiding conflict is relatively easy when the following simple rules are followed. A fiduciary should not:

- *Purchase property from an estate or trust.* Even if the purchase price and terms are fair, the fiduciary puts him- or herself in a position of not getting the best price and terms possible for the estate or trust by not offering the same opportunity to others.
- *Sell property to an estate or trust.* Whether or not the estate received fair value in the transaction will always be open to question.
- *Enter into any transaction where the fiduciary is both the seller and buyer* (i.e., the trust selling property to another trust where the fiduciary is trustee of both trusts). One cannot be loyal to two groups of beneficiaries whose interests are independent of one another.
- *Employ him- or herself to perform special services for the estate or trust.* The fiduciary has the potential of self-enrichment at the expense of the estate or trust.
- *Borrow funds from an estate or trust.* Again, the potential for gaining advantage at the expense of the estate or trust exists.
- *Accept gifts from someone who does business with an estate or trust.* The fiduciary could be in a position that gives an advantage to a friend or colleague in exchange for potential personal gain to him- or herself.

ALERT

Avoid transactions between yourself and the estate or trust you manage. If you feel that you are putting yourself in a compromising position, consider not accepting the fiduciary position in the first place.

Keeping Beneficiaries Informed

One of the most important things a fiduciary must do is keep the beneficiaries informed. These are the people who are going to sue you if something goes wrong and they get hurt in the process. People tend to be forgiving when a mistake is made if they know what is going on and have a good relationship with the executor or trustee. They are much less inclined to let you off the hook if you are secretive and keep things from them.

ESSENTIAL

Keeping beneficiaries informed on a regular basis is paramount to maintaining good relationships with beneficiaries and avoiding lawsuits.

Who do you keep informed? Typically it is the beneficiaries of the estate and, in the case of a trust, the current beneficiaries. That is, those beneficiaries of a trust who are entitled to receive income and/or principal during the term of the trust. However, some state statutes require that a trustee provide information about a trust to remainder beneficiaries upon request.

What kinds of information are you obligated to provide? The trust or estate accounting that is provided to the beneficiaries usually is sufficient to inform them of the routine transactions affecting the administration of the estate or trust. However, the fiduciary is obliged to inform the beneficiaries of any nonroutine transaction before it is consummated if the transaction will have a significant effect on their interest in the estate or trust. The sale of a business or the leasing or sale of a parcel of real estate, for example, would be transactions that fall into this category. A beneficiary may want to acquire the asset or may have some information that is pertinent to the transaction and should be given the opportunity for input.

Serving as Successor, Co-Executor, or Co-Trustee

If you are named a successor executor or successor trustee you should be aware of what will be expected of you before you accept the position. Likewise if you serve as a co-executor or co-trustee you should understand the rules that apply to you as a co-fiduciary.

Successors

The law is fairly clear about what is expected of a successor executor or successor trustee regarding the actions that were taken or not taken by the predecessor. An executor or trustee must not allow a known wrongdoing committed by a predecessor to continue. A fiduciary must take the steps necessary to collect all of the estate or trust property and must take action against the predecessor for any breach, unless there is language in the will or trust document absolving the successor of this responsibility.

Co-Fiduciaries

Serving as a co-executor or co-trustee adds another level of responsibility. A fiduciary is liable for the actions of his or her co-fiduciary and has an obligation to monitor the activities of the co-fiduciary. In general, the following rules apply if you serve as an executor or trustee with someone else:

- Co-fiduciaries must agree to all actions taken in the administration of an estate or trust unless the governing document permits delegation to one or more co-fiduciaries.
- A fiduciary is liable if he or she participates in a breach of trust with a co-fiduciary.
- A fiduciary is liable if he or she allows a breach by a co-fiduciary to continue.
- A fiduciary is liable for not taking proper action to have a co-fiduciary pay for any damages caused by a breach.
- A fiduciary may be liable for improperly delegating a duty or responsibility to a co-fiduciary who has breached his or her duties.
- The court must ultimately settle disputes between co-fiduciaries.

In general, all co-fiduciaries must agree on all acts undertaken in conjunction with the administration of the estate or trust. However, with regard to co-trustees, many states allow discretionary authority to be exercised by a majority when there are three or more trustees. Under these statutes, a dissenting trustee usually will not be held liable for the actions taken by the other trustees if the objection is given in writing to any of the co-trustees.

ESSENTIAL

A will or trust can also contain protective language similar to this: "No co-trustee (co-executor) shall be liable for any act, omission, or default of any other co-trustee (co-executor), provided the co-trustee (co-executor) shall have had no knowledge of any facts that may reasonably be expected to have put the co-trustee (co-executor) on notice in sufficient time to have prevented the act, omission, or default."

Obtaining a release and indemnification from a beneficiary may offer some protection from liability. However, it may not be effective if the beneficiary did not have knowledge of all the facts and circumstances related to the transaction or action taken.

Limiting Your Liability

The duty of loyalty is the basic underpinning of the laws that govern the activities of fiduciaries. This is an obvious connection if you consider the level of trust that is expected with regard to the disposition of one's property after death. Entrusting someone to carry out the wishes of a decedent is to require that he or she act solely in the best interest of the decedent's heirs. The dos and don'ts listed below should be apparent, logical expectations of the way executors and trustees should conduct themselves.

Dos

- Do keep clear and accurate records.
- Do inform beneficiaries of the nature and amount of their interest in the estate or trust.
- Do take possession and keep control of all estate and trust property.
- Do segregate estate and trust property from all other property, and earmark all deposit accounts (bank accounts, brokerage accounts, etc.) as estate or trust property.
- Do exercise reasonable care and skill to make trust property productive.
- Do supervise the activities of all agents.

Don'ts

- Do not allow yourself to be guided by the interests of third parties in administering the estate or trust.
- Do not use estate or trust property for your own benefit.
- Do not allow an agent to do something that is not in the best interest of the estate or trust.
- Do not delegate to others those duties that you can reasonably perform yourself.

- Do not purchase property for yourself if that property is owned or has close connections to the estate or trust.
- Do not disclose confidential information to third parties.
- Do not accept commissions from third parties for work done in connection with the administration of the estate or trust.

Remember

If you remember these things, you will avoid getting yourself into trouble:

- Read the trust document; read the trust document; read the trust document.
- If the terms of a will or trust are misleading or ambiguous, seek clarification from an attorney or instruction from the court.
- Review the standards of conduct that apply to executors and trustees in Chapter 2.
- Retain professionals to assist you with those administration tasks that you do not have time for or for which you lack expertise.
- Communicate with beneficiaries about the administration of the estate or trust on a regular basis.
- Keep complete, accurate, and current records.
- Take possession of and protect all assets of the estate or trust.
- Review and monitor the activities of all professional agents that you hire.
- Do not commingle estate or trust assets with your own.
- Do not purchase assets from or sell assets to an estate or trust if you are the executor or trustee.
- Do not employ yourself to perform special tasks, such as appraisals, accounting services, property management, etc., for a separate fee.
- Do not borrow money from the estate or trust.
- Do not accept gifts or commissions from someone who does business with the estate or trust.
- Do not share confidential information with individuals who do not have an interest in the estate or trust.

CHAPTER 3

Passing Property and the Estate Settlement Process

The term probate literally means the "proving of a will." More commonly it is used to describe the court-supervised process of passing title of one's property, at death, to those legally entitled to it. Probate provides a mechanism for determining a decedent's heirs and settling his or her estate. Even if a decedent had no will, his individually owned property may be subject to probate. It passes under the laws of intestacy of the decedent's state of domicile (where he lived). Whether an individual dies with or without a will, the steps that must be taken to settle an estate are essentially the same.

How Property Passes at Death

Before beginning the administration of an estate, the executor needs to know how property passes at death. This is important to understand because it identifies the assets the executor will be legally responsible for and those that are not subject to probate administration. Property ownership has several different forms and, upon death, passes under laws that are unique to each form of ownership. The three common ways of owning property are individual ownership, joint ownership, and ownership that is subject to the terms of a contract.

FACT

The form of ownership will determine who gets the property and how they get it!

Individually Owned Property

Property, such as real estate, stocks and bonds, mutual funds, bank accounts, automobiles, and other property that is titled in an individual's name, is controlled by the terms of the decedent's will and subject to the probate process, or laws of descent, in the state in which the decedent lived. Tangible personal property owned by the decedent, such as jewelry, furniture, books, stamp collections, paintings, artifacts, etc., even though they are untitled, are also subject to probate. These assets are referred to as *probate property*. The probate laws may or may not require a formal probate court proceeding for distribution of this property, but there will be some form of legal process. Each state has its own rules about how this type of property is handled at death. Probate property passes to the beneficiaries named in a will or, if the decedent did not have a will, to the decedent's heirs at law as described under the laws of intestacy in the state in which the decedent lived. In either case, the property is subject to distribution under some form of probate process.

ESSENTIAL

The executor is responsible for all property that was individually owned by the decedent.

Jointly Owned Property

If the decedent owned any property jointly with others, it is important to know what kind of ownership it is. Property that is registered as joint tenants or as tenants by the entirety passes to the surviving owner(s) by operation of law and is not subject to probate. Ownership as tenants in common, however, does not pass to the surviving owner(s) by operation of law. This form of ownership represents an undivided interest in property that is considered individually owned. Property that is registered as tenants in common is subject to probate and passes by will or the laws of intestacy.

Contract Property

Property that is subject to the terms of a written contract, such as a life insurance policy, an interest in a profit-sharing 401(k) plan or IRA, a revocable living trust, pay on death (POD) account, transfer on death deed, etc., passes to the beneficiary named in the contract. This property is also not subject to probate unless the decedent's estate has been designated as the beneficiary under the contract.

HOW PROPERTY PASSES AT DEATH

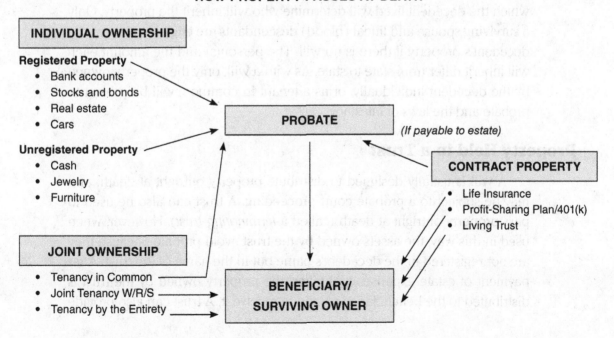

47

What Does a Will Do?

A will is a legally enforceable declaration by an individual with regard to the disposition of his or her assets. It may also address other matters that the will creator (testator/testatrix) wants to be handled at death, such as burial and who will care for minor children. A will only controls the property that is owned by the decedent individually, or as a tenant in common, and may be subject to a probate proceeding. If the value of the property is below a certain threshold (which differs from state to state), it may qualify for a small estate proceeding through probate court or transfer by affidavit without having to go through probate court. If a decedent also has a revocable living trust, typically the trust is named as the residual beneficiary under the will. After the payment of specific bequests, administration expenses, creditors' claims, and taxes, the will distributes to the trust whatever assets remain. This is called a *pour-over will*, and the bulk of the decedent's assets will be distributed in accordance with the terms of his or her trust.

What Happens if Someone Dies Without a Will?

If someone dies without a will and owns property in his or her individual name, or as a tenant in common, the laws of intestacy of the state in which the decedent lived will determine who will inherit the property. Only a surviving spouse and lineal (blood) descendants are eligible to inherit the decedent's property if there is no will. The person(s) and the amount each will inherit differ from state to state. As with a will, only the property owned by the decedent individually, or as a tenant in common, will be subject to probate and the laws of intestacy.

Property Held in a Trust

A will is usually designed to distribute property outright at death, and may be subject to a probate court proceeding. A trust can also be used to pass property outright at death (called a *terminating trust*). However, when used in this way, the assets owned by the trust avoid probate because they are not registered in the decedent's name but in the name of the trust. After payment of estate expenses and taxes, the property owned by the trust is distributed to the beneficiaries named to receive it. A trust can also provide control and management of assets for a specified period beyond death (called a *continuing trust*). The purpose of this type of trust is to protect beneficiaries and/or minimize estate taxes. The trust only controls and disposes of the property to which it has legal title, and the trust assets are not distributed to the named beneficiaries until the final obligations of the decedent are satisfied.

Once the executor identifies all of the assets and determines the form of ownership, the next step is to ascertain how the decedent's property will pass to the survivors. As an example, let's look at how John Porter's estate passes upon his death:

▼ PROPERTY OWNED BY JOHN AND MARY PORTER

	Ownership	Beneficiary
Checking account	Joint with Mary	–
Money market fund	Joint with Mary	–
Savings account	John	–
Stocks and bonds	Living trust	Mary/Children
Mutual funds	John	–
Automobiles	Joint with Mary	–
Furniture	Joint with Mary	–
Residence	Tenants by entirety	–
Condominium	Living trust	Mary/Children
Cash, jewelry	John	–
Life insurance	John	Mary
Profit-sharing plan	John	Mary

John has a pour-over will that distributes his individually owned property (i.e., savings account, mutual funds, cash, and jewelry), after probate, to his living trust. His living trust, which owns his stocks and bonds and condominium, continues for the benefit of his wife, Mary, and their children. All of the property that is owned jointly with Mary passes to her directly by operation of law. She is the named beneficiary under John's life insurance and profit-sharing plan and receives the proceeds directly. As John's executrix, Mary is responsible for passing John's savings accounts, mutual funds, cash, and jewelry to his living trust.

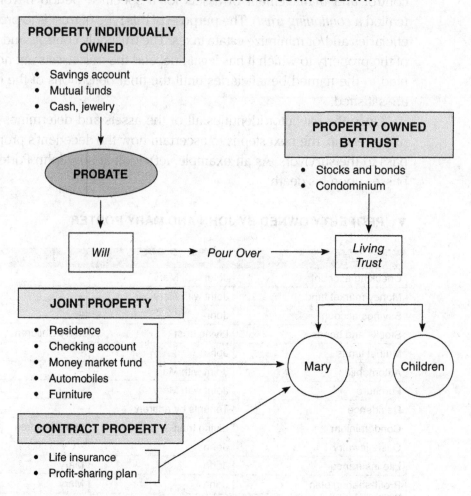

PROPERTY PASSING AT JOHN'S DEATH

PROPERTY INDIVIDUALLY OWNED

- Savings account
- Mutual funds
- Cash, jewelry

PROPERTY OWNED BY TRUST

- Stocks and bonds
- Condominium

PROBATE

Will → *Pour Over* → *Living Trust*

JOINT PROPERTY

- Residence
- Checking account
- Money market fund
- Automobiles
- Furniture

CONTRACT PROPERTY

- Life insurance
- Profit-sharing plan

Mary   Children

Who's Responsible for What?

Technically, the executor is not responsible for transferring everything the decedent owned at death, although as a practical matter, he or she can assist with transferring nonprobate assets. So who is responsible for transferring the various types of assets a decedent may own? Here's a list:

Type of Property	Person Responsible
Individually Owned Property	Executor (Personal Representative)
Joint-Held Property	Surviving Owner(s)
Contract Property (i.e., insurance, IRA, 401(k), etc.	Named Beneficiary
Property Held in a Trust	Trustee

Does the executor have to transfer all assets?
No! Technically, the executor is only responsible for the decedent's individually owned property unless other property, such as life insurance, is payable to the estate.

Assets That Pass under a Will

One of the most difficult and important tasks that an executor has to perform is locating, valuing, and organizing the decedent's property by type of ownership. This requires going through all of the decedent's records and identifying everything the decedent owned outright and property that he or she had an interest in. Once the inventory is sorted by type of ownership (i.e., individually owned, jointly owned, contract property, etc.), the total fair market value of the individually owned property (probate property) will determine the probate procedures required to transfer the property to the decedent's heirs or beneficiaries. Assets that will be covered by a will, and therefore be the responsibility of the executor, fall into two general categories. One category is assets that bear the decedent's individual name in the title, called *registered property*, and the other is called *unregistered property*.

It is essential that you identify all assets that were in the decedent's individual name at death so you know what you are legally responsible for.

Registered Property

Property that is registered in a decedent's individual name is subject to the probate laws. It includes checking and savings accounts, brokerage accounts, stocks and bonds, mutual funds, real estate, automobiles, and other property that has a legal title form of registration. It does not include property that is registered as joint tenants or tenants by the entirety, or property that designates a beneficiary under the terms of a contract.

51

Unregistered Property

Virtually every estate, no matter what its size, includes tangible personal property. This category of assets includes jewelry, paintings, furniture, tools, stamp collections, antiques, clothing, appliances, memorabilia, etc. and is also included as part of the probate assets even if there is no formal registration indicating ownership. The mere fact that the decedent had the property in his or her possession and that ownership was obvious makes it individually owned by the decedent. Also, any items that are referred to in a will are indications of individual ownership and should be included as part of the probate estate.

Digital Assets and Accounts

This is a relatively new category of assets that executors and trustees must deal with. As a result of the digital age, many people now keep digital records and maintain digital financial and other property accounts. These assets may have both monetary and sentimental value to the estate and therefore must be accounted for, especially those digital accounts that have financial value. Some of these accounts may have to be closed because they are automatic bill-paying accounts, and others may have to be closed to avoid identity theft. Others may be useful in gathering financial information. Documents that may be important to the administration of the estate or trust may be in digital form and stored on laptops, flash drives, external hard drives, smartphones, and online storage accounts. A decedent may have had:

- Social media accounts (Facebook, Twitter, LinkedIn, etc.)
- E-mail accounts (AOL, Hotmail, Gmail, etc.)
- Online music accounts (Amazon, iTunes, Pandora, etc.)
- Online video accounts (Netflix, etc.)
- Online data storage accounts (Google, etc.)
- Online retail accounts (Amazon, eBay, Expedia, etc.)
- Financial online accounts (banks, brokerage, insurance, retirement plans, PayPal, etc.)
- Domain names

ALERT

Digital assets are difficult to handle, but they must be accounted for. Following the steps outlined here will help.

The problem with digital accounts is that each service provider has its own Terms of Service agreement and those terms may prevent transfer of the account and the account's user name and password to someone else. This could make it difficult for the executor to access and deal with the account as part of the administration of the estate. If the executor has the user name and password and accesses the account without permission, he or she may not only be violating the Terms of Service agreement but may also be violating the federal Computer Fraud and Abuse Act, the federal Stored Communications Act (privacy law), and any similar state laws that may exist. Although a few states have enacted legislation to allow the executor or trustee to have access to these accounts, it is still not clear as to how much authority an executor has beyond the Terms of Service agreements. The executor should consult with the estate's attorney before proceeding.

ALERT

Be careful when accessing digital asset accounts. Seek legal advice if you're not sure what to do, and don't do anything that you have doubts about.

The executor is still responsible and must manage these assets if they have financial value and are part of the estate, and should also assist beneficiaries with getting access to pictures, e-mails, and other items that have sentimental value. So what is an executor to do? The following steps will help you:

1. Make an inventory of all digital assets that were owned by the decedent along with the names of the accounts, user names, and passwords, if available.
2. Check the decedent's computer and other electronic devices for any important documents and information that may be needed for the administration of the estate. If you don't have access to the device, take it to an electronics technician and have the data transferred to a DVD.

3. Contact the companies for each digital account, preferably in writing, and inform them of the death of the decedent; request a copy of the Terms of Service agreement; provide proof of your role as executor by giving them a copy of the letters testamentary; request any account balance and/or value as of the date of death; and ask what is required to transfer the account to the estate or named beneficiary.

Responses to these inquiries will allow the executor to assess what accounts have financial value and should be included in the estate's inventory, what accounts can be transferred to the estate, and whether or not an account has a named beneficiary and should be dealt with by that beneficiary. As this information is collected, the estate's attorney should also be consulted with regard to any further action that the executor may need to take with respect to a particular digital account.

How Is Probate Handled?

Most people want to avoid a formal probate proceeding. Why? First, it can be very expensive. In most states, the fee is a percentage of the value of probate assets. This is often defined as the gross value and not the net (the gross value less the decedent's debts). In some estates, this fee can be sizeable and result in a smaller inheritance for heirs. Most courts also assess court fees for using their system to probate a decedent's estate.

Another reason to avoid probate is that it can take a long time to complete. Eighteen months to two years is not unusual for completing the process and distributing the property to the decedent's heirs. In some cases it takes even longer. Unfortunately, the executor is often blamed for the delay. Most people do not understand the process or the fact that the executor is required to complete the task in accordance with rules prescribed by law. These rules, both federal and state, can slow the process. Nevertheless, the heirs will want their inheritance immediately and the executor must often spend time explaining why they have to wait.

A Snapshot of the Process

It begins with petitioning the court for a hearing to probate the decedent's will. It can take weeks and sometimes months to get a hearing, depending on the district and how backed up the court calendar is. Under an informal proceeding, this is much quicker and may not require a hearing. Until the hearing and/or formal appointment, the executor has no legal authority to conduct the affairs of the estate. As a practical matter, however, if you intend to accept the position as executor and are reasonably sure that the court will make the appointment, it is wise to begin the process of gathering and safeguarding the decedent's assets. Waiting months for a formal court appointment could jeopardize the proper handling of the estate. It is unlikely that the nominated executor will be criticized for using good judgment in protecting estate assets.

ESSENTIAL

It would be wise to begin the process, such as taking steps to protect estate assets, even before you are formally appointed.

Once appointed as executor, you must prepare an inventory of the decedent's assets. Itemize what the decedent owned at death and establish the fair market value of each. In most jurisdictions, this inventory must be submitted to the court. As the executor, you should also publish a notice to creditors in the legal notice section of the appropriate newspaper(s) for the period specified by local law. The public notice announces the death of the decedent and invites creditors to make claims for any outstanding debts. At the expiration of the notice period, creditors who have not submitted a claim and are unknown to the executor are usually barred from making future claims.

During probate, you manage the decedent's estate as the executor and pay expenses associated with the settlement of the estate. The administration of the estate may include overseeing or being actively involved in the management of the decedent's business. If the decedent owned rental property, management will involve finding tenants, making repairs, paying operating expenses, and collecting rents. Any stocks and bonds or other securities will need to be evaluated to determine which ones, if any, need to be sold either to raise funds to pay taxes and expenses or to protect the portfolio against an extraordinary loss. You must see to it that all income that is due the estate is collected and all verified claims and other expenses are paid. Each of these activities must be recorded and accounted for. Accounting reports must be provided to the court and the beneficiaries prior to closing the estate.

If the estate owes any federal estate tax, the tax return must be filed and taxes paid no later than nine months from the date of death. A state inheritance or estate tax may also be due. It is best not to file the return any sooner than necessary; the estate will be much better off earning interest for as long as it can on the taxes due. This is one reason why it takes longer than a year to settle an estate. An estate is a separate taxable entity and must also file income tax returns to report and pay any taxes due on the income it receives. The probate court will not allow the closing of the estate and discharge of the executor until all taxes have been paid.

ESSENTIAL

You should make a decision to serve or not to serve as soon as possible so an alternate can be appointed and no one will assume you are acting as the executor.

An accounting of the activities of administration is usually presented to the probate court for approval prior to closing. If the beneficiaries desire, or if ordered by the court, a master will be appointed to review the executor's records. The master's job is to perform an audit of the administration of the estate and report the findings to the court. If the review is satisfactory, the master will recommend to the court that the accounting be approved. If a master is not appointed then the court will approve the accounts and order final distribution. At this point the executor prepares to distribute the assets of the estate to the decedent's heirs. A distribution schedule is prepared, listing the property each beneficiary will receive. The assets are then registered in the names of the beneficiaries and delivered to each of them.

Once distribution has been completed and receipts obtained from each beneficiary, you must submit a final accounting (also referred to as a *supplemental final accounting*) to the court along with the signed receipts. This demonstrates to the court that all tasks have been completed and that the decedent's assets have been distributed to those who are legally entitled to them. At this point, the court will issue an order to close the estate and discharge you as the executor. Once the discharge has been ordered, you are relieved of any further responsibilities with respect to the administration of the decedent's estate.

You've Been Named the Executor; Now What?

Uncle Joe just died, and before he passed away he told you that he had named you the executor under his will. Once you discover what might be involved, you are not quite sure you want to serve or can handle the responsibility. However, you might feel that this is the least you should do for Uncle Joe. After all, you were the one person he was willing to trust to handle his affairs. Besides, you should be honored that he chose you over other family members and friends. To serve or not to serve—that is always the question. While this can be an agonizing decision, it must be made within a reasonable period of time.

If your decision is not made promptly, it could cause unnecessary delays in settling the estate. If you decide not to serve, the court will appoint someone else unless the decedent's will designates an alternate executor. If you decide to serve, notify the attorney who drew the will, or an attorney of your choice, to file the petition for probate with your acceptance noted.

To protect the interests of those who are entitled to payment of claims and of those who are legally entitled to receive the property, as executor, you are required to follow the instructions of the decedent's will, or if there is no will, the laws of intestacy in the state of jurisdiction. The laws of intestacy specify the lineal descendants (blood relatives) who legally inherit the decedent's property if there is no will. The probate court issues letters of administration where there is no will, or letters testamentary for an executor who has been named in a will. This is your legal authority to act as executor. Once formally appointed, you assume all of the duties and responsibilities under local law. This includes identifying, taking control of, and safeguarding all probate assets.

Administering an estate should be done in logical steps to ensure that all of the legal requirements are met and the estate is managed efficiently. To do otherwise makes the process more difficult than it needs to be and invites criticism from heirs. The next chapters will walk you through preparing for the administration and the following steps you will need to take in the process:

- Collecting and Protecting Estate Assets
- Preparing an Inventory and Obtaining Appraisals
- Managing Estate Assets During the Period of Administration
- Estimating the Estate's Cash Requirements and Raising the Needed Funds

- Paying Claims and Administration Expenses, Including the Executor's Fee
- Filing Required Tax Returns
- Making Tax and Other Postmortem Planning Elections
- Preparing and Maintaining Accounting Records
- Distributing Assets to the Beneficiaries
- Closing the Estate

SETTLING THE ESTATE

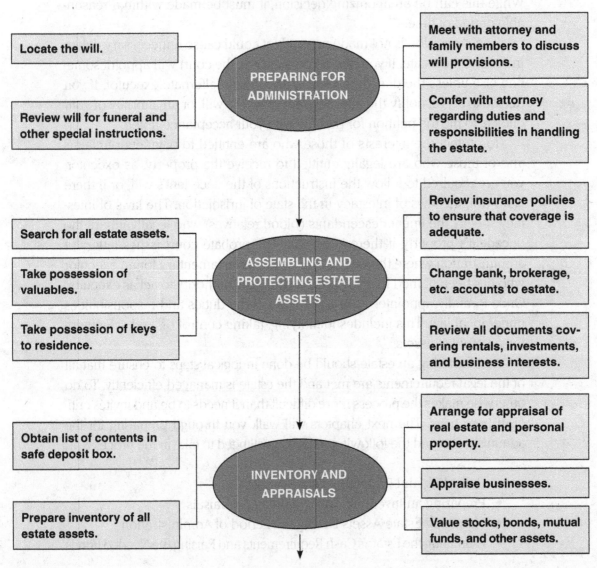

Locate the will.

Review will for funeral and other special instructions.

PREPARING FOR ADMINISTRATION

Meet with attorney and family members to discuss will provisions.

Confer with attorney regarding duties and responsibilities in handling the estate.

Search for all estate assets.

Take possession of valuables.

Take possession of keys to residence.

ASSEMBLING AND PROTECTING ESTATE ASSETS

Review insurance policies to ensure that coverage is adequate.

Change bank, brokerage, etc. accounts to estate.

Review all documents covering rentals, investments, and business interests.

Obtain list of contents in safe deposit box.

Prepare inventory of all estate assets.

INVENTORY AND APPRAISALS

Arrange for appraisal of real estate and personal property.

Appraise businesses.

Value stocks, bonds, mutual funds, and other assets.

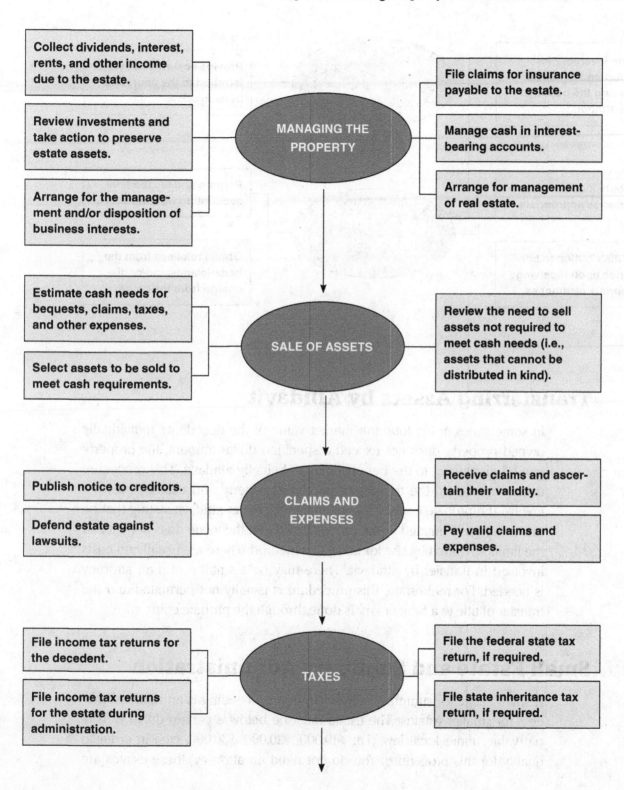

Collect dividends, interest, rents, and other income due to the estate.

Review investments and take action to preserve estate assets.

Arrange for the management and/or disposition of business interests.

MANAGING THE PROPERTY

File claims for insurance payable to the estate.

Manage cash in interest-bearing accounts.

Arrange for management of real estate.

Estimate cash needs for bequests, claims, taxes, and other expenses.

Select assets to be sold to meet cash requirements.

SALE OF ASSETS

Review the need to sell assets not required to meet cash needs (i.e., assets that cannot be distributed in kind).

Publish notice to creditors.

Defend estate against lawsuits.

CLAIMS AND EXPENSES

Receive claims and ascertain their validity.

Pay valid claims and expenses.

File income tax returns for the decedent.

File income tax returns for the estate during administration.

TAXES

File the federal state tax return, if required.

File state inheritance tax return, if required.

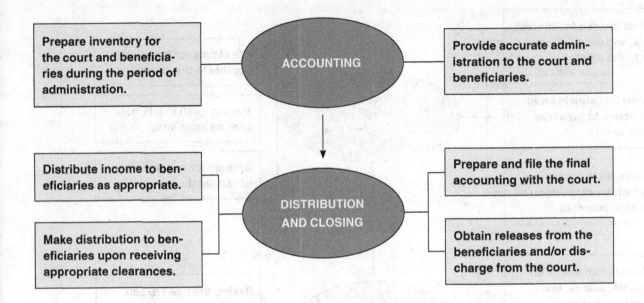

Transferring Assets by Affidavit

In some states, if the total fair market value of the decedent's individually owned property does not exceed a specified dollar amount, the property can be distributed to the beneficiaries or heirs by affidavit. This procedure usually applies to the transfer of personal property and usually does not involve the probate court. The beneficiary signs an affidavit stating that he or she is legally entitled to the property and that the value does not exceed the limits specified by law for using this method. There are usually no costs involved in transfer by affidavit. There may be a small cost if an attorney is needed. For real estate, this procedure is usually not permitted and the transfer of title to a beneficiary is done through the probate court.

Small Estate and Summary Administration

A small estate, or summary, administration proceeding is an informal process for smaller estates. The estate must be below a certain dollar threshold value under local law (i.e., $10,000, $20,000, $30,000, etc.) in order to qualify for this procedure. You do not need an attorney; these estates are typically handled by or through the clerk of the probate court. The procedure requires the executor or a family member to complete some forms provided by the clerk. In some jurisdictions, the small estate proceeding is used to transfer real estate to the decedent's heirs where there is no requirement for a formal probate proceeding.

Informal, Unsupervised, or Independent Probate Proceedings

If the gross value of the decedent's probate assets is greater than the threshold for the small estate proceeding, an informal, unsupervised, or independent probate proceeding is either required or is an option in many states. Some states limit this procedure to a specific range of estate values; others make it an option for any size estate. The court does not directly supervise this procedure, which many states have adopted through the Uniform Probate Code. It simplifies the process, minimizes settlement costs, and is designed to reduce the time it takes to settle the estate.

Once appointed executor, you act independently from the court throughout the administration and settlement of the estate. Some states may require limited reporting to the court at the beginning, during, or upon completion of the settlement process. The cost is significantly less than a formal proceeding because an attorney is not required and court costs, if any, are minimal. At any time under this method, an executor, beneficiary, or any interested party can exercise the option to have the estate handled by the court in a formal proceeding. Although an attorney is not required, the executor should consider retaining counsel for advice on how these procedures work under local law.

Formal, or Supervised, Probate Proceeding

When a decedent's probate assets reach a certain value, some states require a formal, or supervised, probate proceeding. Whether the formal proceeding is required or is elected by those involved, an attorney is usually necessary and often involves extensive supervision by the probate court. Hearings are required throughout the proceeding, and inventories, accountings, and other reports must be filed with the court. Court costs and attorney's fees make the formal probate proceeding more expensive, and it usually takes longer to complete. It is not unusual for the settlement of larger or more complex estates to take two to three years or longer.

A formal probate proceeding is the most costly and time-consuming process for settling an estate. The least time-consuming process is a transfer by affidavit.

Procedures vary from state to state, and it is your duty as executor to find out what the local law requires and what options are available. An estate attorney can tell you, or you can contact the clerk of the probate court for guidance.

CHAPTER 4

Preparing for the Administration of the Estate

Supervision and management of a probate estate can be complex. It requires time, attention to detail, and meeting deadlines. Unanticipated events can change a relatively simple settlement process into a time-consuming job. The key to keeping everyone happy is keeping them informed. Creditors and beneficiaries want to know what's going on and when they can expect to be paid or receive their inheritance. Whether the news is good or bad, they'll want to hear from you. If there's a problem and the probate is delayed, frequent communication will help buffer any unhappiness. Don't wait for the court to issue letters testamentary giving you legal authority as executor. This process may take several weeks, or even months. The responsibility of protecting assets should begin immediately, if you have made a commitment to serve.

Locating the Original Will

You might hear of a decedent's death and your appointment as executor from a family member or, in some cases, learn of the death from an obituary notice. The decedent's attorney may also inform you because you are named under the will. The most important and immediate step once you have been informed of the death is to locate and secure the decedent's original will. Only the original will can be presented to the probate court, although there have been cases where a copy of a will has been probated when the original could not be found.

ESSENTIAL

You cannot begin the process without the last (original) will and all codicils.

One of the obvious places to look is in the decedent's safe deposit box. Most banks will allow the removal of a will from a decedent's safe deposit box when presented with a death certificate. A family member or the estate attorney should be present while the box is being searched for the will; financial institutions will usually require one of their employees also to be present. The search of the safe deposit box is an opportunity to collect information about other assets, such as stocks, bonds, insurance policies, jewelry, etc., that may have to be probated or are otherwise part of the decedent's estate. Make an inventory of the box's contents.

You might also look for the original will in the decedent's home among other important documents. Ask a family member to assist in this search. Like the opening of the safe deposit box, the search of the decedent's home is also an opportunity to begin developing an inventory. The original will may also be held for safekeeping with the decedent's attorney, bank, or other financial institution. Sometimes a business associate or friend will have possession of the original will. The search for the will must be thorough to assure that the most current will and all codicils (amendments) are presented to the probate court.

Locate the original will as soon as possible after death because it may contain burial and funeral instructions and/or directives regarding anatomical gifts. It is obviously critical to notify the decedent's physician, family, and attorney of any organ donations as soon as possible. Most organ donations must be made within hours of death or they may not have value.

ESSENTIAL

Be methodical. Organizing the process and keeping on top of things will save you time, aggravation, and criticism from creditors and beneficiaries. Use the checklist at the end of this book to help you with this process.

Family members need to be notified of any funeral instructions so that burial arrangements can be made in accordance with the wishes of the decedent. The decedent may not have surviving family members and the executor may need to make the funeral arrangements if friends or acquaintances of the decedent are not inclined to assume this responsibility. The original will should be turned over to the attorney for filing with the court.

Selecting an Attorney for the Estate

Although some states may not require an attorney to represent the estate, as executor, you should consider retaining an attorney to guide you through the initial stages. Contrary to popular belief, it is the executor who has the responsibility for hiring the attorney to represent the decedent's estate. The executor will ultimately be held accountable if something goes wrong. Therefore it behooves you as the executor to select an attorney that is qualified to take on the responsibility. Typically, the attorney who prepared the decedent's will is the logical choice. He or she would be familiar with the decedent's expressed wishes and have some knowledge with respect to the decedent's family and financial affairs. However, if the will was drawn many years ago, this familiarity may no longer exist. In addition, the attorney may not have an interest in doing this kind of work, or may not have the expertise to handle probate administration matters.

FACT

The attorney's fee is a proper administration expense and is chargeable to the estate.

If you feel that the attorney is incapable of handling the estate, or if there is a conflict of interest, select another attorney. Look in the yellow pages of the phone book for attorneys who specialize in estate planning and administration, or contact the local bar association for references. A banker or accountant can also be a good reference.

It is always a good idea to discuss this matter with the decedent's family and beneficiaries; they may have someone in mind. Do not, however, get talked into using a favorite uncle or family friend who does not have expertise in this area. An attorney whose practice does not include estate administration may also give the engagement a low priority. The attorney may have to devote the same amount of time and attention to the probate as the executor. Any delays caused by an attorney will become a problem for the executor who is answerable to the decedent's heirs and the court. So choose wisely.

ESSENTIAL

The estate attorney's primary practice should be in the area of estate planning and administration. An online search may help you narrow down the choices in your locale.

What to Cover with the Estate Attorney

Once you select the attorney for the estate, arrange an initial meeting to begin the planning process. If there is a co-executor named in the will, that individual should also be present at this meeting. If someone other than you as the executor is named trustee under the decedent's revocable living trust, that individual should participate in the discussion as well. Turn over the original will to the attorney at this time for filing with the probate court. This first meeting should accomplish the following things:

- Review of the decedent's will and trust
- Assign duties and responsibilities between the executor, attorney, and trustee
- Determine if there is a need for special administration
- Determine if there is a need for family and other allowances

- Discuss the surviving spouse's elective right
- Obtain the necessary documents and information that will be needed to begin the probate process
- Review the initial steps, time frames, and deadlines for administering the estate

Reviewing the Decedent's Will and Trust

A summary of the pertinent provisions of the will and trust should be made. The summary will be helpful when discussing the provisions with the family and as a reference for planning. Funeral instructions and anatomical gifts should be noted, specific bequests should be identified, and any instructions regarding the payment of administration expenses should be reviewed. Determine if the will is a pour-over will that names the decedent's trust as the residuary beneficiary, or if there are any other residuary beneficiaries. Review the trust to determine if it terminates or continues, if death taxes, debts, and funeral expenses are payable from the trust, whether there is a marital and family trust split, and whether there are any generation-skipping transfers.

Duties and Responsibilities of Professional Advisors

At the first meeting, decide what duties and responsibilities you will assume as executor and what tasks will be handled by the attorney. The attorney's principal duty is to serve as legal advisor and counselor to the personal representative. The attorney is also responsible for drafting all legal documents, representing the estate before the probate court, and advising you, the executor, of your duties and responsibilities regarding the administration of the estate.

ALERT

Make sure that the people you hire understand what responsibilities they are assuming. If they don't, you could end up in hot water.

Some attorneys will file the estate tax returns and fiduciary income tax returns for the estate. Others prefer that an accountant or someone else who has specific expertise in this area handle these responsibilities. There may be legal issues that fall outside the expertise of the estate attorney, and he or she may prefer that these matters be referred to attorneys who specialize in those areas. Other duties, such as preparing the inventory, maintaining accounting records, arranging for appraisals, managing the decedent's business interest, etc., can be handled by the attorney, the accountant, a financial advisor, or the executor.

It is very important that you have a clear understanding of who is doing what so nothing "falls into the cracks." A common problem in administering an estate is assuming the attorney has taken responsibility for a particular task while the attorney thinks that the executor is handling it. The solution is simple. Make sure that the assignment of responsibilities is clearly understood by everyone involved. Put it in writing if necessary. The executor should keep a written record of these assignments and monitor the activities of all advisors that are retained.

Determining the Need for Special Administration

You may have to act to protect the decedent's property prior to receiving formal appointment by the court (i.e., issuance of letters testamentary). You may need to manage the decedent's business, attend to a bad investment, deal with pending litigation, or manage some other special situation that requires immediate action. You can apply for the appointment of a special administrator within a few days if you need to deal with these matters. The formal appointment of an executor can sometimes take weeks, and in some cases, several months.

The attorney can help you decide whether special administration is necessary and should file the appropriate petition with the court. Once approved, the court will appoint a special administrator, who may not necessarily be the personal representative named in the will, and give that individual specific limited authority to deal with the particular issue.

Determining If Family and Other Allowances Are Needed

Most states provide a decedent's surviving spouse and minor children with certain allowances from the estate, which is in addition to what has been provided for them under the decedent's will or the laws of intestacy. These allowances generally fall into two categories. One is a monetary allowance, called a *family allowance* or *homestead allowance*, for financial support during the period of administration. The other is a specific dollar value of property, called *exempt property*, which they can receive from the estate. Both types of awards are usually exempt from creditor claims against the decedent and the decedent's spouse. Although these allowances are nominal, you should discuss them with the spouse in terms of eligibility and to make arrangements for payment if needed.

The Surviving Spouse's Rights

Under the probate statutes in many states, a surviving spouse has the right to receive a specified amount of money or property instead of what has been provided, or not provided, under the decedent's will. For example, on her death, Mary leaves all her property to her children. Her husband, John, can elect to receive a portion of the property even though Mary excluded him under her will. This election against the will, referred to as the *elective share*, may be limited only to probate assets in some states. In other states, the right applies to the decedent's "augmented estate," which includes all of the decedent's property, including trusts, joint assets, insurance policies, retirement plans, etc. It may also include property that the decedent had transferred to others prior to death.

ESSENTIAL

Because it can get very complicated, it might be best to have the estate attorney deal with an elective right issue. You will have enough on your plate already.

In some states, the amount of the elective share increases with the number of years of marriage. As the executor, you will need to determine the amount and extent of this right and explain it to the surviving spouse, who will decide whether or not to make the election. The court will usually require that a form be completed or that a petition be filed to exercise the election. In some states, a written declination is also required if the surviving spouse does not wish to take the elective share.

Consideration should also be given to the tax and estate planning implications of making the election. For example, property received by a surviving spouse as a result of the election will normally qualify for the marital deduction unless it is a terminable interest. Dower and courtesy interests (the rights given to a wife—dower, and the rights given to a husband—courtesy, in some states) are terminable interests that would not qualify for the marital deduction. If the elective share is a dower or courtesy interest, it may generate additional estate taxes in the decedent's estate. The surviving spouse should be advised to seek counsel before making the election. This is a complex matter, and as executor, you should have the estate attorney assist you with this issue.

Documents and Information Needed to Settle the Estate

After finding the will, the executor and/or attorney should collect the basic information necessary to begin the probate process as soon as possible. Information can be obtained from the decedent's family, friends, and personal records and should include the following:

- Decedent's Social Security number
- Decedent's home address
- Decedent's date of birth
- Decedent's date of death
- Names, addresses, telephone numbers, and relationships of all beneficiaries named under the decedent's will or of any heirs at law if there is no will
- Birth dates for all minor children

- Birth dates of other individuals whose inheritance is contingent on the attainment of a specified age
- Names and addresses of all witnesses to the will
- Preliminary list of assets that will be subject to probate (i.e., assets in the decedent's name) and estimates of their value
- Preliminary list of nonprobate assets (i.e., jointly owned property, trusts, IRAs, profit-sharing plans, 401(k)s, etc.), estimates of their value, and the names and addresses of co-owners and beneficiaries
- Preliminary list of life insurance policies owned by the decedent, their face value, and the beneficiaries named in the policies
- Preliminary list of known debts of the decedent, including mortgages and other encumbrances on the decedent's real property, outstanding bills, credit cards, notes, etc.; the amounts owed; and account numbers
- Copies of any trusts, including all amendments, which were created by the decedent, or that the decedent was a beneficiary of; the names and addresses of the trustees; and a list of the trusts' assets and estimated value
- Copies of any deeds, leases, contracts, etc.
- Copies of any pension, profit-sharing, 401(k), IRA, or other employee benefit plan documents
- Three years of income tax returns
- Last gift tax return filed, if any (if the decedent made gifts in excess of the annual exclusion amount in any one year, a gift tax return, Form 709, was required to be filed)

Considerable effort could be involved in locating the decedent's heirs. Obviously, the first source should be family members and friends. If that fails, you should make a thorough search of the decedent's records, correspondence, address book, miscellaneous notes, etc.

The more you probe, the more information you will obtain. The more information you obtain, the easier your administration will be.

If an address cannot be found among the decedent's records, you can publish a legal notice in a newspaper where the heir was last known to reside. You can also contact the county department of records or office of vital statistics for an address. Another good source is the Social Security Administration. Although they will not give you an address or phone number, the administration will contact the individual and ask him or her to contact you as the executor. As a last resort, you can hire a professional to locate the missing heir. There are several companies that provide this service, and most will not charge a fee unless the heir is found.

ESSENTIAL

Google search can help you find a lost heir and the web can help you find firms that assist executors with this task.

The decision to hire a professional search firm should be based on the amount of the inheritance. While there is no common formula for making this determination, obviously the estimated cost of locating the heir should not exceed the value of the inheritance. Once an address is found, write a letter notifying the individual of the decedent's death. The letter should describe the interest the individual has in the decedent's estate and include a current address and telephone number where the executor can be contacted.

Hiring Professionals, Due Dates, and Other Issues

The executor has the responsibility to locate and take possession of all assets that belong to the estate, pay all debts and expenses, distribute the assets to the beneficiaries who are legally entitled to receive them, and account to the beneficiaries and the court for these actions. This requires planning, both before the executor's formal appointment and throughout the entire administration. Careful planning will avoid delays and costly administration errors. During the initial meeting with the attorney for the estate, some key issues need to be discussed in preparation for the administration of the estate:

- Hiring an accountant, investment advisor, banker, appraiser, business agent, realtor, etc.—Although the executor may be able to handle many of the administrative tasks alone, you should obtain professional assistance where needed. Be mindful that you are responsible to the creditors and beneficiaries of the estate for any errors that occur, intentional or unintentional. The estate attorney can be a good source for recommending professionals you may need to assist in the administration of the estate.

- Outline key due dates—It is extremely important to anticipate and meet the various deadlines imposed on the estate. First set a target date for final distribution of the estate. Although this is a rough estimate, the target date gives you a point from which other estimates can be made. You can estimate target dates for all aspects of administration. In the absence of target dates, the tendency is to focus on the most pressing problems first, which, in turn, may cause delays in other phases of the administration. Setting target dates and identifying deadlines will keep the administration of the estate on track.

Failure to perform the various administrative functions on time can be costly to the estate. Some of the dates that should be included in the plan for administration are:

Event	Due Date
Court hearing dates	Set by the judge having jurisdiction over the probate proceeding
Filing the inventory of probate assets	Depends on state law; usually 30 days from the date of death
Expiration of the Notice to Creditors*	Depends on the law of each state, but usually 120 days after publishing of notice
Alternate valuation date**	6 months from the date of death
Filing of the Federal Estate Tax Return	9 months from the date of death
Filing the decedent's final income tax returns	April 15, following the year of death
Filing the Fiduciary Income Tax Returns for the estate	3½ months after end of selected tax year
Period for IRS to respond to request for early determination of estate tax***	9 months from the date the request is filed

*The Notice to Creditors is a public notice that invites creditors to make claims against the estate for debts owed. Upon expiration of the notice, creditors are usually barred from making future claims.

**This is a provision under the Internal Revenue Code that allows the estate to use an alternate valuation date that could potentially reduce the estate tax liability.

***A personal representative may be held personally liable for additional estate taxes assessed against the estate. An early determination of the tax by the IRS protects against this possibility.

- Review issues that will require special attention—The contesting of a will can be disruptive to the administration of the estate. Although this is a legal issue that would be decided by the courts or settled among the disputing parties, as executor, you may have to take a position on behalf of the estate. Pending or threatened litigation involving the estate may require hiring an attorney and deciding on a strategy to protect estate assets. If no one was designated to manage the decedent's business, you may need to decide on continuing the business or preparing it for liquidation. You should discuss these issues with the attorney and other professionals in deciding how they will be handled.

Meeting with the Family

A meeting should be held with family members and other beneficiaries. If possible, the meeting with the attorney should take place first so that the plan of administration can be discussed with the heirs. The meeting should be attended by the estate's attorney and trustee, if other than the executor. The meeting will have several purposes:

- To review the terms of the will and trust
- To explain the functions of the attorney, executor, and trustee
- To describe the steps that need to be taken to settle the estate
- To outline a rough timetable for administration of the estate
- To obtain information from family members that is pertinent to the administration of the estate

The heirs will want to know what Uncle Joe left them, so one of the first items on the agenda should be a reading of the will by the attorney or executor. All bequests under the will should be described, as well as the dispositive provisions of the decedent's trust. The decedent's will may also contain precatory language (words or phrases in a will or trust stating that something should be done but not directing that it be done) that expresses the decedent's desires. These expressions should be paraphrased or read to the heirs. The family, and others who have an interest in the estate, are primarily interested in the terms of the will. The reading should be thorough and delivered with compassion.

The executor and trustee are in charge of the decedent's affairs from the date of death through completion of the administration of the estate. The decedent may not have planned for meeting the immediate financial needs of his family, and a determination should be made early in the conversation whether or not a need exists. Funds can be made through a family allowance if allowed under local law, or by obtaining a short-term loan.

This meeting is a good opportunity to gather information. It is important to explain the need for this information, because some family members may be reluctant to provide it if they feel it is personal and unnecessary. The executor or attorney should explain all of the legal rights that the heirs have with respect to the estate and/or trust. To the extent that any elections being considered have tax or estate planning implications, they should be discussed with the family members or their financial advisors.

ESSENTIAL

It is important that you, as the executor, describe the process for administering the estate and provide an estimated time frame for completion. If the trust is a terminating trust, provide the heirs with an estimate for final distribution of the trust assets. This is probably of greater importance to the family than other estate matters. Spending the extra time to explain the process will go a long way toward making family members comfortable with your handling of the estate. The more they understand, the more helpful they can be.

Preparation for Administration Checklist

- Locate the original will and all codicils.
- Review the will and trust with the estate's attorney.
- Develop a written agreement specifying the responsibilities the attorney and other professionals will assume, and which duties the executor will handle.
- Determine if there is a need for special administration.

- Determine if a family or homestead allowance is needed.
- Determine if the surviving spouse will exercise his or her elective share right.
- Obtain basic information, such as names, addresses, dates of birth of beneficiaries, tax returns, a list of assets, etc.
- List and record known key due dates, and estimate when key tasks should be completed.
- Meet with the family and attorney to review the provisions of the will and the trust.
- Outline the probate process for the beneficiaries and give them an estimated time frame for completion.

CHAPTER 5

Phase One of Administering the Estate

Once the preparation steps have been completed, you will be ready to begin the process of administration. The first, and perhaps most important, step is to collect and take control of all estate assets. You cannot manage the estate unless you have possession and legal authority over this property. Just as important is the protection of these assets, not only for the estate and its beneficiaries, but also to protect yourself from liability. The next steps include preparing an inventory, so you clearly know what you are in charge of, appraising assets at their date-of-death value, managing the property in your possession, and paying claims and administration expenses.

Collecting Estate Assets

Assembling and protecting estate assets is one of the most important steps in settling an estate. In addition to locating and accounting for the decedent's property, as executor you are responsible for preventing the destruction, deterioration, or disappearance of these assets. Even before the formal search has begun, items sometimes have a way of disappearing. A beneficiary who does not understand the legal process for passing property at death may take possession of the diamond ring or other valuables that "Mother wanted me to have" when those items have been given to someone else under her will. Taking possession of tangible assets should be done as soon after the decedent's death as possible to prevent them from getting into the wrong hands.

ALERT

Collecting and protecting estate assets is an important task that should be done as soon as possible. Don't put this off!

Where to Look

If you are lucky, the decedent will have left an inventory of the assets he or she owned, making the job of locating them a lot easier. The list may not be up to date, but it is a starting point. More than likely there will be no list and you will need to begin the search. The best place to start is with the decedent's income tax returns. Here, assets that are associated with income from investments, business interests, rental properties, retirement plans, etc., can be identified. Property tax deductions indicate real estate holdings.

Another good source is the decedent's checkbook. Deposits that are made to other bank accounts may be found here in addition to payments for insurance premiums, mortgages, investments, safe deposit boxes, vehicle registration fees, purchase of jewelry, and other payments that can be traced to assets owned by the decedent. The decedent's mail is another source. Dividend, interest, rent, retirement, and other checks are sources for locating assets. Friends and family members may be able to help identify assets and their location. Statements covering brokerage accounts, mutual funds, and other investment accounts will give detailed descriptions of these assets.

If the decedent had a safe deposit box, it should be inventoried. This can be done at the time the box is opened to retrieve the will. The box may contain an inventory of assets, life insurance policies, stock and bond certificates, promissory notes, jewelry, cash, rare coins, and legal documents. Assets located in the safe deposit box are obviously secure and need not be removed immediately.

Searching the Residence

A principal responsibility of a personal representative is securing the decedent's residence. The decedent's home should be searched for valuables, such as jewelry, cash, paintings, art objects, etc. The decedent may have these valuables insured separately and an inventory identifying them (i.e., "scheduled property") may be attached to the insurance policy. The executor should take possession of these items immediately for safekeeping. Once the valuables have been safeguarded and the decedent's documents and other financial records have been collected, the residence should be secured.

Protecting Estate Assets

As executor, you are responsible for the decedent's property and charged with preventing any destruction or deterioration of the assets. As mentioned earlier, this process needs to begin even before the executor is formally appointed. Tangible personal property, particularly jewelry and valuable artifacts, can be intentionally or unintentionally "misplaced." Other steps that need to be taken include:

- *Safeguarding the residence.* The locks should be changed immediately, unless there is a responsible person, such as a relative or close family friend, who can occupy the decedent's residence and protect its contents. This is to make sure that no one with keys obtained from the decedent can gain access. In some cases, it may be necessary to hire a guard service to protect the property until other security arrangements can be made. If the home is a condominium or apartment, a resident manager might be able to assist in keeping an eye on things.

- *Safeguarding personal items.* Consider renting a safe deposit box registered in the name of the estate to store small portable items such as jewelry. Take possession of other valuables and secure them in an appropriate storage facility until they are distributed to the beneficiaries.

- *Protecting automobiles.* If the decedent's automobile was jointly owned, the surviving owner can have full possession and use immediately after the death. If owned by the decedent individually, it should be locked in the decedent's garage or secured in a storage facility until it can be legally transferred to a beneficiary or sold.

- *Change the mailing address.* The mailing address of the decedent should be changed immediately to that of the executor. Statements and other correspondence received in the mail will help you get a handle on the decedent's affairs. Social Security and other checks representing income to the estate should be deposited in a separate bank account in the name of the estate.

- *Get authority over bank and brokerage accounts.* Technically, an executor must have letters testamentary from the probate court in order to exercise legal control over accounts that a decedent has with financial institutions. However, once these accounts have been identified, you should notify the financial institution that you will have authority over those accounts as soon as letters testamentary have been issued. If necessary, you can obtain special letters of administration for anything that needs to be done immediately. All existing accounts should be reregistered in the name of the estate. Some financial institutions will have their own protocols for this, but most will read: "Estate of (name of the decedent), deceased, (name of the executor), executor." All new accounts established for the estate should also be registered this way.

- *Make sure that real estate and other valuable assets are adequately insured.* Contact the decedent's insurance agent and review the insurance coverage on all assets. As executor, you will be held responsible for any losses on assets not adequately covered. Pay particular attention to the coverage on real estate and valuable personal property such as jewelry and paintings.

- *Evaluate securities and other financial assets.* Retain a professional investment advisor to help you review the decedent's financial assets and identify any securities that need to be sold immediately in order to protect the estate. The review should also identify assets that are candidates for liquidation to pay debts and meet the other cash needs of the estate.

Managing the Decedent's Business

If the decedent owned a business, you should take whatever steps necessary to continue the business until it is sold or distributed to the beneficiaries, in order to protect its value. The decedent's partner, employee(s), family member(s), or someone who has expertise in the field may handle the management of the business, but whatever the case, the executor should oversee the management of the business until it is sold or distributed. Depending on the nature of the business, you may need to hire a professional, such as an accountant, to help you monitor the operation.

▼ **CHECKLISTS FOR ASSEMBLING AND PROTECTING ESTATE ASSETS**

Searching for Assets:
Review the decedent's tax returns.
Review the decedent's checkbook.
Inventory the safe deposit box.
Review the decedent's mail. Look for account statements and correspondence that identify other assets.
Conduct a search of the decedent's residence for personal records.
Ask family and friends of the decedent about any assets that they know of that were owned by the decedent.
Protecting Assets:
Change the locks on the decedent's residence.
Collect and put in safekeeping all valuable personal items, such as jewelry, paintings, artifacts, etc.
Secure automobiles in a garage or storage facility.
Change the mailing address to that of the executor.
Reregister all banks, brokerage accounts, and other financial accounts into the name of the estate.
Meet with the insurance agent to make sure that all assets are adequately covered.
Evaluate the securities portfolio.
Arrange for the continued management of the decedent's business or other enterprise.

Preparing an Inventory and Obtaining Appraisals

The basis for the probate proceeding is the list that you made of all assets that were registered in the decedent's individual name or otherwise owned by the decedent. This inventory may have to be filed with the probate court. Other probate assets may include things such as installment sales contracts, powers of appointment, tax and other refund claims, insurance policies on the lives of others, accounts receivable, Social Security benefits, Veterans Administration benefits, etc. The inventory should include unregistered personal property, such as jewelry, paintings, stamp collections, etc., as well. It's important to distinguish those personal items (tangible personal property) that have value from those that have no value at all. You can hire an appraiser to help you make this determination.

ESSENTIAL

The inventory is the most important piece of the administration. It will tell you whether or not probate is necessary, whether estate taxes will be due, and what items you will be responsible for.

Joint tenancy and tenancy by the entirety property, while not subject to probate, must be inventoried for estate taxes. Other nonprobate assets, such as life insurance, retirement plans, IRAs, revocable living trusts, and property subject to a contract, must also be inventoried for estate taxes. While not part of the probate proceeding in the decedent's state of domicile, real property titled in the decedent's name in other states must be accounted for as well. This property will be subject to an ancillary probate proceeding in the state in which it is located.

The descriptions on the inventory should be fairly specific. For each parcel, the real property description should include the property's address, land area, tax, city, county, state, or other identification reference number, an indication of whether or not the property is improved or unimproved, a listing of all encumbrances, and the date-of-death value. All lien holders should be described along with the nature of the lien and the amount that was owed at the decedent's date of death. Record the year, make, model, and vehicle identification number for all automobiles owned by the decedent. For all checking, savings, brokerage, and other accounts owned by the decedent, list the name of the institution, account number, and date-of-death balance. Describe securities by the name of the company, number of shares owned, and date-of-death value.

If the estate is required to file a Federal Estate Tax Return (Form 706), it would be helpful to categorize the assets on the inventory in accordance with the asset schedules on the return:

Schedule A - Real Estate
Schedule B - Stocks and Bonds
Schedule C - Mortgages, Notes, and Cash
Schedule D - Insurance on the Decedent's Life
Schedule E - Jointly Owned Property
Schedule F - Other Miscellaneous Property
Schedule G - Transfers During Decedent's Life
Schedule H - Powers of Appointment
Schedule I - Annuities

Valuation of Assets

All of the decedent's assets must be valued at their fair market value on the decedent's date of death. The Internal Revenue Service generally defines fair market value as "the price at which the property would change hands between a willing buyer and a willing seller, neither being under any compulsion to buy or to sell and both having reasonable knowledge of relevant facts . . ."

ALERT

Where an organized market exists, such as the New York Stock Exchange, the market price on the decedent's date of death is the value for estate tax purposes.

Valuations are based on a hypothetical sale where there is no actual sale in the market place. Valuation of some types of assets, such as a closely held business or a parcel of real estate, can be complex. Although the law does not require formal appraisals, the executor is responsible for substantiating all reported values. An executor should always obtain an appraisal by a qualified expert for assets that are difficult to value or whose value may be challenged by the IRS. Not all property needs to be appraised professionally. The rules for valuing specific types of property are fairly straightforward and covered by IRS regulations:

Type of Property	Required Method of Valuation
Bank Accounts	Account balance on the date of death.
Stocks and Bonds	The average (arithmetic mean) between the high and low trade price on the date of death.
Mutual Funds	The amount that would be received if the shares were redeemed on the date of death (the "bid" price or redemption value).
Real Estate	Fair market value.
Tenants by the Entirety (husband and wife)	One half of the fair market value.
Joint Tenancy (other than spouse)	Entire value of the property less the original contribution of the survivor.
Life Insurance (owned by decedent on his/her life)	Amount received by the estate or by the beneficiary.
Life Insurance (owned by decedent on his/her life)	Amount received by the estate or by the beneficiary.
Life Insurance on Someone Else's Life (owned by decedent)	The cost of buying another policy of the same value and same type on the same insured.
Annuity (joint and survivor contract)	The amount that the same insurance company would require for a single life annuity on the survivor.
Stocks of a Closely Held Company	Value is based on history and nature of business, economic outlook, book value, earnings capacity, dividend paying capacity, goodwill, recent sales of stock, and similar publicly traded company's stock.
Mortgages and Notes	The amount of the unpaid principal plus accrued interest to the date of death.

As executor, you should be aware that the IRS will assess a penalty for any asset that is substantially understated on the estate tax return (Form 706). Substantial understatement is a value that is 50% less than the amount determined to be the correct value.

▼ **CHECKLISTS FOR INVENTORY AND APPRAISALS**

Inventory
Prepare an inventory of all assets owned in the decedent's individual name (probate assets).
Inventory all jointly owned property (for estate tax return).
Inventory all property subject to a contract (for estate tax return).
Appraising the Property
Value all assets as of the decedent's date of death.
Follow the rules for valuing property prescribed by the IRS, or make sure that the appraiser understands the rules.
Obtain professional appraisals for real property, business interests, and other difficult-to-value assets.

Managing Estate Assets During the Period of Administration

An executor is a temporary administrator whose responsibilities are limited in duration. Ordinarily, the executor is not responsible for managing the decedent's portfolio during the period of administration, except for the temporary investment of cash. However, the executor does have the responsibility to preserve the assets for the beneficiaries of the estate. Essentially this means that you must exercise reasonable care and skill to prevent any substantial loss to the estate from occurring. As executor, you will be judged by how you carry out your responsibilities in settling the estate and not on any measure of investment performance.

Securities Portfolio

Contrary to popular belief, the executor is not responsible for making a profit for the estate and its beneficiaries during the period of administration. In addition to selling a security to raise cash, an investment should only be sold if it is apparent that it will lose substantial value if retained. If you are aware that a particular security will substantially diminish in value if held until it is distributed, as executor, you have a duty to sell that asset to prevent the loss. This is obviously a judgment call that requires careful analysis. In situations where the information about the investment is widely known, and suggests that some kind of action should be taken, you should take whatever steps are necessary to protect the estate against a loss. Sell a security in a situation where the probability of incurring a substantial loss is obviously high. Again, the primary duty is to preserve what is there.

ALERT

Decisions regarding the management of the securities portfolio should be motivated entirely by the need to protect these assets. Consulting with a professional investment advisor before you sell a security is a good idea.

Business Interests

If the decedent owned a business, the executor has a responsibility to dispose of it, unless the decedent's will directs that the business be continued. As the executor, you will be held responsible for any losses that occur if the business is managed for retention without authorization; however, you do have a responsibility to protect the business by managing it until it is sold or distributed. If you do not have the skills to properly manage the business, hire someone with the right expertise. This could be an employee of the company or a management firm that has experience in that particular industry or field. Review the financial statements of the business periodically or have a professional evaluate the operations and advise you of the financial condition of the enterprise. If the estate owns the majority, or all, of the outstanding shares of the company's stock, you should, as executor, get a seat on the board of directors and/or be elected a corporate officer of the company, in order to maintain control of the business until it is sold or distributed to the heirs.

Real Estate

The decedent may have owned residential or commercial real estate for investment. As with any other asset, the executor is responsible to preserve the value of these assets during the period of administration. This may entail maintaining rental cash flows, paying operating expenses, and making repairs to the property. If a real estate agent manages the property, you should monitor the agent's activities, including income collections, expenditures, and the other functions that are required under the management agreement. An evaluation of current market rent and rates should be made to determine if the rent or lease needs to be adjusted. Again, as with any other estate asset, the executor is responsible for preserving and protecting any real estate assets. Get advice from a real estate expert if needed.

Investing Cash

During the period of administration, income might be collected from a variety of different sources, including dividends, interest, rents, refunds, proceeds from the sale of assets, etc. Deposit these funds in an interest-bearing account. Operating cash (cash needed to pay day-to-day expenses) should be in a separate interest-bearing checking account. Funds that will not be needed for several months can be invested at higher interest rates in certificates of deposit at a bank or savings and loan institution. The maturity date of these deposits should obviously coincide with the date the funds will be needed to pay expenses or for distribution to the heirs.

Asset Management Checklist

- Invest all cash receipts in interest-bearing accounts.
- Sell only those assets that are needed to raise cash or prevent the estate from incurring an obvious substantial loss.
- If you lack the time or expertise to manage the decedent's property, hire a professional to either perform the task or advise you.

Estimating the Estate's Cash Requirements and Raising the Needed Funds

One of the most important tasks for executors is figuring out what bills and other expenses need to be paid and where the money to pay them is coming from. This will require careful review of the estate's cash flow and analysis of the assets it owns. As part of the process decisions will have to be made about the timing of payments and what assets will need to be liquidated to raise the needed cash.

Cash Requirements

As executor, you must determine the cash needs of the estate at the earliest possible opportunity and decide what assets are to be sold to raise the needed funds. Debts, court costs, taxes, administration expenses, family allowance, funeral expenses, etc. will need to be paid on a timely basis. Estimating the cash needs of the estate and determining when the funds will be needed should be a high priority. Prepare a schedule similar to the following to assist you with this task:

	Amount	Date Needed
Funeral Expense	$_____	_____
Family Allowance	$_____	_____
Creditors' Claims	$_____	_____
Mortgages & Liens	$_____	_____
Court Costs, Publication Fees, Appraisal Fees, & Other Administration Costs	$_____	_____
Executor's Fees	$_____	_____
Packing & Shipping Costs	$_____	_____
Cash Bequests	$_____	_____
Income Taxes	$_____	_____
Probate Fees	$_____	_____
Estimated Federal Estate & GST Tax	$_____	_____
Reserve for Contingencies	$_____	_____
Total Cash Needs	$_____	

Timing is important. Cash may be needed immediately to cover payments such as the premiums on insurance coverage to protect estate assets. The decedent's spouse and children may also need access to cash through the family allowance if other funds are not available. Expenses such as estate taxes should not be paid until the taxes are due, nine months from the date of death. Estimating the timing of these expenses is important in determining which assets are to be sold and when they should be sold.

Raising the Needed Cash

An executor is authorized to sell estate assets to pay expenses and meet other cash needs either under the terms of the decedent's will or local law. The typical language under a will gives the executor fairly broad powers, including the power to borrow funds. Here's an example of a typical provision:

"I authorize and empower my Personal Representative at any time prior to final distribution of my estate, without first selling personal property and without securing the prior approval of any court or judge, to sell and convey all or any part of my estate, real or personal, on such terms as it shall determine, and to borrow money and to mortgage, pledge, or otherwise hypothecate to secure the same, any of the said property, in such amounts, at such rates of interest, and upon such terms and conditions as it shall determine . . ."

ESSENTIAL

Use liquid assets (cash and cash equivalents) to cover the estate's cash needs before you consider selling securities, real estate, or other non-liquid assets.

Once the cash requirements for the estate have been determined, the executor should identify the liquid cash that is available from checking accounts, savings accounts, money market funds, insurance, etc. to pay expenses. Identify assets that need to be liquidated to raise the remaining funds. As the executor, you have the sole authority to select the assets that you deem appropriate for sale. However, before selling any assets, consider reviewing the sell list with the beneficiaries. Although you are not required to do this, a beneficiary may have an attachment to a particular asset and may prefer that another asset be selected for sale. A beneficiary may also want to advance the needed funds to the estate instead of having the assets sold. The executor should not speculate on the timing of the sale of these assets; they should be liquidated as soon as is practical. You cannot be criticized for taking quick and decisive action, even if the market goes up after the sale has been completed.

As an alternative to selling a security immediately, a stop loss order can be placed with a broker to protect the estate against any downside risk from a drop in price. Other assets may have to be sold at a private sale by sealed bid or auctioned through open, competitive bidding. The executor can select any method that is reasonable to obtain the best price. If you need help with these decisions, consult with the estate attorney or a professional financial advisor.

Checklist for Raising Funds

- Make a list of all required cash disbursements, and indicate the date funds will be needed to make the payments.
- Identify the assets that are to be sold to raise the needed funds, and consider discussing the plan with the estate beneficiaries.
- Sell the assets as soon as is practical. Do not try to "time the market."
- Deposit the proceeds in an interest-bearing account until the funds are needed for payment.

Paying Claims and Administration Expenses

There are basically two categories of estate debts: debts that were incurred by the decedent prior to his or her death, such as credit cards, taxes, medical bills, household bills, etc., and expenses that are incurred in the administration of the decedent's estate. The latter category includes items such as executor fees, attorney fees, court costs, appraisal fees, publishing expenses, etc. Under normal circumstances, you should pay claims and expenses as soon as possible to avoid any late-payment charges. However, as executor, you may need to postpone payment until you determine that there are sufficient funds to cover the expenses.

You also need to determine if the decedent had insurance to cover credit cards, mortgages, consumer loans, medical expenses, etc. If the estate's assets are not sufficient to cover all of the claims and expenses, some creditors may not be entitled to full payment. Every state has established priorities for payment when debts and expenses exceed the estate assets available to pay them. The following is the order of priority prescribed by law in most states:

1. Expenses of estate administration, including executor and attorney fees, publication expenses, appraisal fees, court costs, etc.
2. Funeral expenses (must be reasonable)
3. Family allowance in accordance with local law
4. Federal taxes
5. Expenses of the decedent's last illness
6. State taxes
7. All other general debts and expenses (most claims fall into this category)

If there is not enough money to pay all of the claims in a particular category, payment is made on a pro rata basis with the amount available.

Notice to Creditors

Local laws give creditors the opportunity to make a claim against an estate for amounts the decedent legitimately owed prior to death. This process takes two forms. One is a notice to creditors that is published in a newspaper of general circulation. The other is a direct notification by mail to those creditors who are known by the executor to have claims. The published notice to creditors advises unknown creditors of the death of the decedent and gives them the opportunity to submit their claims. It is published with a frequency and time period (i.e., once a week for three or four months, etc.) specified under local law.

ALERT

It's important to publish the notice to creditors as soon as possible. After the notice period expires, the estate will be protected from future claims.

The notice also gives instructions for submitting claims to the executor for payment. If unknown claims are received after the notice to creditors has expired, they are forever barred and payment should not be made. However, the beneficiaries may prefer that these claims be satisfied. Under these circumstances, the executor should obtain written direction from the beneficiaries to pay the claims. Debts that are known to the executor must be paid regardless of the expiration of the notice to creditors.

Payment of Claims

Sufficient information should be submitted with all claims so the executor can make a determination of their legitimacy. The claim should include the name and address of the claimant, the amount owed, the due date, a copy of the bill, and any other documentation to support the claim. Both known creditor claims and unknown creditor claims that are submitted within the notice to creditors period should be paid soon after the public notice to creditors has expired. If a claim is made that involves assets that were held as joint tenants with the decedent, an allocation of the expense incurred prior to and after death must be made. The decedent's estate pays the share of the expense that was incurred prior to death. The portion incurred after the decedent's death is the responsibility of the surviving joint owner(s).

If you reject a claim, you should immediately notify the claimant in writing. The claimant may be entitled to sue the estate if the suit is brought within the time period specified under local law. The executor usually has the authority to compromise and settle claims against the estate, and this should be taken into consideration as an alternative to litigation.

Payment of Expenses

Either through the decedent's will and/or state law, as executor, you have the authority to incur and pay all expenses out of the decedent's property that are incidental to the administration of the estate. These expenses include personal representative fees, attorney's fees, income taxes, estate taxes, real property taxes, appraisers' fees, advisors' fees, assessments, utility bills, insurance premiums, family allowance, court costs, etc. All of these expenses are expected to be paid in a timely manner. Disbursements for the family allowance should be made as soon as funds become available.

FACT

Taxes should be paid only when they are due and not before. This is particularly important with respect to the payment of estate taxes. The tax can be very large and the estate would lose interest on these funds if paid before the tax is due. Other expenses should be paid within a reasonable time after receipt of the bill and once funds are available.

Executor's Fees

Executor fees are usually paid just prior to completion of administration. Executors are entitled to receive reasonable compensation for the services they perform and responsibilities they assume when settling a decedent's estate. The executor's fee is an administration expense and a proper charge against the estate. If the executor is also the sole beneficiary of the estate, charging a fee is a good way to distribute funds to the executor/beneficiary and have it taxed at a lower tax rate. This occurs because the fee is a deductible expense for estate tax purposes. The estate is usually in a higher tax bracket than the executor/beneficiary, and the payment of fees can reduce the tax on these amounts.

The executor's fee is usually set by statute in each state and is often a percentage of the value of the estate assets. Some states allow both a percentage-of-assets fee and a fee based on the income received by the estate. Other states allow the executor to receive "reasonable compensation" instead of a percentage. In these states, the fee will depend on local practice and is usually approved by the probate court. It is a good idea to keep time records to substantiate the charges for the court and/or the beneficiaries of the estate. You may also need these records to justify any extraordinary charges for handling unusual tasks during the period of administration.

In most states, there are separate statutory provisions for trustee fees and the fees that executors are entitled to charge. If the same person is both the executor of the decedent's estate and his or her trustee, fees can usually be charged under both statutory provisions for administering and managing the same property, unless there is an exception in the law. If the will or local statutes call for reasonable fees, check with your local bank, estate attorneys, or other estate practitioners in your area to find out what the customary charges are.

Checklist for Payment of Claims and Expenses

- Publish a notice to creditors in accordance with local law.
- Verify that a claim is legitimate before payment is made.
- Unknown claims that are submitted after the notice to creditors has expired should not be paid. Check local law to verify this.
- Pay all expenses incurred in the administration of the estate promptly.
- If there are insufficient assets in the estate to cover all claims and expenses, refer to local law to determine the priority for payment.

CHAPTER 6

Administering the Estate: Taxes and More

Just because someone dies doesn't mean that the obligation to file tax returns ceases. In fact, even more tax returns and other filings may come into play during the period of administration. The executor needs to be aware of what filings will be required and their due dates. In addition, he or she may be required to make tax and other postmortem elections that will be beneficial to the estate and its beneficiaries. Having a general understanding of what these choices mean and seeking competent professional help to address these matters are prudent steps that the executor should take.

Who Is Responsible for Filing Tax Returns?

As executor, you are responsible for filing tax returns on behalf of the decedent's estate. These include the decedent's final income tax returns, fiduciary income tax returns, and the federal and state estate tax returns. As personal representative, you can be held personally liable for penalties and interest for failing to file these returns on a timely basis. The Internal Revenue Service also will hold a fiduciary personally liable for paying the decedent's debts, other than those that have priority over federal taxes.

ALERT

If you are handling a small estate, many of these tax filings will not apply. However, for larger estates, it's important that the executor be aware of the various forms that may come into play.

If an executor has not been appointed because there are no probate assets, the "executor" for the purposes of filing these returns is "any person in actual or constructive possession of any property of the decedent" (Internal Revenue Code Section 2203). An individual who inherits the decedent's property as a surviving joint owner would have this responsibility under this section of the code, as would the trustee of a trust created by the decedent.

The executor will have a number of postmortem tax planning opportunities when filing these returns and has an obligation to take advantage of them on behalf of the beneficiaries. These are usually very complex planning issues and you should seek competent advice from a qualified tax attorney, CPA, or other professional who specializes in this area.

The executor, or person having possession of the decedent's property, should file IRS Form 56, Notice Concerning Fiduciary Relationship, to inform the IRS of the capacity in which the person who is representing the decedent's estate is serving. The IRS will send all tax notices to this person once it receives the form.

The decedent's estate is a separate taxable entity requiring a tax identification number. The number is obtained by filing IRS Form SS-4, Application for Employer Identification Number. This identification number is required for filing the estate's annual fiduciary income tax returns.

FACT

The IRS Publication 559, "Survivors, Executors, and Administrators" and IRS Publication 950, "Introduction to Estate and Gift Taxes" outline your obligations and will assist you with these tasks. The publications can be downloaded from the IRS website at *www.irs.gov/ Forms-&-Pubs.*

The form can either be mailed or faxed to the IRS. The number can also be obtained by telephone, with the requirement that the form be mailed or faxed within twenty-four hours after the call. However, it may take up to four weeks to get the number. The quickest way is to apply online at *www.irs.gov.* You will get your number immediately upon completion of the application.

The decedent's Social Security number is used as the identification number for the decedent's final income tax returns and federal estate tax return.

Other IRS forms may need to be filed during the administration of an estate. They are outlined in Appendix B.

Decedent's Final Income Tax Returns

The executor is responsible for filing any tax returns that the decedent would have been required to file if living, including his or her final individual income tax returns. However, the surviving spouse shares this responsibility if a joint return is filed. Filing a joint return with the surviving spouse is an election that the executor must make. The following should be taken into consideration in making this choice:

- Will splitting the income attributable to either spouse lower the tax bracket upon which the income is taxed?
- Is there an advantage to using the decedent's medical expenses against the surviving spouse's income, assuming the decedent had not earned substantial offsetting income prior to death?
- Does the decedent have operating losses or a capital loss carryover that can be used against the surviving spouse's income?
- Can the surviving spouse pay more than his or her share of the tax due in order to pass more of the estate on to the children or other beneficiaries?

- Is there a reason to avoid joint and several (individual) liability with the surviving spouse by filing separately?
- Is faster response to a request needed for an early determination of the tax and release from liability?
- Will filing separately allow better utilization of medical, casualty loss, and miscellaneous expense deductions by lowering the threshold amounts at which point these expenses become deductible?

It may be necessary to file federal and state income tax returns if the decedent died before filing these returns for the previous year. For example, if the decedent died in March, but had not filed returns for the previous year, income tax returns will have to be filed for that year and the year of death. The decedent's final federal income tax return is due on the day the decedent would have been required to file the return, April 15. The decedent's Social Security number is used as the tax identification number on this return. The executor should file Form 5495 with the IRS to request an early determination of the tax and a discharge from personal liability.

Fiduciary Income Tax Returns

The executor must file an income tax return for the estate for each year of administration. In general, beneficiaries of an estate are taxed on any income that is paid out to them during the period of administration. All income that is retained during the estate's tax year is taxed to the estate, which has a separate rate schedule. The tax on estate and trust income is higher than for individuals. Since any income in an estate that is not needed to pay estate expenses will ultimately be distributed to the beneficiaries, it almost always makes sense to distribute the excess income to the beneficiaries and avoid having it taxed at the higher rate. This can be done through payment of the family allowance or direct distributions to the beneficiaries.

In most states, early distributions to a beneficiary cannot be made until the notice to creditors has expired (i.e., during the period that claims can be presented for payment). Some states may require prior court approval for any distribution. Distributions that are made prior to closing the estate must be authorized under the decedent's will or local law.

The executor can select a tax year other than December 31 for the estate, for example, May 1 to April 30. This can have tax planning advantages; beneficiaries can defer taxes on any unusually high income during the period of administration. The timing of the payment of deductible expenses can also reduce taxes. For example, if deductions exceed the estate's taxable income for any taxable year other than the final year of administration, the excess deductions are lost. However, if these excess deductions are incurred in the final year for the estate, they can be passed out to and deducted by the beneficiaries on their individual income tax returns.

If the administration of the estate goes beyond two taxable years from the decedent's date of death, the personal representative must make estimated tax payments based on the estimated taxable income projected for those years. These are complicated tax issues that involve some sophisticated income tax planning techniques, and a qualified CPA should be consulted.

65-Day Rule

An executor can elect to treat distributions made within 65 days of the close of the estate's tax year as having been made on the last day of that tax year. For example, if the estate's tax year is December 31, 2013, income can be distributed in the first 65 days of 2014 and reported as if it had been paid in 2014. This rule makes it easier to distribute estate income to beneficiaries and can potentially minimize the income tax liability. The 65-day rule allows the executor to determine with certainty if there would be an advantage to distributing the income to low-bracket beneficiaries in any one year.

Federal Estate Tax Return

Generally, if an estate tax return is required, the executor or trustee is responsible for filing it. If the value of the decedent's gross estate exceeds the exemption equivalent (in 2013 this amount was $5,250,000), a federal estate tax return is due no later than nine months from the decedent's date of death. The Federal Estate Tax Return, Form 706, can be a very complex return to prepare. An executor almost always needs to hire an attorney or CPA who specializes in this area of taxation to complete the return. It is important that the executor identify who will prepare the return, set deadlines for gathering information, obtain appraisals, and begin the preparation of the return no later than thirty days from the due date of the return to allow for timely completion and filing.

A review of the estate's detailed inventory is the first step in determining whether an estate tax return must be filed. The IRS requires that 50% of all property that was owned jointly with the decedent's spouse be included in the estate for tax purposes unless the surviving spouse can prove he or she contributed more than 50% to the acquisition of the property. That amount is deducted from the total value of the asset and what remains is taxable in the decedent's estate. If the property was owned jointly with someone other than the surviving spouse, 100% of the value is included. However, if the other owner can prove that he or she contributed to the acquisition of the property, the amount of the contribution is excluded from the value.

When the value of the gross estate is close to the exemption equivalent, the executor should consider filing a return, even if it does not appear that a return is required. If you do not file a return and the IRS later determines that the value was incorrect and a return was, in fact, required, the IRS will assess penalties and interest. The decision to file a return, under these circumstances, should be based on whether the estate includes assets that are difficult to appraise (e.g., real estate and business interests), and whose value could be called into question by the IRS. The executor could be held personally liable for the penalty and interest if a return is required and not filed.

The decedent's Social Security number should be used as the tax identification number on the return. The surviving spouse's Social Security number cannot be used. If the decedent did not have a Social Security number, the executor must obtain one by filing Form SS-5 with the local Social Security Administration Office. An estimate of the tax should be made as soon as the necessary information is available to allow the executor to raise the needed funds.

The executor (or trustee) is personally liable for correctly filing the estate tax return and paying any taxes that are due. To get relief from this exposure, the executor should file Form 5495, Request for Discharge from Personal Liability under Internal Revenue Code Section 2204 or 6905. The IRS has nine months from the date the request is received to make a final determination that the amount of the tax reported on the return is correct and the executor is no longer liable. If the IRS does not respond within the nine-month period, any additional tax liability will be the responsibility of the beneficiaries and not the executor. Take care when making distributions of the estate's assets to beneficiaries prior to receiving this discharge. As executor, you should withhold sufficient funds to cover any potential additional assessments until the discharge has been received from the IRS or the nine-month period has lapsed.

Right of Recovery of Estate Taxes

In general, if the second-to-die spouse's estate includes a marital trust (i.e., estate trust, power of appointment trust, QTIP trust, or qualified domestic trust) that he or she was a beneficiary of, the second-to-die spouse's estate is entitled to recover from the marital trust the estate tax attributable to that trust. If the executor or trustee does not exercise this recovery right, the amount of the tax will be treated as a gift to the beneficiaries of the marital trust. If the second-to-die spouse's will, or trust, directs that the tax not be recovered from the marital trust, then there is no gift.

QUESTION

What is a State Death or Inheritance Tax Return?
The decedent's state of domicile may require that an estate and/or inheritance tax return be filed. Generally, an inheritance tax is based on what a person inherits from an estate, while an estate tax is based on the value of the decedent's estate. Not all states assess a state death tax, but the executor needs to make sure that a state return is filed and the tax paid if required.

Generation-Skipping Transfer Tax (GSTT)

Executors and trustees have the responsibility to report all generation-skipping transfers made by the decedent and pay any taxes that may be due. Generation-skipping transfers are those that are made to grandchildren, descendants who are at least two generations younger than the decedent, and unrelated persons who are 37½ years or more younger than the decedent. These individuals are called "skip persons."

In addition, transfers to trusts in which all interests (i.e., the right to receive income and principal) are held by skip persons are generation-skipping transfers. While all generation-skipping transfers must be reported, only amounts in excess of the GSTT exemption ($5,250,000 for 2013) are subject to the generation-skipping tax. The tax may be due immediately or sometime in the future, as is the case with transfers through a trust. Transfers that must be reported fall into three general categories:

- *Direct skip*—a transfer, subject to federal gift or estate tax, of a property interest directly to a skip person.
- *Taxable distribution*—a distribution from a trust (during its term) to a skip person.
- *Taxable termination*—the termination of an interest in a trust that results in a distribution to a skip person.

An executor is required to file a gift tax return, Form 709, to report all pre-death direct-skip transfers that the decedent made and had not reported. An executor is also required to report any generation-skip transfers that occur at the decedent's death under a will or trust on the estate tax return, Form 706. Again, a qualified CPA, tax attorney, or other tax professional should handle these tax filing requirements.

Checklist for Filing Tax Returns

- Apply for a tax identification number (employer identification number) using Form SS-4.
- Make a list of the returns that need to be filed and their due dates.
- Estimate the amounts of the tax as soon as possible so the needed funds can be raised.
- Hire a tax attorney or CPA to complete the fiduciary income tax returns, estate tax return (Form 706), and state death or inheritance tax return, and assist with any tax planning matters.
- If the value of the estate is close to the exemption equivalent amount, consider filing the estate tax return even though a return may not be required.
- At the time the estate tax return, if required, is filed, request an early determination of the tax and relief from personal liability by filing Form 5495, Request for Discharge from Personal Liability under Internal Revenue Code Section 2204 or 6905.

Making Tax and Other Postmortem Planning Elections

Executors and trustees have a responsibility to take advantage of tax planning opportunities that will benefit the decedent's heirs. An executor must also consider the effect several tax elections will have on the estate itself. This process can involve lengthy tax analyses. They include the deceased spousal unused exclusion (DSUE) election, the allocation of administration expenses, medical expenses and casualty losses, the qualified terminable interest property (QTIP) election, allocation of the generation-skipping transfer tax (GSTT) exemption, the alternate valuation election, the special use valuation, disclaimers, and extension of time to pay estate taxes. Other issues that can affect a favorable tax result include making the right choice in handling income in respect of a decedent (IRD) and the qualified domestic trust election (QDOT).

Deceased Spousal Unused Exclusion (DSUE)

The executor can make an election to allow the decedent's surviving spouse's estate to use the decedent's unused exclusion (exemption) amount upon his or her subsequent death. This provision under the Internal Revenue Code is commonly referred to as the *portability election*. Typically, an estate plan will incorporate a credit shelter trust provision under a person's revocable living trust to accomplish this (i.e., preserving the exclusion amount for both husband and wife). If there is no such trust provision in the decedent's estate plan, the executor can make this election to "preserve" the exclusion ($5,250,000 for 2013) for use in the surviving spouse's estate. However, the DSUE amount is only available if the executor makes the election on Form 706, whether or not a return is required to be filed. This issue should be discussed with the family's estate planning attorney and a decision made as to whether or not to make this election.

Administration Expenses, Casualty Losses, and Medical Expenses

Administration expenses, such as fees paid to attorneys, accountants, appraisers, and the executor, can be deducted on either the estate tax return (Form 706) or the fiduciary income tax return (Form 1041). This option also applies to casualty losses. The estate tax will be reduced if these deductions are taken on the estate tax return and correspondingly the income tax liability will be higher. If taken on the income tax returns, the reverse is true.

Medical expenses can also be deducted on the decedent's final individual income tax return (Form 1040) or on the federal estate tax return. Normally, these expenses are deductible in the taxable year in which they were paid. However, medical expenses incurred before death can be deducted on the decedent's final return if paid within one year of the decedent's death. The executor should compare the tax savings effect, taking into consideration that medical deductions are limited to the excess over a threshold percentage of adjusted gross income on an individual federal income tax return. If the deductions are claimed on the individual income tax return, the executor must file a waiver of right to claim the deduction on the estate tax return.

Qualified Terminable Interest Property (QTIP) Election

Property that passes to a surviving spouse is deducted from the decedent's adjusted gross estate (marital deduction) to determine the amount of federal estate tax. The IRS allows an unlimited marital deduction for property that passes directly to a surviving spouse or is used for the benefit of the surviving spouse. This does not eliminate the estate tax on the marital deduction assets; it simply defers the tax until the death of the surviving spouse. The most common types of qualifying marital deduction, other than direct transfers to a surviving spouse, are payments to a surviving spouse as a beneficiary of a life insurance policy or pension plan, assets that pass to a surviving spouse as a result of owning property jointly, and transfers of qualified terminable interest property (QTIP). QTIP transfers are usually done through a trust. For a trust to qualify for the marital deduction, four requirements must be met:

1. The property must "pass" from the decedent.
2. The surviving spouse must be entitled to an income interest for life.
3. No other beneficiary may have any rights in the trust during the surviving spouse's lifetime.
4. An irrevocable QTIP election must be made.

The election is made on the estate tax return, which will qualify all or a fraction of the QTIP trust property for the marital deduction. This is done by listing the QTIP property on Schedule M of the estate tax return (Form 706). The advantage of the QTIP trust disposition is that it allows a partial marital deduction election. This permits the executor to elect an amount that will result in some tax being paid at the decedent's death, if it will be tax-cost effective to both the decedent's estate and that of the surviving spouse. Again, hiring a CPA or other tax expert to assist with this analysis is wise.

Allocation of the Generation-Skipping Transfer Tax (GSTT) Exemption

Every individual who transfers property subject to the GSTT is entitled to an exemption ($5,250,000 for 2013). The exemption can be allocated during the individual's lifetime or at death. The executor or trustee has the responsibility to allocate the GSTT exemption to any property transferred by the decedent to a "skip person." Where transfers are made by the decedent through a trust, the allocation needs to be coordinated with the trustee to allow proper funding. Ideally, the allocation should be made to those assets that have the highest potential for growth, since the appreciation will also be protected from the tax.

The GSTT exemption must be allocated at the time of death and no later than the due date of the Gift and Generation-Skipping Tax Return (Form 709) for gifts that were unreported prior to the decedent's death. For transfers made under the decedent's will or trust, the exemption is required to be allocated no later than the due date for the estate tax return (Form 706). With respect to QTIP trusts that distribute assets to skip persons at the death of the surviving spouse, the spouse is considered the transferor of these assets for GSTT purposes, which could "waste" the decedent's exemptions. The executor can remedy this by making a "reverse QTIP election" on the decedent's estate tax return. This would have the effect of treating the decedent as the transferor of the funds instead of the decedent's spouse.

If the executor does not make an election, the GSTT exemption is first allocated to direct skips made by the decedent prior to death, then to generation-skipping transfers made at death, and finally to trusts created by the decedent that will result in generation-skipping transfers.

Alternate Valuation

An executor can elect to use an alternate date for valuing the decedent's assets to determine the federal estate tax. This alternate date is six months from the decedent's death. This election gives relief to estates that experience a decline in value of assets shortly after the decedent's death. If the decline is large enough, the estate could have difficulty paying the tax. The election has the effect of lowering the estate tax by allowing the use of the lower market value upon which the tax is based. Using the lower value for estate taxes also lowers the cost basis on the property inherited by the heirs. If the alternate value is used, the result will be a higher income tax upon sale of these assets at some future date. If property is sold or distributed within six months of the decedent's death, the asset(s) will be valued as of the date of sale or distribution if the alternate (i.e., six month) valuation election is made. The election can only be made if it has the result of reducing the value of the gross estate and therefore the estate tax.

Special Use Valuation

An executor can elect to value real property that is used for farming or other trade or business at its current use value rather than at its highest and best use value. For example, if a farm were located in an area that could presently or sometime in the future be used for residential, commercial, or industrial development, the highest and best use value would be considerably higher than its current use as a farm. There is a limitation, however. The total value of the property may not be decreased from its fair market value by a specific amount ($1,070,000 in 2013). This provision permits a lower value to be used for estate tax purposes and is intended to allow the decedent's family to continue operating the business rather than forcing its sale to pay taxes. To qualify for the special use valuation (Internal Revenue Code Section 2032A) option, several conditions must be met:

1. The decedent must have been a U.S. citizen or resident at the time of his or her death.
2. The property must be located in the United States, passed by the decedent to a "qualified heir," and used for a "qualified use."
3. The value of the business (i.e., the real property plus supplies, equipment, etc.) must comprise 50% or more of the decedent's gross estate

adjusted by any mortgages or other indebtedness on the property ("adjusted value").

4. The real property, by itself, must be 25% or more of the adjusted value of the gross estate.
5. The property must have been used by the decedent, or a member of his or her family, for a qualified use (i.e., farming or a trade or business) for five of the eight years prior to the death of the decedent.
6. The decedent or a member of his or her family must have "materially participated" in the operation of the business for five of the eight years preceding the decedent's death.
7. The heir(s) must receive a present interest in the property.
8. The executor must make the irrevocable election on the Estate Tax Return, Form 706.
9. Anyone with an interest in the property must sign an agreement accepting personal liability for any taxes that may be due as a result of the failure of the property to qualify for the special use valuation.
10. One or more of the decedent's heirs must continue to meet the material participation requirement for at least ten years.

Another election available to a decedent's estate concerns the payment of taxes on a closely held business interest. If the closely held business interest represents more than 35% of the decedent's adjusted gross estate, the estate tax attributable to the business can be paid over fourteen years (Internal Revenue Code Section 6166). This tax can also be paid at a favorable interest rate. Making the special use valuation election could disqualify the estate from making use of this option because it may lower the value of the closely held business below 35%.

If the value of the decedent's incorporated business is 35% or more of the adjusted gross estate, the IRS allows favorable tax treatment for sale of the company's stock to pay the estate tax (Internal Revenue Code Section 303). The special use valuation election could disqualify this option by reducing the value below the 35% threshold. Again, the executor needs to compare the benefits of each option before making the choice.

Disclaimers

If an heir legally declines (through a disclaimer) his or her inheritance under a will, trust, life insurance policy, or as a survivor on jointly held property, that interest passes to someone else. The use of disclaimers is primarily an estate tax planning election, but they are also used to correct drafting errors in wills and trusts and to achieve other dispositive objectives. Someone making a qualified disclaimer of property is deemed to have pre-deceased the decedent, and the property interest passes to the successor in interest under a decedent's will or trust, by operation of law, under the terms of a contract or under the laws of intestacy. For example, John's will says that his entire estate is to go to his wife, Mary, if she survives him. If she does not survive John, then his estate is to go to their two children. If Mary disclaims her interest under John's will, she is deemed to have predeceased John and the children inherit John's estate. A qualified disclaimer removes the ownership of the property from the estate of the person disclaiming the interest and can reduce the estate tax for the person making the disclaimer. A disclaimer is an irrevocable refusal to receive an interest in property.

A disclaimer can save taxes in a variety of situations. It can be used to pass property to someone without incurring a gift tax. In the previous example, Mary, in effect, has made a tax-free gift to her children by disclaiming her interest under John's will. Assuming that John's estate is under the exempt amount (i.e., $5,250,000 in 2013), and therefore no estate tax is due, his property would pass tax-free to the children. If Mary took her inheritance and then gave it to the children, she would have to pay a gift tax on the amount over the annual gift tax exclusion.

Correcting adverse conditions is another use of disclaimers. For example, if the special use valuation would be beneficial to the decedent's estate, but the property does not qualify because it passes to a nonqualified heir, the heir can disclaim the interest and qualify the property to minimize the estate tax.

To maximize sheltering assets from federal estate tax in the estate of the second to die, the family trust should be funded with the exemption equivalent (i.e., $5,250,000 in 2013). Underfunding can occur if most or all of the assets in the decedent's estate are owned jointly. For example, if a decedent had $3,000,000 in his revocable living trust and the rest of his assets, which were valued at $4,000,000, were owned jointly with his wife, his family trust would be underfunded. In other words, if the exemption equivalent amount is $5,250,000 (year 2013), the trust would be underfunded by $2,250,000 ($5,250,000 less $3,000,000). She could disclaim enough of her interest in the joint assets (i.e., $2,250,000) to fully fund the trust. Those assets would be deemed to be his alone at the time of his death and would pass under his pour-over will to fund the family trust for the full amount of the exemption equivalent.

Disclaimers can also be used to correct drafting errors in wills and trusts. For example, a marital-deduction trust will not qualify for the marital deduction if it allows either income or principal to be paid to someone other than the decedent's spouse. If a trust, for example, permits distributions to the decedent's children, they could disclaim their interest in the trust to correct the problem and qualify the trust for the marital deduction.

If a surviving spouse is the trustee of a family trust (i.e., credit shelter trust) and the trust provides that the surviving spouse can distribute principal to herself in accordance with an "ascertainable standard" (i.e., health, education, maintenance, and support), the trust assets are not subject to estate taxes upon her death. However, if the "ascertainable standard" language is flawed because it contains a disqualifying word, the surviving spouse could disclaim her right to receive a distribution under that word, thus correcting the flaw.

Income in Respect of a Decedent (IRD)

Income earned by a decedent, but not actually or constructively received by the decedent prior to death, is called *income in respect of a decedent*, or *IRD*. Examples of IRD include unpaid salary, deferred compensation, retirement plan benefits, accrued interest and dividends on securities, royalties, installment obligations, and accounts receivable. This income is not reported on the decedent's final income tax return (Form 1040), but instead is reported on the estate income tax return (Form 1041) or the individual income tax return of the beneficiary who receives the IRD. IRD is also included in the decedent's estate for estate taxes, but does not get a step-up in basis as other assets do. However, an offsetting income tax deduction is allowed for the estate tax that is attributable to the inclusion of IRD in the decedent's gross estate.

The executor, and trustee, should attempt to distribute IRD to satisfy a charitable bequest or to lower tax bracket beneficiaries. If a trust is involved in the decedent's estate plan, the executor could distribute an interest in IRD, before it is received, to the trust. In turn, the trust could, if it permitted, distribute the IRD to multiple beneficiaries who may be in lower tax brackets. The income tax deduction for the estate tax paid on the IRD can be passed through the trust for use by the trust's beneficiaries.

The income tax impact on IRD can be reduced by choosing an appropriate tax year for the estate. If the receipt of IRD is known, you can split the income between two or more tax years. This might result in less tax than if the income was reported in one year. Taxable IRD can also be offset by electing to take deductions on the estate's income tax return instead of the estate tax return. The taxation of IRD can also be minimized by timing deductible expenses to coincide with the receipt of IRD.

Accrued interest on Series E and EE U.S. Savings Bonds, which is normally reportable upon redemption of the bonds, is IRD. The executor can elect to report the accrued interest on the decedent's final income tax return, thereby eliminating it as IRD. If the decedent's final return has a small amount of income and/or large deductions, including this interest on the decedent's final return could significantly reduce the overall tax liability. A comparative analysis of the various options is necessary to determine the right course of action.

Qualified Domestic Trust (QDOT)

The marital deduction is not allowed if the surviving spouse is not a U.S. citizen. From the government's point of view, if the marital deduction were allowed in this case, the non–U.S. citizen surviving spouse could move back to his or her country and the tax on the marital assets would be difficult, if not impossible, to collect. There are two ways to achieve the marital deduction if the surviving spouse is a non–U.S. citizen.

The deduction will be allowed if the surviving spouse is a resident at all times following the death of the decedent and becomes a citizen before the decedent's estate tax return is filed.

The deduction is also available if the marital deduction property is transferred to a qualified domestic trust (QDOT) by the decedent's will or trust, or if the QDOT was designated as a beneficiary under property subject to a contract. The surviving spouse can also transfer to the QDOT any property that he or she received as a joint owner or beneficiary, if the transfer is made before the decedent's estate tax return is filed.

The basic requirements for qualifying a power of appointment trust, QTIP trust, and charitable remainder trust for the marital deduction also apply to the QDOT. However, there are other requirements that specifically apply to the QDOT:

1. The trust must require that at least one trustee be a U.S. citizen or domestic corporation.
2. The trust must require that no distributions of principal be made unless the trustee, who is a citizen or a domestic corporation, has the right to withhold the estate tax on the distribution.
3. The executor must make the QDOT election on the decedent's estate tax return.

Sale of Closely Held Stock

If an estate owns a closely held company, liquidating the stock can have adverse consequences. If a closely held stock is redeemed to pay estate taxes, it will be treated as a dividend and subject to ordinary income tax. However, if the closely held stock represents more than 35% of the adjusted gross estate, less certain allowable deductions, and only enough shares are redeemed to pay estate taxes and funeral and administration expenses, the redemption will not be considered a dividend. This is called a Section 303 stock redemption, which is a reference to the Internal Revenue Code section that allows the exclusion (IRC Section 303.) If the redemption represents all of the decedent's holdings, or if after the redemption the estate will own less than 50% of the voting power of the company, the sale will be tax-free. This exception is covered under Section 302 of the code.

Partnerships

If the estate owns a partnership interest, an election (IRC Section 754) can be made on the partnership return that allows the "internal partnership account value" to receive a step-up in basis. This will be advantageous for the individual or trust that receives the partnership interest from the decedent's estate in terms of depreciation and the allocation of future partnership earnings. The "outside ownership value," or the value that is carried by the individual or trust that inherits the partnership interest, is the value (date of death or alternate value) reported on the decedent's estate tax return. If no return is required, then it is the date-of-death value. This value is also the cost basis to determine gain or loss upon sale of the partnership interest.

Extension of Time to Pay Estate Taxes

The federal estate tax is due nine months from the decedent's date of death. However, there are four provisions under the Internal Revenue Code that allow the executor to defer the payment, which may be useful if the estate or trust has assets that cannot be easily liquidated:

1. The executor may apply for an extension of twelve months for the amount of cash shortage in the estate to pay the tax. The request may be granted only for a "reasonable cause," as to why the tax cannot be paid when due.
2. If the executor can show "reasonable cause," an extension of ten years may be granted for the payment of the tax. However, the extension will only be granted for one year at a time (IRC Section 6161).
3. If the decedent's estate is entitled to a reversionary or remainder interest in property, the executor can elect to postpone the tax attributable to that interest until six months after the present interest in the property terminates (IRC Section 6163).
4. If the estate owns a closely held business interest (defined as 45 or fewer shareholders/partners or 20% or more of the interest included in the gross estate) which represents more than 35% of the adjusted gross estate, the personal representative can elect to have the tax attributable to that interest paid over fourteen years. The estate can make interest-only payments for the first five years, but must begin making principal payments after that (IRC Section 6166).

These elections require a thorough analysis of the interest costs associated with deferring the payment of the tax. For some deferral elections, such as the deferral of tax on a closely held business interest, a special interest rate is available. Other elections assess a higher interest rate. The executor may also want to elect for deferral so assets that need to be sold to pay the tax can be liquidated in a timely manner. Obviously, the economic benefit of deferring the sale of assets should be evaluated before any election is made.

Tax Elections Checklist

Determine which tax issues and elections may apply to the estate (and trust):

- Allocation of administration and medical expenses and casualty losses
- QTIP election
- Allocation of the GSTT election
- Alternate valuation
- Special use valuation
- Disclaimers
- Taxation of IRD
- QDOT election
- Section 302 and 303 stock redemption
- Partnership step-up in basis election
- Extension of time to pay estate taxes election

Once the elections have been identified:

- Determine the marginal estate and estate income tax rates.
- Obtain the marginal income tax rate of all beneficiaries.
- Discuss the elections with a CPA or tax attorney.
- Evaluate the cost/benefit of each option.
- Discuss the choices with the beneficiaries and/or their financial advisors.
- Make the appropriate election.

CHAPTER 7

From Maintaining Records to Closing the Estate

Keeping thorough and accurate records of the administration is a must. You cannot properly manage the estate and keep track of what you are doing if there is no record of administrative activities. In addition, you need good records to inform beneficiaries about the administration. The executor is also required to follow special accounting rules. He or she should have a general understanding of these rules even if an accountant is hired to handle the recordkeeping, because some administration decisions may be based on how they are accounting. The final administering steps are closing the estate and distributing what's left to the beneficiaries. This process requires attention to detail to make sure that each beneficiary receives exactly what he or she is entitled to under the will.

Preparing and Maintaining Accounting Records

The executor must maintain and make available to beneficiaries and other interested parties, such as the estate's creditors, a detailed record of all activities pertaining to the administration of the estate. The court may also require an accounting for its approval. Most jurisdictions have a prescribed format for court accountings. Although a court accounting is a matter of public record and available to interested persons, it is primarily prepared for review by the court.

ESSENTIAL

One of the unique characteristics of estate accounting is the need to distinguish income from principal. The decedent's will and/or state law will determine how the executor accounts for, and separates, the two. Most states have adopted the Uniform Principal and Income Act in one form or another. The purpose of the Act is to standardize the accounting rules for both estates and trusts.

The decedent's will is the first source of authority for how estate transactions are to be handled. If the will is silent with respect to how a particular accounting transaction is to be handled, the executor should look to state law and the Uniform Principal and Income Act for guidance. Although an individual's will may have some specific directives on how particular transactions are handled, accounting rules for estates have some common characteristics:

- All income accrued but not received prior to the decedent's death must be allocated to principal.
- For any property specifically bequeathed under a will (or trust), net income earned after the will maker's death belongs to the beneficiary. This is true even if the property is not distributed until the estate is settled. Income and expenses that are associated with the property should be accounted for separately from the other estate assets.
- Where a sum of money is bequeathed under a will (i.e., a pecuniary bequest), the beneficiary is not entitled to the income earned during

the period of administration. That is, if a bequest of $10,000 is made, the beneficiary gets $10,000, not $10,000 plus interest.

- All expenses incurred in connection with the settlement of the estate, including debts, funeral expenses, family allowances, attorney's fees, personal representative's fees, accountant's fees, court costs, and estate taxes, are charges against principal.
- Generally, the beneficiary who receives what is left after specific bequests, payment of expenses, etc. is entitled to the income earned during the period of administration.
- If a decedent bequeaths his or her residuary estate to a trust, the income earned during the administration of the estate is allocated to and becomes attributable to the trust.

Estate accounting covers only those assets that are under the direct control of the executor (i.e., probate assets) and all receipts and disbursements in connection with the administration of the estate. Joint assets and property subject to a contract (i.e., life insurance, trust assets, retirement plans, etc.), although inventoried for federal estate tax purposes, are not part of the decedent's probate estate and therefore not included in the estate accounting. The inventory of assets owned by the decedent individually is the basis of the probate estate. It must reflect all changes that take place during the course of administration. The inventory will change as new assets are discovered, property is sold to raise funds to cover expenses, and when distributions are made to beneficiaries.

FACT

In preparing the estate accounting, the executor should obtain the reporting format required by the probate court that has jurisdiction over the estate. Although the format may differ slightly from state to state, estate accountings do have a common structure.

All financial activities that take place during the administration must be reported to the probate court, the estate's beneficiaries, and other interested parties. Income and principal transactions are reported separately.

Accounting Checklist

- Identify all assets and sources of income that will be subject to probate.
- Determine if an estate accounting must be filed with the probate court, and obtain the court's required accounting format.
- Review the decedent's will, Uniform Probate Code, and Uniform Principal and Income Act in the jurisdiction where the estate is being administered for guidance in maintaining the accounting records.
- If necessary, retain a qualified accountant.
- Establish a tickler to provide periodic accounting reports to the beneficiaries of the estate.

Distributing Assets to the Beneficiaries

Estate assets can and should be distributed to the decedent's beneficiaries as soon as estate expenses have been paid. However, if there is the possibility of additional taxes as a result of an audit of the estate tax return, you should withhold sufficient funds to cover the estimated assessment. The reason for this should be obvious. If there is an additional estate tax and the executor cannot collect the tax due from the beneficiaries, he or she is personally liable for the tax. If the Internal Revenue Service does not respond within nine months from the date of the request, the executor is relieved of personal liability.

ALERT

You should consider making partial distributions before the clearance is received if it is unlikely there will be an additional tax, but retain sufficient assets to cover unpaid expenses.

Nonprobate assets, such as jointly owned property, insurance proceeds, trust assets, retirement plan proceeds, etc., pass by the terms of the contract or by operation of law. If they are not subject to creditor claims and not needed to cover debts, administration expenses, and taxes, they should be allowed to pass to the surviving owners or beneficiaries. Personal effects and certain specific bequests can also be distributed shortly after death if they will not be needed to pay expenses.

Joint Assets and Contract Property

Joint assets must be valued for estate tax purposes. Once this is done, the executor can assist the surviving owner(s) to transfer the asset into the name(s) of the new owner(s). The property should be retitled so the survivors can sell or otherwise take full control of the property. The survivor must present a certified copy of the death certificate to the bank, brokerage firm, or other financial institution where the account is located. If the property is shares of stocks and bonds, the death certificate is sent to the transfer agent for the company that issued the stock or bond along with the certificate. Real property is transferred to the surviving joint owner(s) by recording a certified copy of the death certificate with the local real property recordation office.

In regard to contract property, if the decedent's estate is named as a beneficiary under a contract, the executor is responsible for making the claim. The role of the executor, if someone other than the estate is named, is to inform the beneficiary that he or she is the beneficiary and, if appropriate, assist with making the claim. To make claims on life insurance policies, the beneficiary needs to obtain and complete a claim form from the insurance company that issued the policy. Every insurance company has its own form and will usually require that the insurance policy and a certified copy of the death certificate accompany the completed form when the claim is submitted. It is a good idea to submit it by registered or certified mail. Keep a copy of the claim form. Other types of property subject to a contract, such as retirement plans, may also require a claim form and a certified copy of the death certificate. The beneficiary should contact the plan administrator for the forms and claim procedures. Several payment options may be available under a retirement plan. A beneficiary would be well advised to consult with a tax advisor before selecting an option and making the claim.

Personal Effects

As a practical matter, unless otherwise specified in the decedent's will, household items are considered the property of the surviving spouse or other joint owner of the decedent's residence. However, a decedent's will usually provides for the disposition of this property. A typical will provision covering personal property might read like this:

"I give all my personal and household effects, such as jewelry, clothing, automobiles, furniture, furnishings, silver, books, pictures, and any insurance on such property, to my wife, if she survives me; or, if she does not survive, I give my tangible personal property to my children who survive me in equal shares as they shall agree, or if they do not agree, as my personal representative shall, in my personal representative's discretion, determine."

ALERT

Distributing personal effects "equally" can sometimes be tricky. If there are disagreements, you can use different methods that will be fair to all beneficiaries.

Distributing personal property to the decedent's surviving spouse under this sort of dispositive language is a nonevent, since she would already have possession. Valuable items, however, do need to be inventoried for tax purposes. In the event that the spouse does not survive, the will calls for distributing the decedent's personal property to the children in equal shares as they agree, as in the previous example. Distributing assets this way does not usually present any difficulties. However, if there are disagreements, the executor can assure fairness by handling the distribution using any of the following methods:

- *Pick and choose.* Children are given the right to pick and choose the assets they want ("as they shall agree"). Even without this specific direction, they should be allowed to select the items they want. The value of the items selected should be tallied and adjustments made to the share of each beneficiary so that each receives an equal value.

- *Auction.* The pick-and-choose method works only if all of the beneficiaries agree on who gets what. If the items have substantial value, or if there is disagreement, the personal property can be auctioned among the beneficiaries. The highest bidder would receive the item and the bid amount would be deducted from that beneficiary's inheritance.
- *Sale.* The items that have not been selected should be sold and the proceeds distributed in equal shares to each beneficiary.

Unwanted items (property with little or no value) can be donated to a charity, or given away to friends of the family by the surviving spouse, the children, a family friend, or by the executor.

Specific Bequests

A decedent's will may direct that an individual or charity be given a particular item or a specified dollar amount. These are referred to as *specific bequests.* Examples:

- "I give, devise, and bequeath to my daughter, Sally, my 15 carat diamond engagement ring."
- "I give my son, John, $25,000.00."
- "I give $100,000 to the University of Pennsylvania to provide scholarship assistance for deserving young men and women as the University shall determine in their discretion."

Unless the specific bequest is needed to pay debts, administration expenses, and taxes, distribute it to the beneficiaries as soon as practical. If the specific bequest asset is income producing, such as a rented apartment or stock paying a dividend, the beneficiary is entitled to all of the income attributable to the asset from the decedent's date of death. If the bequest is a specific dollar amount, called a *pecuniary bequest*, the executor may have the option to satisfy the bequest by making a distribution in kind (i.e., distributing property itself). However, the property must have a value equal to the dollar amount of the bequest at the time the distribution is made. Income earned during the period of administration on the amount of the pecuniary bequest is not payable to the beneficiary.

ESSENTIAL

You must take the time to understand the terms that define who gets what to make sure you distribute the right amount to each beneficiary.

The Residuary Estate

The property that remains after distributing specific bequests and paying estate debts, administration expenses, and taxes is referred to as the *residuary estate* (i.e., what's left). The decedent's will may instruct that the residuary estate be distributed to a single individual, several individuals, a trust, or to one or more charitable organizations. The beneficiaries of the residuary estate may receive a specific dollar amount, a percentage of the residue, or a combination of the two. The decedent's will may also direct that distribution of the residuary estate be made per capita, per stirpes (each branch of the family is to receive an equal share of an estate), or per capita at each generation. These are legal terms that define how property passes if one or more named beneficiaries does not survive the decedent. The executor must understand the meaning of these terms to assure that the decedent's property is distributed to the right persons and in the right amounts:

Per Capita

A per capita provision in a decedent's will distributes property equally to all beneficiaries living at the time of the decedent's death—share and share alike. This means that the surviving descendants will inherit equally, regardless of their generation. For example, let's assume that a decedent had three children, John, Sally, and Fred. John had one child (Kerry); Sally had two children (Ron and Mary); and Fred had three children (Judy, Mike, and Ruth). If Sally predeceased her decedent father, John, Fred, and Sally's two children (Ron and Mary) would receive an equal share of the estate.

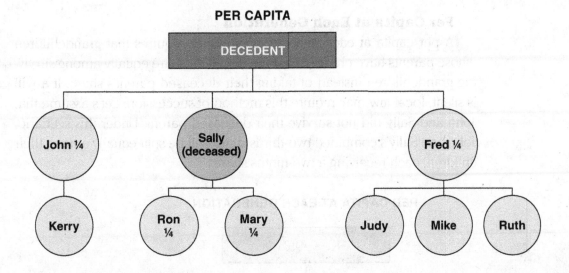

PER CAPITA

Per Stirpes

A per stirpes provision first divides property among the first-generation beneficiaries (children of the decedent) with a deceased child's share passing to that child's children (the decedent's grandchildren) and so on down the line. In other words, the property passes along bloodlines in each generation by right of representation. Using the previous example, Sally's share, under a per stirpes provision, would pass to her two children, Ron and Mary, each receiving half of Sally's one-third share, or one-sixth share each.

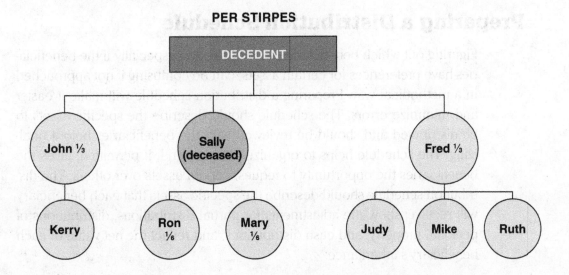

PER STIRPES

Per Capita at Each Generation

A per capita at each generation provision requires that grandchildren whose parents have predeceased the decedent share equally among surviving grandchildren instead of taking their deceased parent's share. If a will is silent, local law may require this method of succession. Let's assume that John and Sally did not survive their deceased parent. Under this scenario, John and Sally's combined two-thirds share will be split equally among their children, each receiving a two-ninths share.

PER CAPITA AT EACH GENERATION

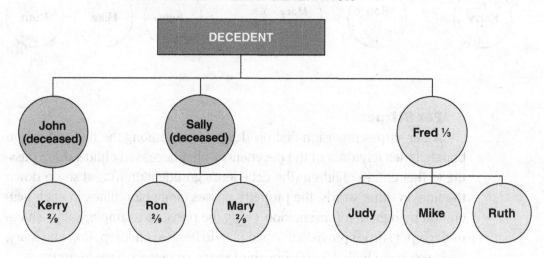

Preparing a Distribution Schedule

Figuring out which beneficiaries get what assets, especially if the beneficiaries have preferences for certain assets, can be confusing if not approached in a methodical way. Preparing a distribution schedule will make it easier and minimize errors. The schedule should describe the specific assets to be distributed and should be reviewed with the beneficiaries before finalizing. The schedule helps to organize the plan and, if permitted, gives the beneficiaries the opportunity to request certain assets over others. The distribution schedule should describe the specific assets that each beneficiary will receive; show the adjustments for partial distributions, distributions of personal property, and cash distributions; and reflect the net value of each beneficiary's inheritance:

▼ **DISTRIBUTION SCHEDULE**

	Total Value		Bill Doe (⅓ share)		Jane Doe (⅓ share)		Harry Doe (⅓ share)
25 shares ABC Co.	$12,520.00	8 shares	$4,006.40	8 shares	$4,006.40	9 shares	$4,507.20
500 shares XYZ Co.	80,658.20	167 shares	26,939.84	167 shares	26,939.84	166 shares	26,778.52
	93,178.20		30,946.24		30,946.24		31,285.72
Cash	28,320.60		9,440.20		9,440.20		9,440.20
Personal property	10,230.00		4,750.00		2,730.00		2,750.00
	131,728.80		45,136.44		43,116.44		43,475.92
Cash to equalize			-1,226.84		+793.16		+433.68
	131,728.80		43,909.60		43,909.60		43,909.60
Less: partial distribution	-6,000.00		-1,000.00		-3,000.00		-2,000.00
Total	**$125,728.80**		**$42,909.60**		**$40,909.60**		**$41,909.60**

The distribution schedule is used to figure out how many shares of stock each beneficiary is to receive and how much of the remaining cash each is to be paid. The cash balance is first allocated in accordance with what each beneficiary is to receive under the will. Adjustments are then made (i.e., additions and subtractions of cash) to equalize the shares. Deduct any partial distributions that were made during the course of administration to arrive at the amount distributable to each beneficiary.

ESSENTIAL

A written schedule is essential to making sure you distribute exactly what each beneficiary is entitled to.

Distributing the Property

The executor does not usually need authorization to distribute estate property, although some jurisdictions may require approval of the plan for distribution (the distribution schedule) by the court. Once the assets are ready for distribution (retitled in the names of the beneficiaries), delivery can proceed. Securities should be delivered in person, by registered mail or through the beneficiaries' banks along with a schedule of the cost bases of the property, which is the value used for estate tax purposes (the date-of-death or alternate value).

If an estate tax return was not required, the cost basis is the date-of-death value. Most banks will arrange for their customers to receive assets from an estate upon request by the executor. If a beneficiary lives out of state or in a foreign country, this is a way to assure that the property is delivered to the right person and that the estate receipt will be signed and returned. The executor should obtain a receipt and release from each beneficiary, which should be prepared by the estate's attorney. The following is an example of a receipt and release:

RECEIPT AND RELEASE

The undersigned, being one of the beneficiaries of the estate of (name of the decedent), hereby acknowledges receipt of the balances of income and principal distributable to me under the terms of the last will and testament of (name of decedent). The said balances consist of:

(Itemize securities, cash balances in income and principal, and other assets that are being distributed)

Further, in consideration of the payment to me of the balance of the estate assets, I hereby release and discharge the personal representative of any further liability in connection with the estate or its administration.

In witness whereof I have executed this instrument this _____ day of _____, 20____, with the intention of being legally bound.

_____

Distributions to a minor must be made to the child's legal guardian. If a beneficiary is incompetent, the distribution must be made to a conservator or guardian (appointed by the court) of the property (or estate) of the incompetent person.

If a beneficiary cannot be located, the probate court will determine the disposition of the property payable to that beneficiary and issue instructions to the executor.

Closing the Estate

The last step in the administration of the estate is to prepare a final accounting and close the estate. The probate court may require that a final accounting be submitted to the court, along with receipts from the beneficiaries, before it discharges the executor. Each state has its own closing procedures, which may or may not involve a court proceeding. However, before this final step is taken, the executor should check to see that all of these required administration tasks have been completed:

- Have all debts, administration expenses, and taxes been paid?
- Have all required tax returns been filed?
- Has the release from personal liability for the federal estate tax been received or the nine-month period for an IRS response lapsed?
- Has the final accounting been prepared and copies provided to the beneficiaries and other interested parties?
- Have all the assets been distributed and receipts and releases obtained from all beneficiaries?

Some states allow an informal closing. Under this procedure, the executor files a statement with the court that the administration of the estate is complete and an accounting has been provided to the beneficiaries and unpaid claimants, if any; after a specified period from the filing date (usually one year under local law), the executor is discharged from any further responsibility.

FACT

When you receive the order of discharge from the probate court, your job as executor is done.

In a formal probate proceeding, the final accounting is submitted to the probate court for approval. A master (auditor) may be appointed by the judge to review the accounts and advise the court as to whether or not the estate was properly administered. The appointment and expense of the master can usually be avoided if all beneficiaries approve the accounting prior to the hearing and waive their right to have a master appointed. If the court is satisfied that all of the requirements for settling the estate have been completed and the administration has been handled properly, it will issue an order of discharge relieving the executor from any further responsibility. The order of discharge is the formal closing of the estate.

Distribution Checklist

- If possible, make partial distributions to beneficiaries prior to the closing. Retain sufficient assets to cover final expenses.
- Distribute personal assets to family members. Conduct an auction for these items, if necessary.
- If a beneficiary does not survive a decedent, ascertain whether his or her share will be distributed per capita, per stirpes, or per capita at each generation.
- Prepare a distribution schedule. Discuss with the beneficiaries before finalizing.
- If a beneficiary resides outside the city where the estate is being administered, distribute that beneficiary's share through his or her bank.
- Obtain a receipt and release from every beneficiary.
- If required, submit the final accounts and receipts to the court and request the court to issue an order for discharge.

CHAPTER 8

Definition of a Trust and the Responsibilities of a Trustee

Trusts come in many different forms. Some are created during a person's lifetime, and others come into existence after death. The most common, and perhaps most popular, is the revocable living trust, which is created while someone is still alive. These trusts can be changed or revoked at any time by the creator. An irrevocable trust can also be created during one's lifetime, which cannot be changed or revoked, usually. A trust can be created under a will as well and thus comes into being at death.

The Basic Components of a Trust and What They Mean

Whether created before or after death, trusts are designed to achieve estate planning objectives that are unique to the individual who created it. Basically, trusts are legal arrangements that carry out specific instructions and allow someone to manage property for the benefit of others. A trustee essentially steps into the shoes of the creator of the trust either before or after the death. This is not always an easy thing to do. The creator may have left legal and financial problems that would challenge even the most knowledgeable and experienced individual.

How well a trustee manages the trust will determine if the estate planning objectives will be achieved. Understanding the general structure of a trust is a key first step to proper management of it. Regardless of the type of trust, they all have the same basic components:

- *Settlor.* The creator of a living trust (either revocable or irrevocable, established while someone is still alive); trustor or donor.
- *Testator* (male), *Testatrix* (female). The author of a will. A trust could be created under the will.
- *Trustee.* The person or institution (i.e., bank or trust company) that takes title to property and agrees to manage it, subject to the terms of a trust agreement or trust provisions under a will.
- *Income beneficiary.* The person(s) for whose benefit the trust was created and whose interest is limited to the income earned by the trust assets.
- *Principal beneficiary.* The person(s) for whose benefit the trust was created and whose interest is in distributions of principal.
- *Remainderman.* The remainderman is the beneficiary, individual, or organization that receives what's left in the trust upon its termination.
- *Income.* Income is the return on trust property, such as dividends, interest, rents, profits, royalties, etc., as opposed to principal.
- *Principal.* Principal is the property of the trust other than the income from the property. Principal is also referred to as *corpus* or *capital*.

A trustee's responsibilities may differ from trust to trust, depending on the type of trust and the particular purpose for which it was established. A revocable living trust is usually managed by its creator, the settlor, during his or her lifetime. A settlor of a revocable living trust may choose to appoint a trustee to manage his or her trust because the settlor may lack management expertise, wants to travel, or simply does not want to be bothered with the management of his or her property. In this situation, the trustee usually manages the trust property under direction of the settlor. The trustee is typically limited in the amount of discretion he or she can exercise. As a practical matter, the trustee's responsibilities are similar to that of an agent. The settlor has the power to amend or revoke the trust and therefore retains total authority and dominion over the trust and the trustee. The primary difference between a true agency and a trust relationship is that the trustee holds title to the trust property and has an obligation to act even without receiving direction from the settlor if failure to act would be harmful to the settlor.

FACT

Trusts come in a wide variety of shapes and sizes. Some are revocable and can be terminated or amended at any time. Others are irrevocable and can only be changed by court order.

Should the settlor become incapacitated, the successor trustee named in the trust is responsible for taking control and managing the trust property for the benefit of the settlor. At this point, the trustee makes all of the decisions and must observe the standards of care that would be expected of a prudent person dealing with the property of another. The trustee must manage the trust solely for the benefit of the incapacitated settlor and not the settlor's heirs. This level of responsibility continues until the settlor recovers or until the settlor's death.

Upon the death of the settlor, the trust becomes irrevocable. Likewise, a trust created under a decedent's will is also irrevocable. Under an irrevocable trust, the trustee has total authority and responsibility to carry out its provisions. While similar to managing a trust for an incapacitated settlor, the trustee's responsibilities under an irrevocable trust are far greater.

ALERT

The assets and obligations of the decedent should be evaluated to ascertain if there are any problems that would make management difficult for the nominated trustee. For example, environmental problems, like contamination from a leaking fuel storage tank, can be especially challenging and time consuming for a trustee and could expose the trust to liability.

The management of trusts is a serious responsibility and will be difficult if the trustee does not understand the basic rules. As trustee, you may put yourself at risk and jeopardize the purpose and intent of the trust if you do not know what the duties are and what is expected of you. In order to successfully carry out the provisions of a trust, you should possess good financial and business skills and/or hire financial advisors to provide the needed expertise. If you accept the role of a trustee without fully understanding the responsibilities, you not only expose yourself to personal liability but could also bring harm to the beneficiaries you serve.

Standards of Care

As previously discussed, every trustee has certain responsibilities under the law. In carrying out these responsibilities, trustees are subject to established standards of conduct under common law and the principles of equity. Most states have incorporated these rules, in one form or another, under their local statutes. The rules focus on the trustee's fundamental duty to carry out the directions of the trust's creator. The standards of care that apply to trustees have deep roots that can be traced to biblical times. Courts have been fairly consistent in describing and upholding the concept of prudent standards for trustees.

Whether a trustee has been reasonable in carrying out his or her responsibilities is not based entirely on the particular action taken by the trustee, but on the standards of care that ordinary prudent persons are expected to perform under similar circumstances. In managing the trust's affairs, a trustee will be held accountable for failure to apply the standards of care and skill. The standard of care that applies to trustees is often referred to as the *prudent person rule*. The Uniform Trustees' Powers Act, which many states have adopted, defines a prudent person as:

"A trustee whose exercise of trust powers is reasonable and equitable in view of the interests of income or principal beneficiaries, or both, and in view of the manner in which men of ordinary prudence, diligence, discretion, and judgment would act in the management of their own affairs."

In an 1883 court case (Speight v. Gaunt), the presiding judge, Lord Blackburn, articulated the standard for trustees: "as a general rule a trustee sufficiently discharges his duty if he takes in managing trust affairs all those precautions which an ordinary prudent man of business would take in managing similar affairs of his own. . . . It would be both unreasonable and inexpedient to make a trustee responsible for not being more prudent than ordinary men of business are."

This does not mean that a trustee can speculate with trust funds because he or she speculates with his or her own investments. Safeguarding income and principal, as ordinary persons of prudence would do, is what is expected. Being honest and well-intentioned is not sufficient and will not excuse a trustee who does not apply prudent practices in administering the trust.

A trustee must understand that he or she cannot personally profit from the administration of the trust. The duty of loyalty is perhaps the most important rule for trustees. It mandates, among other things, a full and frank disclosure of any transactions in which the trustee may have a personal interest.

In administering the trust, a trustee must be impartial. This is fundamental and perhaps one of the most difficult responsibilities a trustee has. A trustee cannot favor current beneficiaries over remainder beneficiaries or one beneficiary over another. The trustee must be fair to all beneficiaries when making decisions about investments, distributions of income and principal, and paying expenses, or with any other decisions in which the trustee uses discretion. This does not mean that distributions of income and/or principal to beneficiaries must be equal; however, the trustee must consider the individual needs and interests of each beneficiary and distribute funds in accordance with those needs and the terms of the trust.

ALERT

> A trustee must keep beneficiaries informed by providing them with accurate accounting records and other information that is pertinent to their interests.

A trustee is usually given the authority under the trust document to sell, invest, and reinvest the principal of the trust. To remain impartial between current beneficiaries and remainder beneficiaries and to protect the trust property, the trustee has a responsibility to distribute the risk of loss by diversifying the assets of the trust. When allocating deductible expenses between the federal estate tax return and the fiduciary income tax returns, the impartiality duty also comes into play. The remainder beneficiaries benefit if the deduction is taken on the estate tax return. If the deduction is taken on the fiduciary income tax returns, the income beneficiaries benefit.

Discretionary decisions should take into consideration what is equitable for all beneficiaries and in the best interest of the trust as a whole. If a trust document gives the trustee discretion in crediting a receipt or charging an expenditure to income or principal, the trustee needs to make the allocation with the duty of impartiality in mind.

Trustees are expected to be proactive and use initiative in managing the trust. To remain passive or take no action at all is not defensible if something goes wrong. It is also imperative that a trustee seek qualified professional assistance where needed and make informed decisions regarding the management of the trust.

The Trustee's Responsibilities If a Settlor Becomes Incapacitated

A revocable living trust provides for the management of the settlor's financial affairs in the event that the settlor becomes incapacitated. Without a trust, a court-supervised guardianship—or conservatorship—would be necessary to handle the financial affairs of the incapacitated person. A durable power of attorney (one that remains in effect upon incapacity) can also be used for this purpose, but only for the property that is not in a trust. A trust provides significant advantages over a guardianship proceeding or conservatorship. It is more flexible because handling financial transactions for the incapacitated person does not require the court's permission. Costs are lower because there are no attorney fees or costs for filing accountings in court. Upon the settlor's death, the trust also avoids probate and may reduce or eliminate estate taxes. These financial and estate planning opportunities are not available in a guardianship or conservatorship situation.

Every revocable living trust document names a successor, or backup, trustee. If the settlor, who is the primary trustee, becomes incapacitated, the successor trustee takes over.

The trust provision that brings the successor trustee into the picture upon the settlor's incapacity might look like this:

"The determination of whether the Settlor is competent, for the purposes of this trust, shall be made by two physicians licensed to practice medicine in the state of the Settlor's residence, one of whom shall be his or her family physician, stating that the Settlor is incapable of physically or mentally managing his or her financial affairs and is expected to remain so unable indefinitely or for the foreseeable future."

On the incapacity of the settlor, the trustee must follow the terms of the trust and exercise the standards of care that apply. At this point, the trustee should not take any directions from the settlor in managing the trust.

FACT

Older trust documents may not make any reference to incapacity at all. However, it would be reasonable for a trustee to rely on a medical doctor's statement that the settlor is incapacitated and unable to manage his or her financial affairs as sufficient authority to step in as successor trustee.

Once the successor trustee assumes the trusteeship, he or she has the authority, right, and power to do anything and everything that the settlor could do before his or her incapacity. The trustee is now acting in a fiduciary capacity and must use the trust property exclusively for the benefit of the settlor and individuals who relied on the settlor's support before he or she became incapacitated. Expenditures can be made for any purposes that the trustee determines are suitable and proper.

The administration of the trust during the period of the settlor's incapacity is similar to managing an irrevocable trust. The trustee's responsibilities take effect immediately upon acceptance of the trusteeship and include:

- Taking control of all trust property
- Collecting, holding, managing, investing, and reinvesting the assets of the trust
- Paying the legitimate obligations of the settlor
- Using the trust property for the exclusive benefit of the settlor

As in any other fiduciary role, the trustee is expected to observe the standards of care that would be observed by a prudent person dealing with someone else's property. The trustee must keep the trust property separate from all other property of the settlor and maintain records of all transactions during the period of the settlor's incapacity.

As long as the settlor is incapacitated, the trustee is responsible for the management of the trust unless the trustee resigns and a successor trustee takes over, or the settlor dies. Should the settlor die, the trustee carries out the provisions of the trust, which will either call for the trust to terminate or continue. If the settlor recovers and is no longer incapacitated, the trustee can continue to manage the trust at the settlor's direction or can resign and turn the management of the trust back to the settlor or an alternate trustee.

Revocable Living Trust That Terminates at Death

Managing a trust that terminates at death is significantly different than one that continues beyond the death of the settlor. Under a terminating trust, a trustee's responsibilities are very similar to those of an executor, without the necessity of a probate proceeding. The administration of this type of trust has a relatively short duration.

Revocable living trusts that are established for the purpose of providing protection in the event of incapacity, avoiding probate, and distributing property outright to heirs usually terminate at the death of the settlor. This type of trust serves a similar purpose as a will; its principal function is to distribute the trust property to the beneficiaries named in the trust document upon the death of the settlor.

Although the trust is the principle means of passing property to heirs, a will is also used to distribute personal belongings and handle any property that was not transferred to the trust prior to death. In this case, the will is drafted as a companion to the revocable living trust (this is the pour-over will that we've previously discussed). Such a will transfers any assets in the decedent's individual name at death to the revocable living trust for ultimate distribution to the decedent's heirs. Hopefully, the value of the personal property and the property in the decedent's own name is small enough to avoid a probate proceeding. The trustee's responsibilities under a revocable living trust that terminates at death include:

- Assembling and protecting trust assets
- Preparing an inventory and acquiring date-of-death appraisals of the trust property
- Providing limited management of the trust property
- Estimating cash requirements and raising the needed funds
- Paying claims and administration expenses
- Filing the required tax returns and paying any taxes due
- Making tax and other elections
- Preparing a distribution schedule
- Preparing the accounting covering the administration of the trust
- Making final distribution of the trust assets to the beneficiaries and closing the trust

ESSENTIAL

Using a trust instead of a will has the added benefit of avoiding probate and guardianship in the event of incapacity.

The executor of a decedent's estate is usually the same person as the trustee under his or her revocable living trust. In a well-planned estate, all of the individually owned assets will have been placed in the trust and, therefore, there will be no probate. The trustee, in this case, has total control of the decedent's property and is responsible for settling the affairs of the decedent. These include filing the decedent's final income tax returns, filing fiduciary income tax returns, filing the estate tax return (if required), paying the decedent's final bills, taking possession of and distributing the decedent's personal property, and dealing with other financial matters. If there is a probate, some of these functions, such as filing the estate tax return, need to be coordinated with the executor.

The major benefit in handling someone's estate through a revocable living trust is that the trustee does not have to deal with the probate court. In most states, court hearings or filings are not necessary if all the decedent's property is in his or her trust. This means that the estate can be settled quicker. However, the time that it takes to settle any estate depends on whether federal estate taxes are payable, the nature of the assets owned, and the decedent's instructions regarding the handling of his or her affairs.

If the decedent has a taxable estate, the federal estate tax return (Form 706) is not due until nine months after death. The trustee has an obligation to wait until the due date before filing the return and paying the tax; interest can be earned on the amount of taxes for the full nine-month period. This of course means delaying settlement of the estate until then. Settlement might also be delayed if the decedent leaves specific instructions to sell a particular asset. If the trust owns a business, has commercial real estate interest, has limited partnership interest, or has some other illiquid asset, it could take additional time to consummate the sale. Matters being litigated or disputes among the heirs can also delay distribution and the closing of the trust.

Checklist for Managing a Terminating Trust

- Notify the beneficiaries that the trust has terminated and describe the provisions of the trust that relate to their inheritance. This should be done as soon after the settlor's death as practical.
- Publish a notice to creditors.

- Obtain security reissue instructions from all beneficiaries, including how the securities are to be registered, current addresses, Social Security numbers, and the name and address of a local bank through which delivery can be made if assets cannot be delivered in person locally.
- Value the securities, real estate, and other assets for the purpose of ascertaining any estate tax that may be due and the amount to be distributed to the beneficiaries.
- Prepare a distribution schedule and tax cost basis schedule, and review them with the beneficiaries before finalizing.
- Have the attorney for the trust prepare new deeds for any real property distributable to beneficiaries.
- Arrange for the preparation and filing of the decedent's final individual income tax returns.
- Arrange for the preparation and filing of the fiduciary income tax return(s) required; arrange for the preparation and filing of the federal estate tax return and state inheritance return. Reregister all securities in accordance with the instructions of the beneficiaries.
- Prepare an accounting for the period from the settlor's date of death through and including all transactions prior to making final distribution of the assets to the beneficiaries.
- Deliver the assets and obtain approval of the final accounting, receipts for delivery of the assets, and a signed release of liability from all beneficiaries. The following is an example of a combined approval of account, receipt, and release:

APPROVAL OF ACCOUNT

RECEIPT AND RELEASE

I, the undersigned, being a beneficiary of the (name of trust), for the purpose of receiving distribution without a court order:

I. Acknowledge that I have examined the account of the trustee for the period from (beginning date) to and including (ending date) and approve the same, which approval shall have the same effect as if the account had been approved by the court;

II. Acknowledge receipt of income and principal as itemized therein, and release and discharge the Trustee from any liability in connection with the above trust or its administration;

III. Agree to indemnify and save the Trustee harmless against all liability, loss, or expense (including but not limited to costs and counsel fees) which may ever be incurred as a result of the settlement of its account and/or the distribution herein referred to upon this Receipt and Release.

In witness whereof I have executed this instrument this _____ day of _____, 20____, with the intention of being legally bound.

_____

- Prepare a supplemental final accounting from the end date of the last accounting through and including the final distribution of assets and cash. Provide each beneficiary with a copy of the supplemental final accounting.

Like a probate estate, as soon as the expenses, taxes, and other obligations of the trust have been satisfied, the assets can be distributed to the beneficiaries. Once the assets have been distributed and the final accounting has been delivered to the beneficiaries, the trust can be closed. Unlike a probate proceeding, in most jurisdictions the trustee is not required to seek a discharge from the court. The trustee can submit accountings to the court if the trustee wants to have the court approve the administration. However, having the beneficiaries approve the accountings and sign a release is less costly and allows the trust to close sooner. If a beneficiary refuses to approve the accountings and sign a release, the trustee has the option of seeking court approval at the expense of the trust. The final distribution of assets and closing of the trust effectively discharges the trustee of his or her responsibilities.

REVOCABLE LIVING TRUSTS THAT TERMINATE AT DEATH

Will → PROBATE

Pour Over

Payment of claims, taxes, administration expenses, etc. ← Revocable Living Trust

Distributed outright to . . .

Beneficiaries

Trust That Continues after Death

The responsibilities under a continuing trust are significantly greater than under a terminating trust and extend over a much longer period. Revocable living trusts that continue after death fall into two general categories. The first is the trust that is designed to protect beneficiaries for a period beyond the settlor's death. Some individuals want to control their wealth after death by denying their heirs direct access to their fortunes. Others may have a nobler objective of protecting those they feel need to be protected. Instead of directing the trustee to distribute the trust's assets outright at death, as in a terminating trust, this type of trust continues until the beneficiary reaches a certain age, or sometimes until the beneficiary's death. This type of trust will usually require the trustee to exercise discretion in distributing income and principal for the benefit of the beneficiary for the term of the trust. Upon termination, the trust property is distributed to the named remaining beneficiaries.

ALERT

The credit shelter or bypass trust is sometimes referred to as the *family trust* or *"B" trust.*

The other category of continuing trust is probably the more common one. This is a revocable living trust that has as one of its primary purposes the reduction or elimination of the federal estate tax. The key feature under this type of trust is the so-called credit shelter or bypass trust. The credit shelter trust is a separate trust created under the terms of the revocable living trust upon the settlor's death. It is funded with assets having a value equal to the exemption amount ($5,250,000 for 2013). The income and principal from this trust are used primarily for the benefit of the surviving spouse and often include the decedent's children.

The credit shelter trust is sometimes also referred to as the family trust, where children and grandchildren are included, because it benefits all family members. Typically, on the death of the surviving spouse, the credit shelter trust terminates and the assets are distributed to the children, grandchildren, or other named beneficiaries. Under the Internal Revenue Code, this trust will not be subject to estate tax in the surviving spouse's estate. In other words, the assets in this trust avoid estate taxes altogether and pass directly to the children or other named beneficiaries. Hence it is sometimes referred to as the bypass trust.

The assets that are not transferred to the credit shelter trust are either distributed outright to the surviving spouse or retained in the marital trust, another type of trust created under the decedent's revocable living trust. The marital trust qualifies for the marital deduction, thereby avoiding any estate tax in the estate of the first to die. Although there is no tax on the marital trust assets at the first death, the tax is merely postponed. The marital trust assets will be subject to estate tax in the surviving spouse's estate and taxed accordingly.

The surviving spouse gets the benefit of the marital trust for life. On the death of the surviving spouse, the assets will either pass as the surviving spouse directs in his or her will or as the settlor directs in the trust. In either case, the assets usually will be distributed to the children. The marital trust must direct that all of the trust income be paid to the surviving spouse in order to qualify it for the marital deduction. The trust may provide that principal be paid to the spouse at the discretion of the trustee or at the surviving spouse's direction. Upon the death of the surviving spouse, the assets of the marital trust are included in his or her estate for federal estate tax purposes. If the marital trust along with the other assets owned by the surviving spouse exceeds the exemption equivalent amount, the excess will be taxed.

In a continuing trust, the trustee's initial responsibilities are the same as with a trust that terminates at death. That is, the final affairs of the decedent's estate must be settled. Then the trustee must:

- Review and exercise tax and other elections.
- Set up the trust(s) for administration.
- Fund the marital and bypass trusts.

Once these initial steps have been accomplished, the trustee will be responsible for managing the trust until it terminates. The trustee's duties will include:

- Managing the trust's investment portfolio
- Managing real estate assets
- Managing business interests
- Making discretionary distributions to beneficiaries
- Maintaining fiduciary accounting records
- Filing fiduciary income tax returns for the trust(s)
- Making final distribution of the trust assets upon its termination

Trusts can continue for many years, and it is important that the trustee be aware of and understand these ongoing responsibilities. Also, he or she should be aware of the time commitment involved. To accept the trusteeship of a continuing trust without this knowledge is foolhardy and does nothing but expose a trustee to personal liability. Familiarity with the standards of care and the basics of trust administration discussed in this chapter is essential for a trustee of a continuing trust.

REVOCABLE LIVING TRUSTS THAT CONTINUE AFTER DEATH

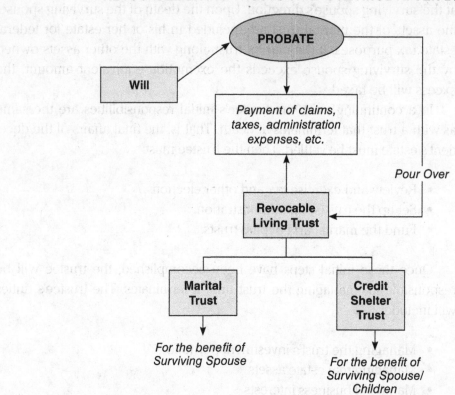

CHAPTER 9

Preparing for the Administration of the Trust

Whether you are managing a trust that terminates at death or one that continues, there are numerous details that need to be attended to. As with any other business activity, a well-established plan will help manage the numerous administrative tasks of a trust more efficiently. Organizing, collecting, and establishing proper trust records in the beginning will minimize administration problems later on. There are several initial steps necessary to properly set up a trust for administration. Once these steps have been taken, a plan for administration should be developed and a sound management system established. Many of the initial steps can be performed concurrently with the settlement of the decedent's estate.

Taking the Initial Steps

The initial steps involve such things as reviewing the trust document, collecting and safeguarding trust assets, preparing an inventory, and other tasks that need to be addressed at the beginning of your administration. These need to be done methodically so you don't miss anything.

Trust Set-Up Checklist

- Examine the trust document and determine if the trust is terminating or continuing.
- Determine if income accrued to the date of death but not received as of the date of death is payable to the estate of the settlor. There should be a provision in the trust that covers this.
- Check the trust document to see if estate taxes are payable from the trust.
- Check the trust document to see if medical, funeral, and other debts associated with the death of the settlor are payable from the trust.
- Have an initial conference with the beneficiaries and/or notify them of the trust provisions that affect their interests. A copy of the trust should also be provided to the beneficiaries.
- Identify and take control of all assets belonging to the trust.
- Arrange for safekeeping of all tangible assets.
- Prepare an inventory of all trust assets using the values as of the date of death.
- Apply for a tax identification number for the trust (Form SS-4).
- Identify all encumbrances and liabilities.
- Acquire appropriate insurance coverage for all real estate assets and other trust property, such as jewelry, paintings, coin collections, etc. If the property is covered by an existing policy, review the policy to see that the amount of the insurance is adequate.
- Collect any life insurance proceeds payable to the trust.
- If rental property is an asset of the trust, notify tenants to mail all future rent payments to the address of the trustee.
- Notify all debtors to mail future payments to the trustee.
- Notify or have the attorney for the trust inform the surviving spouse of her legal rights with respect to the trust.

- Determine if there are any alien or nonresident beneficiaries. Arrangements will have to be made with regard to delivery of assets, income and principal distributions, and the withholding of U.S. tax, if required.
- Determine how much needs to be reserved for taxes and other expenses.
- Carry out any initial instructions in the trust document, such as a directive to sell a specific asset, payment of specific bequests or allowances, etc.
- Prepare and sign an acceptance as trustee letter/form. Many financial institutions will require this before they accept your authority under the trust to take control of accounts. Sample:

ACCEPTANCE AS TRUSTEE

Under the terms of the (name of trust), dated, (date original trust was signed), the undersigned is nominated as trustee (or successor trustee).

(name of trustee), whose address is (address of trustee), hereby accepts the nomination as trustee (or successor trustee) and agrees to perform all of the duties and accepts all of the obligations imposed upon (him/her) as trustee (or successor trustee), such acceptance to be effective as of this date.

(Signature of trustee)

Date

Establishing a Management Plan

Before administration of the trust begins, develop a plan of action that includes how specific administrative tasks are to be performed and by whom. Some of the more important issues to be addressed in the planning process include:

- Will a division of the trust into a marital, credit shelter, and/or generation-skipping share be necessary? If so, who will advise the trustee how the splits are to be made and what assets will be used to fund the trusts?

- Who will handle the trust's investments?
- Who will handle the management of any real property owned by the trust?
- Who will maintain the accounting records for the trust and prepare accounting reports for the trustee and beneficiaries?
- How often will accounting statements be sent to the beneficiaries?
- If there are individuals referred to in the trust who are to be consulted with in regard to investments, an agreement should be established outlining the procedures that will be followed to implement this directive.
- Once the income needs of the trust and the short-term, intermediate-term, and long-term cash requirements have been determined, an investment policy with goals and objectives needs to be established. Who will do this and when?
- How often will the investments be reviewed and when?
- Who will prepare the fiduciary income tax return(s) for the trust?
- The investments of the trust need to have an initial review by a qualified investment professional to determine if immediate action needs to be taken with respect to any individual securities in order to protect the portfolio. Who will do this and when?
- If the trust owns closely held stock, does the ownership interest warrant the trustee serving as a member of the board of directors and/or an officer of the company?
- What tax elections need to be made and who will be retained to advise the trustee in this regard?
- If there is a co-trustee, agree in writing on the division of duties and the procedures that are to be followed in the joint exercise of discretionary decisions.
- What will be required of beneficiaries when considering discretionary payments? These requirements should be communicated to the beneficiaries as soon as is practical.

Setting Up the Documents and Records

Keeping good records is essential to the efficient administration of a trust. There is probably no other aspect that is more important for minimizing errors and maintaining management control. Trust record keeping falls into three general categories. First is the creation and maintenance of the "document" or "pertinent information" file. The second is the "correspondence" or "work" file, and the third is maintenance of accurate accounting records.

ESSENTIAL

The document file is a critical reference of the pertinent records of the trust that will be referenced throughout the entire period of administration.

Trust Documents Checklist

- Copy of the original trust document and all amendments
- Copy of the decedent's original will
- Certified copy of the death certificate
- Copy of all real estate deeds
- Copy of the federal estate tax return (Form 706), if one was filed
- Date-of-death inventory of trust assets
- Family tree
- List of the current beneficiaries, their addresses, birth dates, marginal (highest) tax bracket, Social Security numbers, and interest in the trust
- List of the remainder beneficiaries
- Synopsis of trust that includes:
    1. A quote of the provision that covers distribution of income from the trust
    2. A quote of the provision that pertains to the distribution of principal
    3. A quote of the provision that triggers the termination of the trust
    4. A quote of any provision that prohibits a particular action
    5. A quote of any provision that requires the trustee to take a particular action

- Other documents that are important to the ongoing administration of the trust.

The correspondence file, or work file, should contain all correspondence and other written materials related to the day-to-day administration of the trust. This file should also contain memorandums that outline and document important phone calls and meetings. The more documentation you have, the better.

ESSENTIAL

Keep written notes of meetings with attorneys, accountants, etc. Trusts can last for many years and without good historical records, it will be difficult to recall the details of a particular action taken during the course of administration.

Fiduciary trust accountings are records that cover all of the financial transactions of the trust. These accountings are permanent records and can be useful as a reference and guide in handling future transactions. One of the important functions of fiduciary accounting is to keep income and principal funds separate. All trust documents make specific reference to how, when, and under what circumstances income and principal are to be distributed to the beneficiaries of the trust. It is essential that these records be accurate in order to properly identify the interests of all beneficiaries at any given point. Accountings are also the tool needed to monitor investment performance, income production, and plan payments from the trust and assess how the financial resources of the trust can meet the current and future needs of the beneficiaries.

Tax Considerations and Other Election Choices

As discussed earlier, the executor and/or the trustee should make tax elections that are advantageous to the beneficiaries. Some may not apply, but others are essential to carrying out the decedent's estate plan. Proper postmortem tax planning can result in significant tax savings. For the trustee, the planning process may involve close coordination with the executor and advice from qualified tax professionals. If there is no probate, tax elections will be the responsibility of the trustee.

FACT

The trustee may be solely responsible for making tax advantaged elections.

The QTIP Election

The Qualified Terminable Interest Property, or QTIP election, allows the use of certain qualified property as a marital deduction in determining the decedent's estate tax. A trust can qualify for the marital deduction if the following requirements are met:

- The property must "pass" from the decedent
- The surviving spouse must be entitled to an income interest for life
- No other beneficiary may have any right in the trust during the surviving spouse's lifetime
- An irrevocable QTIP election must be made

A trust that requires all of its income to be distributed to a surviving spouse and no one else would qualify for the QTIP election, assuming that principal is not available to anyone other than the surviving spouse during his or her lifetime. Under the typical QTIP trust, a surviving spouse is not given the right to direct who receives the principal of the trust at his or her death. Instead, the trust is typically distributed to the children upon the spouse's death.

Under the Internal Revenue Code, a partial QTIP election can be made, giving the trustee, or executor, a great deal of tax planning flexibility. For example, a partial election could be made to have some estate tax paid at the first death. This could have a beneficial effect if the surviving spouse's estate will be in a high tax bracket. Many estate planning attorneys recognize the advantages of having this flexibility and will include a provision in the trust that directs the trustee to make the appropriate election.

The following is an example of such a provision, which gives the trustee fairly specific direction:

"The trustee(s) of the Qualified Terminable Interest Property Trust are hereby authorized, at the sole discretion of the trustee(s), to determine whether to elect (under Section 2056(b)(7) of the Internal Revenue Code) to qualify all or a specific portion of the Qualified Terminable Interest Property Trust created herein for the federal estate tax marital deduction. The trustee(s) of the Qualified Terminable Interest Property Trust, in exercising such discretion, shall attempt to minimize, or eliminate if possible, the federal estate tax payable by my estate at the time of my death.

"If, however, the trustee(s) of the Qualified Terminable Interest Property Trust determine that it is in the best interest of the persons who may receive any assets after my death and my spouse's death to pay some federal estate tax in my estate, taking into consideration any other tax that is to be paid because of my death and my spouse's death, and any income tax liability that may be affected by the election, the trustee(s) of the Qualified Terminable Interest Property Trust may elect to take a marital deduction that does not reduce the tax to zero if the payment of the tax will not jeopardize the ability of the Qualified Terminable Interest Property Trust to provide my spouse with the level of support and maintenance contemplated by this Declaration of Trust. The decision of the Qualified Terminable Interest Property trustee(s) to make this election shall be final and binding on all persons."

Even without specific language like this, the trustee should take whatever actions necessary to reduce taxes and preserve the trust property for the benefit of the beneficiaries and other interested parties who would be affected by payment of the tax. Obviously, this election involves some sophisticated tax planning, including an analysis of the surviving spouse's estate tax liability, an evaluation of whether there would be any advantage to paying some tax now (i.e., at the first death), the impact of the election on the beneficiaries' interest in the trust, and the overall tax and economic benefits of the various alternatives.

Disclaimers

The use of disclaimers can achieve significant tax advantages and can also be used to correct trust agreements that contain drafting errors. Once an interest is disclaimed, the person disclaiming the interest is considered to have predeceased the settlor, in the case of a trust, and the interest passes to the person(s) who would be legally entitled to receive it. For example, let's say that a settlor provided in his living trust that his surviving spouse was to receive income for life if she survived him, and if she did not survive him, the income would be paid to the settlor's children. If the surviving spouse disclaimed her interest in the trust, she would be considered to have predeceased the settlor and the income would be paid to the children. This is a good way to transfer property, or an interest in property, to others. Gift taxes are avoided because the person making the disclaimer, in this case the surviving spouse, is considered to have predeceased the settlor and therefore is not making a gift to the children.

Disclaimers can also be used to maximize the amount that can be sheltered through the credit shelter trust of the first to die. If a decedent's credit shelter trust holds less than the allowable amount, and there are other assets such as jointly held property that passes to the surviving spouse by operation of law (automatically), the surviving spouse can disclaim some of the joint property to allow the credit shelter trust to be funded with the full value of the exemption equivalent amount.

If a trust is not drafted properly, it may fail to qualify for the marital deduction and create a tax liability in the estate of the first to die. The failure might be the result of the trust allowing distributions to individuals other than the surviving spouse during his or her lifetime, which would disqualify the trust for the marital deduction. This can be remedied by having the disqualifying person disclaim his or her interest. Before suggesting a disclaimer, the trustee should have the individual seek advice from a financial counselor or attorney to advise the beneficiary of the consequences of giving up their rights under the trust. Disclaimers should be considered as soon after death as is practical, since the election must be made within nine months from the time the interest is created and it may take some time to complete the process. Also, the longer it takes to make the decision, the greater the chances are that the person having the interest will inadvertently receive benefits from the interest (i.e., income distributions), thereby disqualifying the person from making the disclaimer.

Generation-Skipping Transfer Tax (GSTT) Exemption

The generation-skipping transfer tax is assessed for all gifts and transfers to skip persons that exceed the GSTT exemption ($5,250,000 for 2013). These transfers may occur after death through a credit shelter trust and/or QTIP trust. For example, a credit shelter trust might provide that the decedent's surviving spouse receive income and/or principal during her lifetime, and upon her death, continue for the benefit of her children. The trust might also provide for distributions to grandchildren for their education, and upon the death of the last to survive of the settlor's children, that the remaining assets be distributed to the grandchildren as remaindermen. Any distributions to grandchildren (skip persons) during the term of the trust, and distribution of the assets to the grandchildren upon termination of the trust, are generation-skipping transfers subject to the generation-skipping transfer tax (GSTT). The trustee needs to allocate the GSTT exemption at the decedent's death in a way that maximizes, or leverages, its tax sheltering effect. This is done on Schedule R of Form 706, the United States Estate (and Generation-Skipping Transfer) Tax Return.

ALERT

A word of caution: the trustee should never allow additional assets to be deposited to the protected trust(s) once the allocation has been made. This could expose the trust(s) to the generation-skipping transfer tax.

If the election to allocate the GSTT exemption is not deliberately made by the trustee at the time the trust(s) are established, the exemption will be applied to the distributions when they are made, based on the then value of the distributions. However, if the trustee allocates the exemption to the trust(s) at the time the trust(s) are created, the assets in those trusts are "protected." That is, the amount allocated, plus the appreciation on the assets in the trust(s), will pass free of the generation-skipping transfer tax. All distributions to grandchildren, or any other skip persons, should first be made from the protected trust(s), since the assets plus any appreciation in value are exempt from the generation-skipping transfer tax.

The inclusion ratio. If some of the GSTT exemption had been used prior to the death of the decedent, only a portion of distributions made to skip persons will be exempt from GSTT. For example, let's say the decedent used $1,250,000 of her exemption prior to death, leaving only $4,000,000 left ($5,250,000 minus $1,250,000). Let's also assume that her credit shelter trust was funded with the full estate tax exemption amount of $5,250,000. If the trustee elected to allocate the full amount of what was left of her GSTT exemption (i.e., $4,000,000), only a portion of distributions from the credit shelter to the skip person would be exempt from GSTT. The portion of the distributions from the trust that are subject to the tax is expressed as a percentage of the total value of the credit shelter trust and is referred to as the *inclusion ratio* under the Internal Revenue Code. The inclusion ratio is determined by dividing the unused portion of the exemption by the funding value of the credit shelter trust and subtracting the result from 1 (one). In this example, the inclusion ratio for credit shelter trust distributions from the trust would be:

$$1 - \frac{\text{Unused exemption (i.e., } \$5{,}250{,}000 - \$1{,}250{,}000 = \$4{,}000{,}000)}{\text{Value of credit shelter trust upon funding}}$$

$$1 - \frac{\$4{,}000{,}000}{\$5{,}250{,}000} = .2381 = 23.81\%$$

For every principal distribution made to a grandchild, or other skip person, from the credit shelter trust in this example, 23.81% (the inclusion ratio) of the amount distributed would be subject to the generation-skipping transfer tax (GSTT). The intent here is to make the trustee aware that these elections are important to the administration of the trust, and not to give specific direction as to how these elections should be made. Again, the trustee should seek advice from a qualified attorney or tax accountant in dealing with these matters.

CHAPTER 10

Setting up a Continuing Trust for Administration

The basic technique for deferring federal estate tax when the first spouse dies is to maximize the marital deduction. Property that qualifies for the marital deduction is not taxed until the surviving spouse's death. Transfers to a surviving spouse will qualify for the marital deduction if made outright by specific bequest under a will or trust; through joint ownership; under the terms of a contract, such as a life insurance policy, profit-sharing plan, 401(k), or Individual Retirement Account (IRA); or through a qualifying trust. There are four basic types of trusts that qualify for the marital deduction: the estate trust, the power of appointment trust, the QTIP trust, and the qualified domestic trust (QDOT). The other component trusts in the estate plan include the credit shelter and generation-skipping trusts, the credit shelter trust being the device for preserving the exemption amount in the estate of the first to die.

Estate Trust

An estate trust, which is created by a provision under a will or trust, is one that does not require all of its income to be paid to the surviving spouse. However, in order to qualify for the marital deduction, the estate trust must provide that upon the death of the surviving spouse, all of the accumulated income and principal of the trust be distributed to the surviving spouse's estate. Unlike the other types of trusts that qualify for the marital deduction, the estate trust can be funded with unproductive property; that is, property that does not produce income. This type of trust is not used in estate plans very often, but is mentioned here so you are aware that it is one of the variations that qualify for the marital deduction. If you have any doubts as to whether or not you are managing an estate trust, you should consult with a trust attorney or accountant who is familiar with marital trusts.

ESSENTIAL

A trustee will need to establish separate component trusts if required under the terms of a continuing trust.

Power of Appointment Trust

Until the QTIP trust was introduced in 1981 by the Economic Recovery Act, the power of appointment trust was the most commonly used form of marital deduction trust. Although the QTIP trust provides more tax planning options, the power of appointment trust is still used in some estate plans. In order to qualify for the marital deduction, the terms of the power of appointment trust must provide that all of the trust's income be paid to the surviving spouse for life. It must also give the surviving spouse a general power of appointment by which the surviving spouse, under his or her will, can appoint the trust property to his or her estate or to any other person(s) upon death. The power of appointment trust cannot allow any other person to benefit from the trust during the surviving spouse's lifetime. Unlike the estate trust, in a power of appointment trust, the trustee must obtain consent of the surviving spouse to fund it with, or invest in, non-income-producing (i.e., unproductive) property. Also, an election is not required to be made on the estate tax return in order to include the trust for the marital deduction. Qualification and use of the power of appointment trust for the marital deduction is automatic.

Qualified Terminable Interest Property (QTIP) Trust

The QTIP trust is a popular marital trust provision. Like the power of appointment trust, the QTIP trust income must be paid to the surviving spouse and no one else. However, unlike the marital trusts discussed previously, a general power of appointment need not be given to the surviving spouse. This allows the settlor to decide the ultimate disposition of the property upon the surviving spouse's death. The surviving spouse is the only one who can receive principal during his or her lifetime. As with the power of appointment trust, the trustee cannot fund the trust with unproductive property unless authorized to do so by the surviving spouse. An election must be made on the estate tax return (Form 706) by the executor or trustee to use all or a portion of the trust for the marital deduction. Once the election is made, it is irrevocable.

Qualified Domestic Trust (QDOT)

Many couples have a spouse that is not a U.S. citizen. When the U.S. citizen spouse dies the IRS prescribes certain rules in order for the deceased spouse's estate to qualify for the marital deduction. The Qualified Domestic Trust (QDOT) is used to meet these requirements. It is the only way to obtain a marital deduction in this situation. To qualify for the marital deduction, at least one trustee must be a U.S. citizen or domestic corporation (a bank or trust company). The trust must provide that all income be paid, at least annually, to the non–U.S. citizen spouse unless an estate trust is being used. No principal can be paid unless the U.S. trustee has the right to withhold from the distribution the estate taxes that would be due at the time the distribution is made. The trustee must make sure that the tax is withheld and paid so that the marital deduction that was taken is not jeopardized. As with the QTIP trust, an election to use the trust for the marital deduction must be made on the decedent's estate tax return (Form 706).

Credit Shelter Trust

As part of the plan to minimize or avoid estate taxes, the credit shelter trust provision is used to preserve the decedent's exemption amount ($5,250,000 for 2013) from taxation in the surviving spouse's estate. The credit shelter trust typically will provide that the income and principal be used for the benefit of the decedent's surviving spouse and children. Unlike marital deduction trusts, there is no requirement for the credit shelter trust to distribute income to the surviving spouse. Upon the death of the surviving spouse, the assets of the credit shelter trust, including any appreciation in value from the date of funding to the date of death of the surviving spouse, are not included in the surviving spouse's estate. The trust passes, estate-tax free, to the children or other named beneficiaries in the trust. One of the principal planning objectives in funding the credit shelter trust is to use assets that will appreciate in value over time, since the initial value of the assets plus the appreciation will pass tax free to the children or other beneficiaries named in the trust.

Funding the Trust(s)

Funding-allocation decisions are only necessary if both marital and credit shelter trusts are established. If the estate value is under the exemption amount ($5,250,000 for 2013), only the credit shelter trust will be established and all assets will fall into this one trust. If both trusts are established because the estate value exceeds the exemption amount, the marital and credit shelter trusts (and any other trust) should be funded after the estate tax return (Form 706) has been filed and there is reasonable assurance that the return is correct and that the trustee is using the right amounts to fund each trust. Funding the various trusts created under a decedent's revocable living trust can be a challenging task for a trustee. A decedent's revocable living trust, in addition to creating a marital trust and credit shelter trust, may also create a generation-skipping trust or a combination of all three to facilitate the estate plan. There are many issues to be considered in funding these trusts. The decisions that are made will have income tax, estate tax, and trust management implications.

FACT

Funding should be based on the final determination of the values for estate tax purposes, the formula clause in the trust, and the value of the surviving spouse's estate. This information will not be available for many months after the decedent's death. However, the trustee should fund the trusts as soon as possible to minimize any income tax consequences.

There are two basic funding formula clauses under marital and credit shelter trust provisions: One is the pecuniary formula clause and the other is the fractional formula clause. It is important for the trustee to understand these formulas and their basic characteristics; it is also important to understand the consequences of these funding choices.

Pecuniary Formula Clause

The pecuniary formula clause is the most flexible of the two types of funding formulas and gives the trustee several planning opportunities. A pecuniary formula gives (bequeaths) a specific dollar amount to either the marital trust or the credit shelter trust. If the specific dollar amount is given to the marital trust, the excess trust asset value over this amount, or residue, is distributed to the credit shelter trust. If the specific dollar amount is given to the credit shelter trust, the residue is distributed to the marital trust. A pecuniary gift to the credit shelter trust is referred to as a *reverse pecuniary bequest*. Pecuniary formula clauses are used more often than fractional formula clauses because they are easier to administer and are more flexible. There are three funding methods under pecuniary formula clauses. The formula clause in the trust will specify the particular funding method that is to be used:

- "True worth" funding
- "Minimum worth" funding
- "Fairly representative" funding

All three variations allow the trustee to "pick and choose" the assets that will be used to fund each trust, whether it is the marital or credit shelter trust. The trustee must read the terms of the trust carefully to determine what funding method is to be used.

True Worth Funding

This is the most common and flexible of the three types of pecuniary funding variations. It gives the trustee the greatest latitude in choosing the assets that will fund each trust. A pecuniary formula clause that makes a gift to the marital trust with the residue going to the credit shelter trust is the most common type of true worth funding provision. This method guarantees that the surviving spouse, who is the beneficiary, will not be affected by any depreciation in value of the estate assets from the date of death to the date of funding, since the amount that funds the trust is a fixed dollar amount. Also, any assets that have appreciated from the date of death can be allocated to the credit shelter trust, thereby avoiding taxation of those assets in the surviving spouse's estate. The following is an example of a gift (bequest) to a marital trust with a true worth pecuniary formula clause:

"The trustee shall retain and administer as the marital trust an amount equal to the settlor's gross estate for tax purposes, reduced by the maximum dollar amount that, without considering the federal estate tax marital deduction in effect at the time of the settlor's death, can pass free of estate taxation. The trustee shall hold the remaining trust estate as the family trust (i.e., credit shelter trust). Each asset distributed in kind to the marital trust shall be valued at the date of distribution thereof."

The true worth pecuniary formula clause has several characteristics with income tax consequences that the trustee needs to understand before funding the trusts:

- Assets used to fund the trusts must be valued as of the date of funding.
- Assets used to fund the pecuniary amount are considered a sale of those assets for income tax purposes. Therefore, all trust assets must be revalued as of the date of distribution. Capital gains will be real-

ized on any asset used to fund the trust. For this purpose, the capital gain is the difference between the value used on the estate tax return (Form 706) and the date of funding value. The capital gains taxes are paid by the nonpecuniary trust or the credit shelter trust. For this reason, the sooner the funding takes place, the better. The longer it takes to fund the trusts, the greater the potential capital gains.

- Distribution of assets to the marital trust carries with it any taxable income that is classified as distributable net income (DNI) and taxes it to the marital trust.
- Distribution of assets to the trust that represent income in respect of a decedent (IRD) accelerates the reporting of the IRD in the year the trust is funded. This results in the income taxation of the IRD.

Other issues that the trustee should consider before funding the trust include the type of marital trust that is being funded, the intended use of the assets, the income requirements of the surviving spouse and other beneficiaries, and the need to shelter assets from taxation in the surviving spouse's estate. The value that goes into the marital trust is the amount used on the estate tax return, Form 706. High-growth assets should be distributed to the credit shelter trust to maximize the amount that will be sheltered and minimize taxes in the surviving spouse's estate. The assets that are not used to fund the marital trust will automatically fund, or fall into, the credit shelter trust. The assets that have grown, and are expected to grow in value in the future, should be allowed to fall into the credit shelter trust. This maximizes the estate tax sheltering effect of the credit shelter trust and also avoids triggering capital gains tax on the appreciation of these assets.

Some formula clauses require that the credit shelter trust be funded first, with the residue passing to the marital trust. This so-called reverse pecuniary bequest is used primarily when the marital portion of the estate is expected to be very large and capital gains that may be incurred upon funding of the marital trust are a concern. A reverse pecuniary bequest might read as follows:

> *"If the settlor's spouse survives the settlor, then at the settlor's death the trustee shall retain and administer as the family trust an amount equal to the maximum dollar amount that, without considering the federal*

estate tax marital deduction in effect at the time of settlor's death, can pass from the settlor's gross estate free of estate taxation, taking into consideration the value of all available credits against estate tax and all taxable transfers that pass outside of this trust."

The amount used to fund this trust is based on the exemption amount applicable at the decedent's date of death.

Minimum Worth Funding

The minimum worth funding method also allows the trustee to pick and choose the assets to fund the pecuniary bequest trust (marital or credit shelter). In selecting the assets, the trustee must use the date-of-death value (or alternate value if it was used on the estate tax return) or date-of-funding value, whichever is lower. No capital gain is recognized upon funding, because the assets used to fund the pecuniary bequest trust will never exceed their tax cost basis. The following is an example of a minimum worth funding provision:

"My trustee shall select and distribute the cash, securities, and other property, including real estate and interests therein, that will constitute the marital bequest, employing for the purpose of valuation the lesser of the adjusted basis of the asset for federal income tax purposes or current value of the asset at the time of distribution."

The following are characteristics of this type of funding formula:

- No capital gain is realized upon funding of the trust.
- Only those assets that have diminished in value from the date of death need to be valued as of the date of funding. This formula avoids revaluing all of the assets and the time and expense of appraising difficult assets such as business interests and real estate.
- A capital loss cannot be used by the trust unless the funding is from an estate to a trust (i.e., testamentary trust).
- DNI is also taxed to the trust that is being funded with the pecuniary bequest amount and IRD issues associated with the true worth funding method also apply.

- This method gives the trustee the flexibility of favoring the surviving spouse by funding the marital trust with assets that have appreciated in value or by underfunding it with depreciated assets. No capital gains will be realized upon funding. Growth assets should be allocated to the credit shelter trust to shelter future gains.

Fairly Representative Funding

This method of funding is also not as common as true worth funding, because it does not give the trustee as much flexibility. Although it allows the trustee to pick and choose assets to fund the trusts, this is limited because assets selected must be fairly representative of the gains and losses that have occurred from the date of death to the date of funding. The following is an example of a fairly representative funding formula clause:

"The trustee shall fund the marital trust with that pecuniary amount which is equal to the value of my estate as finally determined for federal estate taxes reduced by the largest amount, if any, which if allocated to the family trust would result in no increase in federal estate tax payable at my death. In funding the marital trust, the trustee shall distribute assets in such a manner that they have an aggregate fair market value fairly representative of the appreciation or depreciation in the value to the date or dates of distribution of all assets then available for distribution."

The following are characteristics of this type of formula:

- The values used for funding are the values used on the federal estate tax return.
- No gain or loss is realized upon funding.
- Assets used to fund the bequest must be fairly representative of gains and losses from the date of death to the date of funding. Therefore, all trust assets must be valued as of the date of distribution to make this determination.
- DNI is carried out to the trust that is being funded with the pecuniary bequest resulting in tax at the trust level, although the amount is smaller than with the true worth funding method.

- Income will be accelerated on IRD assets that are used to fund the pecuniary bequest trust.

Fractional Bequest Formulas

One of the disadvantages of a pecuniary formula clause that uses the true worth funding method is that it generates capital gains upon funding, whether it is the marital or credit shelter trust. As with the minimum worth and fairly representative funding methods, this problem is avoided under a fractional bequest formula, which is one reason it may be used in a trust. Under a fractional formula, the marital and credit shelter trusts receive a fractional share of the trust assets. The fraction is based on the values used on the decedent's estate tax return. The following is an example of a fractional bequest formula:

"The trustee shall retain as the marital trust a fraction of the trust property, of which the numerator shall be the largest amount, if any, that can pass free of federal estate tax. This shall take into account the unified credit and the state death tax credit (provided use of the latter credit does not require an increase in the state death taxes paid) but no other credit reduced by the value (as finally determined for federal estate tax purposes) of all other property included in my gross estate passing thereunder, other than property which passes under this item and does not qualify for the federal estate tax marital deduction or charitable deduction, or any charges to principal that are not deducted in computing the federal estate tax on my estate, and the denominator of which shall be the value of my residuary estate as finally determined for federal estate tax purposes."

The following are the principal characteristics of this type of formula clause:

- No gains or losses are realized when funding the marital and credit shelter trusts.
- Income is not accelerated on IRD items upon funding.
- DNI (taxable income) is taxed to the trust if the income is retained, or to its beneficiaries if income is distributed to them.

There are two variations of the fractional formula. One is a pro rata method; the other allows the trustee to pick and choose the assets that will fund the trusts.

Fractional Pro Rata Formula

The pro rata method allocates a fractional share of each trust asset to the marital and credit shelter trusts. The fraction is based on the value of the trust assets and the marital deduction used on the decedent's estate tax return:

Marital deduction attributable to trust

Date-of-death value of trust assets

Fractional "Pick and Choose" Formula

The fractional "pick and choose" method begins with determining the fraction that applies to each trust, as in the previous example. The additional language that would allow a "pick and choose" fractional bequest might read as follows:

"Assets may be allocated to this fractional share by either pro rata or non–pro rata division, in cash or in kind . . ."

The following must be taken into consideration when using this method of funding:

- Gains must be allocated proportionately between the two trusts in the same way that the pecuniary bequest, "fairly representative" funding, method requires.
- Each time a "pick and choose" asset is selected and allocated to the trusts, the fraction must be recomputed. This is because the computation of the fractional formula is based on the estate tax value, and the "pick and choose" asset is allocated at its date-of-funding value.

There are income tax planning issues with all of these formulas, in addition to the obvious estate and generation-skipping tax sheltering opportunities, which the trustee must consider. Funding decisions must also consider the kind of assets being allocated. For example, special use valuation property should be allocated to the marital trust to qualify for the special use valuation in the surviving spouse's estate. These are complex planning issues and, again, the trustee would be well advised to seek competent professional advice before making these funding decisions.

Trust Funding Checklist

- Determine the type of funding formula under the trust and review the formula's characteristics.
- Do not fund any of the trusts until you are sure the estate tax return has been filed correctly.
- Consult with the surviving spouse, and/or the surviving spouse's financial advisor, regarding the surviving spouse's potential estate tax liability.
- Obtain written consent from the surviving spouse if the marital trust will be funded with non–income producing (unproductive) assets.
- Seek professional assistance from a certified public accountant (CPA), or the attorney for the trust, before making funding decisions.

CHAPTER 11

Income Tax Returns and Other Related Issues

Trustees are required to file income tax returns for the trusts they manage and may also have the responsibility to file other returns. Generally, the executor is responsible for filing the decedent's final income tax returns, the federal estate tax return, and fiduciary income tax returns during the period of estate administration. However, if there is no probate and therefore no reason to have an executor appointed by the court, "any person in actual or constructive possession of any property of the decedent" (IRC Sec. 2203) is responsible for filing the returns. The trustee of the decedent's trust is typically in charge of the decedent's property and therefore would have this responsibility. Others who may be "inadvertent executors" and have this responsibility include surviving joint tenants, the decedent's heirs, and any individuals who have possession of the decedent's property.

Filing the Decedent's Final Income Tax Returns

If an executor has not been appointed, the trustee has the responsibility for filing the final income tax returns for the decedent. The trustee should consult with the surviving spouse regarding income tax and other planning issues. The surviving spouse and trustee have the option of filing a joint final return as was outlined in Chapter 6 (Administering the Estate: Taxes and More).

ALERT

The decision to file joint or separate returns involves important tax planning considerations. Unless a trustee has sufficient experience in income tax planning, he or she should seek advice from a competent tax professional before making these decisions.

To protect against future IRS tax claims, the trustee should file Form 5495, Request for Discharge from Personal Liability under Internal Revenue Code Section 2204 or 6905. Within nine months after receipt of the request, the IRS will notify the trustee that the tax liability has been satisfied and the trustee will be discharged from personal liability for any future deficiencies. If the IRS has not notified the trustee, he or she will be discharged at the end of the nine-month period.

FACT

In administering a trust, the trustee must make sure that all taxes are paid before any other expenses are paid. The Internal Revenue Service holds a trustee personally liable for any federal taxes due if the trustee, prior to satisfying any tax obligations, makes other payments. However, the trustee is not liable if debts, such as the decedent's funeral expenses and administration costs, have priority over federal taxes under local law. Also, there is no liability if the trustee paid the decedent's debts and was not aware that any federal taxes were due.

Fiduciary Income Tax Returns

Irrevocable trusts are treated as separate taxable entities and the trustee is required to file a federal fiduciary income tax return each year. Many states also require that a state fiduciary income tax return be filed.

FACT

Trustees are required to file income tax returns for their trusts annually.

There are special rules under the Internal Revenue Code that apply to the taxation of trusts. These rules are very complex and a trustee should not attempt to file the trust return(s), at least initially, without the assistance of a CPA who is experienced in this area of taxation.

Generally, the trust receives a deduction for income distributions that are made from the trust to beneficiaries, and the beneficiaries are required to report the income distributions on their individual income tax returns. Any taxable income that is not distributed to beneficiaries is taxed to the trust.

TAXABILITY OF TRUST INCOME

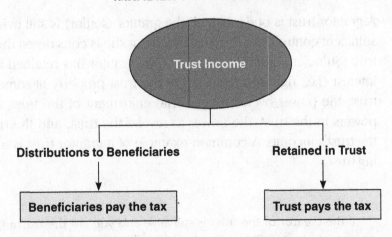

171

The trustee is required to file Form 1041, U.S. Income Tax Return for Estates and Trusts, if:

1. The trust has any taxable income for the tax year.
2. The trust's gross income is $600 or more (regardless of taxable income). or
3. Any beneficiary is a nonresident alien.

Every trust that is required to file Form 1041 must have a tax identification number, which is an Employer Identification Number (EIN). The Employer Identification Number (EIN) can be obtained from the IRS online at *www.irs.gov*, or by completing Form SS-4, Application for Employer Identification Number, and either mailing it or faxing it to them. Information concerning the income and expenses of the trust are reported on Form 1041. The income reportable by the beneficiaries is shown on Schedule K-1, which is part of Form 1041. The Schedule K-1 form must show the income taxable to the beneficiary along with the beneficiary's name, address, and Social Security number. A copy of Schedule K-1 must be provided to each beneficiary who receives income from the trust for his or her reporting purposes.

What Is a Grantor Trust?

A grantor trust is one in which the grantor (settlor) is still living and retains sufficient control over the trust that he or she is considered the owner of the trust. Sufficient control means that the grantor has retained a reversionary interest (i.e., right to receive all of the trust property at some point) in the trust, the power over the beneficial enjoyment of the trust, administrative powers in the trust, the power to revoke the trust, and the right to receive the trust's income. A common example of a grantor trust is a revocable living trust.

FACT

If the creator of the trust is still alive and you are the trustee, you are not required to file a trust tax return, Form 1041.

172

A grantor trust is not considered a separate taxable entity. All income, deductions, and credits are reported on the grantor's (settlor's) individual income tax returns. Generally, Form 1041 is only required to be filed for a grantor trust if the settlor is not the trustee or co-trustee. In this situation, income and deductions, etc. are not reported on the return. Instead, a detailed statement outlining the income, deductions, and credits that are taxable to the grantor is attached to the return. Form 1041 is not required to be filed for a grantor trust if the grantor is the trustee or co-trustee, as in the case of a self-trusteed revocable living trust.

In this case the trust income, deductions, and credits are reported directly on the grantor's Individual Income Tax Return, Form 1040. The grantor must furnish all payers of income with his or her social security number and the payers will report the income just as if it had been paid directly to the grantor. If the grantor is not the trustee or co-trustee of the grantor trust, a trustee has two alternative ways of reporting:

1. The trustee can provide the name and Social Security number of the grantor, along with the address of the trust, to all of the payors of income during the taxable year. If this option is used, the trustee is not required to file a Form 1041 return with the Internal Revenue Service.
2. The trustee can provide the name, address, and tax identification number of the trust to all payors of income. The trustee must then file with the Internal Revenue Service appropriate 1099 forms that report each type of income, show the trust as the payor, and show the grantor as the payee.

If the trustee uses either of these alternatives, he or she must furnish to the grantor a statement that reflects all income, deductions, and credits attributable to the grantor along with any other information necessary for computing the grantor's taxable income. As a practical matter, it is easier to file the Form 1041 return.

What Is Distributable Net Income (DNI)?

Basically, trust income is taxed where it ends up. A trust can either be a conduit, passing all of its income out to beneficiaries, or it can retain some or all of the income, as is the case in a discretionary trust. Taxation of income that is distributed to a beneficiary is based on a concept called *distributable net income* (DNI), a principle that is unique to the taxation of estates and trusts.

FACT

DNI determines the amount that is taxable to a beneficiary, and how much of a distribution deduction is allowed on the trust's fiduciary income tax return (Form 1041). Deductible expenses may include charges against principal. DNI does not include the personal exemption deduction or capital gains and losses allocated to principal. However, it does include tax-exempt interest.

DNI is not the same as trust accounting income. Trust accounting income is the actual income received and recorded by the trust, less all expenses charged against income. Trust accounting income is usually what is distributed to beneficiaries. DNI can differ from trust accounting income because deductible expenses, which are part of DNI, may be charged against principal and therefore would not reduce the trust accounting income distributed to beneficiaries. Here is an example:

	Income	Principal
Dividends	$4,000	
Interest	$6,000	
Trustee Fees	(500)	(500)
	$9,500	$(500)
Trust Accounting Income =		
Income	$10,000	
Expenses	(500)	
Distribution to Beneficiaries	$9,500	
Distributable Net Income (DNI) =		
Income	$10,000	
Deductions	(1,000)	
DNI	$9,000	

In the previous example, the beneficiary reports taxable income of $9,000 (DNI) instead of the $9,500 of actual income he or she received from the trust (trust accounting income.) On the tax return(s) for the trust, the trustee deducts the amount of DNI distributed to beneficiaries. Generally, the taxable income remaining after the DNI deduction is taxed to the trust.

What Are Simple and Complex Trusts?

A trust is classified as either a simple trust or a complex trust for tax purposes. A simple trust, by its terms, requires all of its income to be distributed during the taxable year. It does not provide for charitable distributions and does not distribute any principal during the tax year of the trust. A simple trust is allowed an exemption of $300. A beneficiary of a simple trust must include DNI in his or her gross income, even if the income is not actually distributed during the tax year. A trust may be a simple trust in one year and a complex trust in a year in which the trust makes a distribution of principal to a beneficiary. The trustee is required to file Form 1041 for this type of trust.

A trust that is not a simple trust in any one year is a complex trust. A complex trust provides for discretionary distributions of income, can make distributions to a charity, or can be a simple trust that distributes principal during the taxable year of the trust. Form 1041 is also required to be filed for this type of trust and is allowed an exemption of $100. The deduction for distributions to beneficiaries cannot exceed DNI and any tax-exempt income must be subtracted from the deduction. In a complex trust, allocation of DNI to beneficiaries is based on a "tier system." This system exists to assure that a beneficiary who receives mandatory distributions under the trust receives the maximum amount of DNI before allocating the balance, if any, to other beneficiaries. The system has two tiers:

- *Tier 1 distributions*—Distributions of income that are required by the terms of a trust to be made to a beneficiary.
- *Tier 2 distributions*—Distributions of either income or principal that are in the discretion of the trustee.

Complex trusts can make discretionary distributions from income, principal, or both. Discretionary distributions are Tier 2 distributions and will carry out taxable income to the beneficiary only to the extent that DNI has not been allocated to Tier 1 distributions. For example, if all of the DNI has been allocated to Tier 1 distributions, any beneficiary receiving a Tier 2 distribution will not be taxed on that distribution. If Tier 1 distributions do not exceed DNI, the beneficiaries who receive Tier 2 distributions will be taxed proportionately on the remaining DNI.

Tier 1 and Tier 2 distributions are very complex computations, and the only reason they are mentioned here is to alert the trustee to the fact that distributions of principal may not be exempt from income tax. Trustees should consult a CPA before making a principal distribution that is intended to be tax-free.

The federal tax paid by an estate or trust is normally higher than for an individual because the taxable income threshold for the maximum rate is lower. For example, income retained in a trust that exceeds $11,950 is taxed at the maximum federal rate of 39.6% (2013 rates). For an individual, the maximum rate of 39.6% does not apply until the individual's taxable income exceeds $400,000 (2013 rates). If the trust had taxable income of $12,000, it would be taxed at 39.6%. If that income were distributed, the beneficiary would be taxed at a rate of 15%. This should not be a reason for the trustee to distribute all of the trust's income to beneficiaries who may be in a lower tax bracket. The trustee's first duty is to follow the terms of the trust and carry out its purpose.

Delaying Distributions—The 65-Day Rule

A trustee of a complex trust may elect to treat distributions paid within 65 days after the close of a trust tax year (December 31) as having been made on the last day of that tax year. This gives a trustee some flexibility as to when a beneficiary is taxed on trust income. It also gives the trustee time to compute distributions that will carry out DNI in a complex trust and possibly allocate the distribution to a year in which it does not. Once it is made, the election is irrevocable and cannot be in excess of the greater of trust accounting income or DNI for the tax year. The 65-day rule does not apply to simple trusts, since all of its income is taxable to the beneficiaries in the year it is required to be distributed, regardless of whether it is actually distributed or retained in the trust.

The Generation-Skipping Tax

A trustee may be required to report generation-skipping transfers from a trust and pay any taxes that are due. Transfers subject to the tax fall into three general categories:

- *Direct skip*—a transfer, subject to federal gift or estate tax, of a property interest directly to a skip person.
- *Taxable distributions*—any distribution from a trust to a skip person.
- *Taxable termination*—termination of an interest in a trust that results in a distribution to a skip person.

A skip person is one who is two or more generations below the transferor (settlor/decedent). This is typically the settlor's grandchild. If the parent of a skip person predeceased the settlor, that person moves up a generation and is not considered a skip person. For example, John's daughter, Mary, has two children. Mary dies before her father, John. Distributions to Mary's two children therefore would not be generation-skipping transfers.

If an executor has not been appointed, a trustee may be required to file a United States Gift (and Generation-Skipping Transfer) Tax Return, Form 709, to report a pre-death direct-skip transfer that the decedent made but did not report prior to his or her death. A trustee may also be required to report on the United States Estate (and Generation-Skipping Transfer) Tax Return, Form 706, any generation-skipping transfers that occur at the decedent's death by bequest under the decedent's will or trust. Distributions from a trust to a skip person during the term of the trust, and at the termination of the trust, must be reported on Form 709.

	Who files the return:	Who pays the tax:
Direct Skip	Transferor	Transferor
Taxable Distribution	Trustee	Beneficiary
		(Transferee)
Taxable Termination	Trustee	Trustee

Retirement Plans Payable to the Trust

The rules regarding the taxability of retirement plans (IRA, 401(k), profit-sharing, etc.) payable to trusts are complex. In general, there are two sets of rules that apply to these distributions. One set applies when the decedent dies before the required beginning date. The required beginning date is April 1 of the year following attainment of age 70½. In general, if a decedent dies prior to the required beginning date, all of the plan benefits must be distributed by the end of the fifth year following the death. The distributions do not have to be even, as long as the entire amount in the plan is distributed before the end of the five-year period. This is referred to as the *five-year rule*. If the decedent had named a nonspouse "designated beneficiary" under the retirement plan, including a qualified trust, the designated beneficiary can elect to have the distributions paid over his or her life expectancy, which is called the *life expectancy method*.

ALERT

The rules for retirement plans payable to a trust are complex, and a trustee should get competent advice when handling these transactions.

The second set of rules applies when the decedent dies after the required beginning date. If a decedent named a designated beneficiary, including a qualified trust, under his or her retirement plan, the distributions must continue to be made over the balance of the joint life expectancy of the decedent and the designated beneficiary. If a qualified trust is the designated beneficiary, life expectancy is based on the age of the oldest beneficiary of the trust. A trust will qualify as a designated beneficiary for the purpose of these taxability options if:

1. The trust is valid under state law.
2. The beneficiaries are identifiable under the trust document.
3. The trust is irrevocable or, by its terms, will become irrevocable upon the death of the participant.
4. Certain documentation is provided to the plan administrator.
5. All beneficiaries of the trust are individuals.
6. No person has the power to change a beneficiary after the participant's death.

Under rule 4, the trustee is responsible for fulfilling the documentation requirement. The trustee is required to provide the plan administrator with either of the following:

1. A final list of all of the beneficiaries of the trust (including contingent and remaindermen beneficiaries), with a description of the conditions on their entitlement as of the date of death. Certify that, to the best of the trustee's knowledge, the list is correct and complete; the trust is valid under state law; the trust is irrevocable as of the decedent's death; and the beneficiaries are identifiable. The trustee must also agree to provide a copy of the trust document to the plan administrator upon demand.
2. A copy of the actual trust document.

The trustee must provide documentation to the plan administrator within nine months after the date of death. If rules 1 through 6 are not complied with in the case of a decedent who dies before the required beginning date, all of the benefits must be distributed to the trust within five years (the five-year rule) of the decedent's death. The life-expectancy method will not be available. If the rules are not complied with in the case of a decedent who dies after the required beginning date, the distributions will be based on the decedent's life expectancy only and not on the joint life of the decedent and the oldest beneficiary of the trust. If the decedent's spouse is the primary beneficiary of the trust, the more favorable rules that apply to spouse-beneficiaries may be available. Complying with the rules will give the trustee the option of maximizing the deferral of the tax. Again, these rules are complex, and the trustee should seek guidance from a qualified professional.

CHAPTER 12

How to Manage the Trust's Investments Portfolio

A trustee has the responsibility for managing the trust's investments until the assets are ultimately distributed to the beneficiaries. The trustee's authority for investing trust assets varies from trust to trust. The trustee may be given sole authority under the trust document or may be required to consult with a designated individual in making investment decisions. Even if the trust document directs the trustee to consult with others before making investment decisions, the trustee is ultimately responsible unless there is language in the trust that protects the trustee from any liability that may result from a consultant's advice.

Investment Responsibilities under a Terminating Trust

The investment responsibility of a trustee falls into two general categories. One is managing investments in a terminating trust where the investment responsibility is relatively passive. The other is the responsibility under a continuing trust, which requires ongoing decision-making in managing the portfolio.

FACT

The trust document may direct the trustee to invest in specific stocks or restrict investments to certain asset categories like insured bank deposits or U.S. Treasury obligations, for example. If a trust document is vague or does not give a trustee sufficient powers, the trustee can look to local law for guidance.

A trustee's investment responsibilities under a trust that terminates at the death of the settlor are the same as for an executor. The trustee's responsibility is to preserve the assets and raise the cash needed to pay estate expenses, taxes, cash bequests, etc. as soon as is practical. If investments are to be sold to raise cash, an analysis needs to be made to determine which securities are the best candidates for liquidation. Preserving assets does not require the trustee to manage the investments for the purpose of making more money for the beneficiaries. Preservation, in this context, means that the trustee should take whatever action is necessary to prevent known and obvious losses from occurring, beyond those that are the result of normal market fluctuations. For example, let's say a particular stock's value is rapidly dropping because the company's president has been fired, or the company is being sued for a billion dollars and it is obvious that the company is not likely to recover from these events anytime soon. The trustee should consider selling the stock to preserve what is left of its value for the beneficiaries.

ESSENTIAL

Any cash should be deposited in interest-bearing accounts and, if possible, rents collected from real estate assets.

Investment Responsibilities under a Continuing Trust

In a continuing trust, the trustee's investment duties are active and ongoing. The ongoing management must take into consideration the terms of the trust, the income requirements of the beneficiaries, the need to make distributions of principal, and other circumstances of the trust that affect investment decisions as they occur.

In managing the trust's investments, the trustee must also take into consideration the inherent conflict between the objectives of the current income beneficiaries and the remaindermen. The income beneficiaries want the trustee to invest in securities that will maximize the current income they receive, and the remaindermen want maximum growth to increase the value of their inheritance when the trust terminates. Balancing these objectives presents special challenges for trustees. The trustee must produce enough income to meet the needs of the income beneficiaries and cover administration expenses, as well as provide some growth to the portfolio as a hedge against inflation, and to protect the interests of the remaindermen.

What Investment Standards Apply to Trustees?

Trustees are required to adhere to certain investment standards when managing trust assets. The origins of these standards date back to the early 1800s. The so-called "prudent man rule" statutes were developed from the Harvard v. Amory (1830) case in which the court described how trustees should conduct themselves when managing the trust's investments. The court said that:

> *"All that can be required of a trustee to invest is that he shall conduct himself faithfully and exercise a sound discretion. He is to observe how men of prudence, discretion, and intelligence manage their own affairs, not in regard to speculation, but in regard to the permanent disposition of their funds, considering the probable income, as well as the probable safety of the capital to be invested."*

Under the law of trusts (The Restatement of Trusts 2d (1959)), the same theme prevails as in the Amory case:

"In making investments of trust funds the trustee is under a duty to the beneficiary . . . to make such investments and only such investments as a prudent man would make of his own property having in view the preservation of the estate and the amount and regularity of the income to be derived . . ."

The standard measures a trustee's actions against the actions of others. That is, the law asks the question, "Did the trustee behave in a way that other trustees would have behaved under similar circumstances?" The rules of trust law are default rules. This allows the creator of a trust to direct the trustee, under the terms of his or her trust, to manage the trust in a manner that would not necessarily be permitted under the standards of prudence. However, absent any specific investment directive, a trustee is expected to follow the standards of conduct established under the law.

The Uniform Prudent Investor Act

The National Conference of Commissioners on Uniform State Laws has drafted standards of conduct for trustees who manage trust investments in an attempt to bring uniformity to each state's statutes. The Uniform Prudent Investor Act, which reflects the new guidelines for trustees under the Restatement of Trusts 3d: Prudent Investor Rule, has been enacted by most states. It recognizes that the old rule is outmoded and describes a modern portfolio theory standard for managing trust assets. Although the Uniform Prudent Investor Act is a default rule—that is, the trust document can alter or abrogate the rules under the Act—trustees should refer to it as a guide in managing trust assets as long as the terms of the trust do not give a contrary directive.

Uniform Prudent Investor Act Information

Section 1. Prudent Investor Rule

(a) Except as otherwise provided in subsection (b), a trustee who invests and manages trust assets owes a duty to the beneficiaries of the trust to comply with the prudent investor rule set forth in this [Act].

(b) The prudent investor rule, a default rule, may be expanded, restricted, eliminated, or otherwise altered by the provisions of a trust. A trustee is not liable to a beneficiary to the extent that the trustee acted in reasonable reliance on the provisions of the trust.

Section 2. Standard of Care; Portfolio Strategy; Risk and Return Objectives.

(a) A trustee shall invest and manage trust assets as a prudent investor would, by considering the purposes, terms, distribution requirement, and other circumstances of the trust. In satisfying this standard, the trustee shall exercise reasonable care, skill, and caution.

(b) A trustee's investment and management decisions respecting individual assets must be evaluated not in isolation but in the context of the trust portfolio as a whole and as part of an overall investment strategy having risk and return objectives reasonably suited to the trust.

(c) Among circumstances that a trustee shall consider in investing and managing trust assets are such of the following as are relevant to the trust or its beneficiaries:

> *general economic conditions;*
>
> *the possible effect of inflation or deflation;*
>
> *the expected tax consequences of investment decisions or strategies;*
>
> *the role that each investment or course of action plays within the overall trust portfolio, which may include financial assets, interests in closely held enterprises, tangible and intangible personal property, and real property;*
>
> *the expected total return from income and the appreciation of capital;*
>
> *other resources of the beneficiaries;*
>
> *needs for liquidity, regularity of income, and preservation or appreciation of capital; and*
>
> *an asset's special relationship or special value, if any, to the purposes of the trust or to one or more of the beneficiaries.*

(d) A trustee shall make a reasonable effort to verify facts relevant to the investment and management of trust assets.

(e) A trustee may invest in any kind of property or type of investment consistent with the standards of this [Act].

(f) A trustee who has special skills or expertise, or is named trustee in reliance upon the trustee's representation that the trustee has special skills or expertise, has a duty to use those special skills or expertise.

Section 3. Diversification. A trustee shall diversify the investments of the trust unless the trustee reasonably determines that, because of special circumstances, the purposes of the trust are better served without diversifying.

Section 4. Duties of Inception of Trusteeship. Within a reasonable time after accepting a trusteeship or receiving trust assets, a trustee shall review the trust assets and make and implement decisions concerning the retention and disposition of assets, in order to bring the trust portfolio into compliance with the purposes, terms, distribution requirements, and other circumstances of the trust, and with the requirements of this [Act].

Section 5. Loyalty. A trustee shall invest and manage the trust assets solely in the interest of the beneficiaries.

Section 6. Impartiality. If a trust has two or more beneficiaries, the trustee shall act impartially in investing and managing the trust assets, taking into account any differing interests of the beneficiaries.

Section 7. Investment Costs. In investing and managing trust assets, a trustee may only incur costs that are appropriate and reasonable in relation to the assets, the purposes of the trust, and the skills of the trustee.

Section 8. Reviewing Compliance. Compliance with the prudent investor rule is determined in light of the facts and circumstances existing at the time of a trustee's decision or action and not by hindsight.

Section 9. Delegation of Investment and Management Functions.

(a) A trustee may delegate investment and management functions that a prudent trustee of comparable skills could properly delegate under the circumstances. The trustee shall exercise reasonable care, skill, and caution in:

selecting an agent;

establishing the scope and terms of the delegation, consistent with the purposes and terms of the trust; and

periodically reviewing the agent's actions in order to monitor the agent's performance and compliance with the terms of the delegation.

(b) In performing a delegated function, an agent owes a duty to the trust to exercise reasonable care to comply with the terms of the delegation.

(c) A trustee who complies with the requirements of subsection (a) is not liable the beneficiaries or to the trust for the decisions or actions of the agent to whom the function was delegated.

(d) By accepting the delegation of a trust function from the trustee or a trust that is subject to the law of this State, an agent submits to the jurisdiction of the courts of this State.

Section 10. Language Invoking Standard of [Act]. The following terms or comparable language in the provisions of a trust, unless otherwise limited or modified, authorizes any investment or strategy permitted under this [Act]: "investments permissible by law for investment of trust funds," "legal investments," "authorized investments," "using the judgment and care under the circumstances then prevailing that persons of prudence, discretion, and intelligence exercise in the management of their own affairs, not in regard to speculation but in regard to the permanent disposition of their funds, considering the probable income as well as the probable safety of their capital," "prudent man rule," "prudent trustee rule," "prudent person rule," and "prudent investor rule."

The old "prudent man rule" statute places greater emphasis on specific security selection in the portfolio than the new Uniform Prudent Investor

Act law does. The Uniform Prudent Investor Act applies the standard of prudence to an investment as part of the entire portfolio, rather than on the individual investment.

Total Return

The Uniform Prudent Investor Act allows a trustee to make investments on a total return basis. The total return concept takes into account both the growth (capital appreciation) of an investment and the income earned (dividends and interest) to determine the merits of a particular investment or the portfolio strategy as a whole. For example, a particular stock may pay a dividend that equates to a current yield of 1%, which on the surface may appear to be a poor investment. However, in a twelve-month period the stock may have increased in value by 15%, or a total return (the dividend yield plus capital appreciation) of 16%. This gives the trustee the opportunity to earn a higher return for the trust than could be achieved by investing in a security with a high current yield, such as a bond or high-dividend-paying stock. In addition to being the best measure of investment performance, the total return approach gives a trustee more flexibility in managing the trust's portfolio.

Several states have also adopted the new Uniform Principal and Income Act, which complements the total return approach to investing trust assets. The act will allow transfer of some of the appreciation from principal to income for distribution to the income beneficiaries. This provision is intended to assure that the trustee will distribute adequate returns to the income beneficiary even if the portfolio does not produce high income.

ESSENTIAL

The total return concept under the Uniform Prudent Investor Act gives a trustee more latitude in investment decisions than the old law. In managing the portfolio, trustees can take advantage of investment opportunities that rely primarily on returns from appreciation rather than from income. Trustees should review the trust document and local law before applying this technique in managing the trust's portfolio.

Modern Portfolio Theory

Modern portfolio theory holds that a trustee should purchase investments based on how a security is expected to perform relative to the risk and return of the entire portfolio, not necessarily how that investment will perform by itself. It allows a trustee to include riskier securities in a portfolio as well as conservative ones. The theory requires the trustee to carefully monitor the individual investments in the portfolio and notice how they influence the trust's overall investment strategy. Modern portfolio theory defines two types of risks: compensated and uncompensated. A start-up company has greater risk to an investor than a large well-established corporation. Investing in this type of company offers a potentially higher rate of return for assuming the higher risk. In modern portfolio theory, this is referred to as *compensated risk*. A particular security, which if taken alone might be very risky, may be prudent when purchased in the overall context of the portfolio, under this theory.

Uncompensated risk is created when the trust does not contain a sufficient number of companies and industries in its makeup. In this situation, the portfolio is not being compensated by the company or market for the risk. Diversification of the portfolio minimizes uncompensated risk. Those states that have incorporated modern portfolio theory in their statutes emphasize that diversification within a trust portfolio is expected and a trustee must justify lack of diversification.

General Categories of Investments

Managing a trust portfolio involves the prudent allocation of investments that are suitable to the needs of the beneficiaries and overall investment objectives of the trust. It is important for the trustee to understand the basic asset allocation choices (equities, fixed income, and cash), the reasons for using a combination of each asset, and the investment characteristics of each type. The trustee's job is to select and allocate a mix of equities, fixed income securities, and cash to meet the investment objectives of the trust, while staying within acceptable risk levels. Let's review some investment basics ("Investments 101").

Equities

Equities are investments in the common stock of a company. The investor holds an ownership interest and shares in the company's profits through shareholders' dividends. As the company grows and becomes more profitable, the investor is also rewarded through appreciation in the price of the company's stock. As a general rule, dividends that are paid on common stocks represent a relatively small part of the return on equity investments. Current dividend yields (dividend ÷ price of the stock) may typically be in the 1% to 2% range. The primary reason for investing in equities is the expectation of future appreciation in the price of the stock, which is driven by the profitability of the company. The justification for investing in equities is their record of long-term growth and earnings, which, in addition to providing some income to the income beneficiaries, can help protect the portfolio from the eroding effect of inflation. Equity investments are not without risk. Stocks are subject to business, interest rate, and market risks; however, in most cases, using equities in a trust portfolio makes sense and is a reasonable way to manage the trust's investments.

ALERT

The amount allocated to equities should, of course, take into account the need for income; the liquidity requirements in the short, intermediate, and long term; the estimated termination date of the trust; the need to protect the portfolio from unnecessary risk; and the overall investment objectives of the trust.

Types of Stocks

Stocks fall into several categories and the terms used to describe them are the common jargon of investors. Trustees should be familiar with some of these terms. The capitalization of a company is determined by multiplying the number of shares outstanding by the price of the stock. For example, let's say IBM had approximately 1,795,760,770 shares outstanding on its books at a given date. Let's also say that the closing stock price was $109 on that same day. Multiplying 1,795,760,770 by $109 equals a capitalization of more than $195 billion.

Generally, if a company has a capitalization over $5 billion, it is considered a large cap (i.e., large-capitalization) stock. A capitalization between $1 billion and $2 billion is a mid-cap stock, and below $1 billion is considered a small-cap stock. Generally speaking, large-cap stocks are established companies that usually pay dividends. Also called *blue-chip stocks*, they tend to be more liquid. Mid-cap stocks, because of their size and maturity, have a little more risk than large-cap stocks. Small-cap stocks are the riskiest of the three categories. Their price tends to be very volatile and they have relatively few shares outstanding. This makes small-cap stocks less liquid.

Some stocks are purchased because the stock is selling at a bargain price. These are called *value stocks*. They are purchased at their lower price by investors that are looking for the stock to return to its fair market value. Value stocks are usually purchased by investors who are more conservative and willing to wait for a longer period of time to reap the potential rewards. Growth stock investors look for companies whose earnings will grow. As long as earnings keep growing, the price of the stock is expected to increase. Growth stocks tend to be more volatile and usually have a higher risk than value stocks.

FACT

Another category of stocks is *cyclicals*, which react to changes in the economic cycle. For example, as the economy is expanding, new buildings and production equipment are needed. Companies that produce construction materials and sell manufacturing equipment will benefit. While these companies will do well in an economic expansion, the price of that stock will be adversely affected when the economy begins to contract.

Fixed Income

Fixed income securities are debt obligations issued by corporations and state, city, and federal governments. These obligations are generally referred to as bonds, but include notes, debentures, and mortgages. Bonds are purchased primarily for their interest income and the security of their full face value if held until maturity. The interest paid is generally considerably higher than the dividends paid on common stocks.

Investments in fixed income securities are not without risk. Because the interest rate on a bond is fixed for the term of the obligation, any market interest-rate fluctuations will affect the price, or value, of the bond prior to its maturity. Market interest rates have an inverse relationship to the price of a bond. If market interest rates are higher than the rate paid (the "coupon rate") on a bond, the price of that bond will drop. If market rates are lower, the price of the bond will be higher. However, if a bond is held to maturity, the investor gets the full face value back.

There are basically three types of bonds: Corporates, Municipals, and Treasuries. Corporate bonds pay interest that is subject to federal and state income taxes. The interest from municipal bonds (i.e., debt obligations issued by government entities) is federally tax-exempt. If owned by a trust in the state or municipality that issued them, the interest is also exempt from local taxes. However, municipal bond interest paid to a beneficiary from a trust will only be dual tax-exempt if a municipality in which the beneficiary resides issued the bond. Interest from U.S. Treasury obligations is subject to federal income tax and in some states is exempt from state income tax. In selecting any fixed income document for the portfolio, the trustee should consider liquidity needs, income requirements, and the marginal income tax bracket of the beneficiaries. If some or all of the income is retained and taxed to the trust, the tax bracket of the trust should be taken into consideration.

The choice between a taxable bond and a tax-free bond is determined by converting the current yield on the tax-exempt bond (municipal bond) to its taxable equivalent. The following formula can be used for this purpose:

$$\frac{\text{Nontaxable return (\%)}}{(1 - \text{marginal tax bracket})} = \text{Taxable Equivalent}$$

Example: Taxable bond yield – 4.25%

Nontaxable yield – 3.25%

Marginal tax bracket – 28%

$$\frac{3.25\%}{(1 - 28\%)} = \frac{.0325}{.72} = .0451 = 4.51\%$$

In this example, the nontaxable bond has the higher taxable yield and is the better choice. The taxable bond would have to yield 4.51% to equal the before-tax return on the nontaxable bond. U.S. Treasury obligations are generally viewed as having less risk than corporate and municipal bonds, because they are backed by the full faith and credit of the federal government.

Cash Equivalents

Cash equivalent investments are highly liquid and include interest-bearing savings and checking accounts, money market funds, some certificates of deposit (CDs) and short-term U.S. Treasury bills. In the context of managing a trust portfolio, these are used to meet known short-term cash needs and for temporary investment of funds awaiting investment in more permanent securities. The rate of return is usually lower than other fixed income investments because there is little or no risk, and in the case of a checking account, savings account, or money market fund, the full amount of the principal is available upon demand. The principal on other short-term vehicles such as CDs and treasury bills can be recovered in a short period, usually less than a year. Trustees cannot let cash sit idle and must keep trust funds properly invested at all times. Cash receipts should be invested in an appropriate short-term investment until the funds are paid out or more permanently invested in a longer-term vehicle.

Mutual Funds

A mutual fund is a pool of money from individual investors that is invested in stocks, bonds, short-term money market documents, and a variety of other investments. Some mutual funds invest in a combination of these investments. A mutual fund provides ongoing professional management and diversification to minimize investor risk. There was a time when investment in a mutual fund by a trustee could be viewed as an unauthorized delegation of the trustee's investment duty. At issue was the fact that the mutual fund manager, not the trustee, made the investment choices for the trust. In addition, the trustee could not closely oversee the activities or ratify the actions of the fund manager. Other issues included the unauthorized commingling of trust assets with others and double management fees. The trustee would be charging a trustee's fee based on the value of the trust assets, including the mutual fund, while the fund manager is charging the mutual fund investors a management fee.

This is not an issue if the trust document authorizes the trustee to invest in mutual funds, and most modern trusts do. Even if authority is not given under the terms of the trust, most state statutes allow trustees to invest trust money in mutual funds. If state statutes do not specifically authorize the use of mutual funds in trusts, Section 227 of the Restatement (Third) of Trusts (1992) indicates that such an investment is permissible:

"In the absence of restrictions imposed by statute or by the terms of the trust, mutual funds and other pooling arrangements are clearly permissible investments and that they tend to facilitate diversification."

If there is any doubt, the trustee can obtain written authority to invest in mutual funds from the beneficiaries of the trust.

Deferred Annuities

Although deferred annuities are not considered investments in the classical sense, they are viewed that way by many investors. A deferred annuity is a contract between the owner of the annuity and an insurance company. The owner invests a lump sum with the insurance company or makes payments over a period of time. The insurance company invests the funds and pays out a benefit to the annuitant for a specified time or the lifetime of the annuitant. There are two types of deferred annuities: a fixed annuity and a variable annuity. A fixed annuity pays a set rate, or payment, and is the more conservative investment of the two types. A variable annuity allows the owner to choose how the funds will be invested, which is usually from a group of mutual funds. The payout is based on the investment return—the better the return, the higher the payout; the lower the return, the smaller the payout.

The major advantage of deferred annuities is that the earnings are tax deferred until paid out to the annuitant. In a trust context, an annuity may not always be an appropriate investment. In general, if a non-natural entity, like a trust, owns an annuity, the annuity may not receive tax-deferred treatment on its earnings. If a trustee purchases an annuity for a beneficiary, it may be viewed as favoring that beneficiary over other beneficiaries of the trust. This could be a violation of the duty of impartiality. However, annuities may be appropriate in addressing a specific trust need. For example, if a trust has limited resources, the trustee may want to purchase an annuity to guaranty income payments to a particular beneficiary.

Minimizing Risk to the Trust's Portfolio

Trustees have a responsibility to prudently manage the investment risk in a trust portfolio. This does not mean that the trustee can invest the entire portfolio in very safe investments, such as U.S. Treasury bills, CDs, etc. to avoid risk. In most circumstances, this would be considered imprudent. The trustee's responsibility is not to avoid risk entirely, but to assume a reasonable amount of risk consistent with achieving the investment objectives of the trust.

ALERT

There are several things that need to be considered in minimizing risk in the trust's portfolio. They include avoiding improper investments, the terms of the trust, types of investments selected, allocation of assets, diversification, dollar cost averaging and laddering of maturities when investing in bonds.

Improper Trust Investments

Under the Uniform Prudent Investor Act, trustees are evaluated by the total performance of the portfolio and not necessarily by the results of a single investment. However, each individual investment decision that is made must still be prudent. A poor investment could materially affect the overall results of the portfolio and therefore might be deemed improper. Some investments that may be considered improper investments for trustees include:

- Investments in which the trustee has a personal interest
- Proprietorships and general partnerships
- Short-term investments made for quick turnover and high potential profit
- Unproductive property
- Unsecured loans
- Investments whose value will diminish over time (i.e., wasting assets)

In general, while these investments may be considered improper, they are not prohibited in all cases. Under certain circumstances their use would not be imprudent. For example, the use of family limited partnerships has become an important estate planning tool. Holding these interests in a trust would not be considered imprudent, assuming that the underlying assets in the partnership are reasonable investments.

ALERT

Don't jeopardize the trust or yourself by making imprudent investments.

Terms of the Trust

Most investment managers agree that investing in stocks and bonds for a short time is considerably more risky than using those vehicles for the longer term. Stocks and even bond prices can drop substantially within a given year. If a trustee is forced to liquidate these assets in a down market, losses could be realized. As a general rule, the shorter the term of the trust, the less exposure it should have to equities. If a trust, let's say, will terminate in less than five years, the portfolio should be more conservatively structured to maintain stability and preserve value. While the construction of every trust portfolio takes into account the cash needs of the beneficiaries, capital gains, and other factors, the allocation of assets should also take into consideration the time frame of the trust.

Types of Investments

Trustees are usually given broad authority to invest funds as the trustee deems proper for the trust. Understanding the characteristics of each type of investment and its respective risk level is essential to this decision-making process. The investment pyramid is a good place to start:

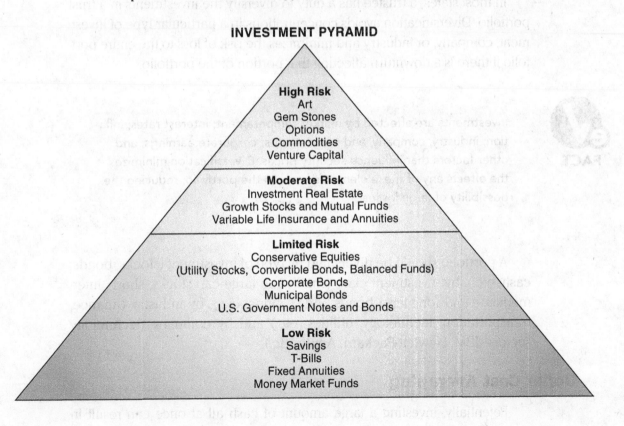

INVESTMENT PYRAMID

High Risk
Art
Gem Stones
Options
Commodities
Venture Capital

Moderate Risk
Investment Real Estate
Growth Stocks and Mutual Funds
Variable Life Insurance and Annuities

Limited Risk
Conservative Equities
(Utility Stocks, Convertible Bonds, Balanced Funds)
Corporate Bonds
Municipal Bonds
U.S. Government Notes and Bonds

Low Risk
Savings
T-Bills
Fixed Annuities
Money Market Funds

Asset Allocation

The objective of asset allocation is to minimize the risk associated with market volatility yet meet the current return and long-term growth objectives of the trust. The trust's portfolio should be diversified among general asset categories (stocks, bonds, cash, etc.) consistent with the amount of income that needs to be generated for trust beneficiaries, the trust's long-term growth objectives, its liquidity needs, and the income tax brackets of the beneficiaries and the trust. The trick in asset allocation is not to overweight the portfolio toward one asset category and underweight in another. The asset mix and weightings should be consistent with the overall investment objectives of the trust.

Diversification

In most states, a trustee has a duty to diversify the investments in a trust portfolio. Diversification avoids concentrations in a particular type of investment, company, or industry and minimizes the risk of loss to the entire portfolio if there is a downturn affecting that portion of the portfolio.

FACT

Investments are affected by market temperament; interest rates; inflation; industry, company, and world events; corporate earnings; and other factors that influence security prices. Diversification minimizes the effects any of these elements have on the portfolio, reducing the possibility of large losses.

A portfolio should be diversified by type of investment (stocks, bonds, cash, etc.), by investment class (small- and large-cap stocks; short-, intermediate-, and long-term bonds; index funds; etc.), by industry (finance, transportation, technology, utilities, etc.) and by company (technology sector—IBM, Hewlett-Packard, Apple, etc.).

Dollar Cost Averaging

Potentially, investing a large amount of cash all at once can result in paying the highest price for a particular investment. To minimize this risk, particularly with investments in common stocks, use the dollar cost averaging approach when making the investment. An equal amount of the investment is purchased over a period. It can be months or years, depending on market conditions and the amount to be invested. Dollar cost averaging spreads the cost of the security over time, thereby spreading the risk of paying too much for the investment.

Ladder of Maturities

Bond prices are affected by fluctuations in interest rates. The price of the bond will fall if interest rates rise relative to the rate (coupon rate) paid on the bond. If interest rates are lower than the rate paid on the bond, the price of the bond will rise. The problem, of course, is that a loss can occur if the trustee is forced to sell a bond at a low price in order to meet a cash need, such as a principal distribution to a beneficiary. If a bond is held until it matures there is no risk, since the entire amount of the principal is returned to the investor. If bonds are purchased so that they mature at different times over a period of years ("laddering"), the risk of loss can be significantly reduced. Another advantage of laddering over shorter periods is to maintain current market interest rates of return in the portfolio. That is, as interest rates rise, the proceeds of maturing bonds can be reinvested in bonds that pay current market rates.

Setting Up an Investment Process for the Portfolio

The prudent investor rule and Uniform Prudent Investor Act focus on the courts' long-held position that the way a trustee manages a trust portfolio is more important than the investment results that he or she achieves. A prudent trustee should have a well-defined process in place to manage the trust's portfolio. Policies and procedures should be established and all portfolio reviews and actions should be documented. The trustee must also consider the duty of loyalty and impartiality to the beneficiaries in whatever actions he or she takes in managing the portfolio. While the investment process may vary slightly from one trust to another and from one trustee to another, it should contain those components necessary to effectively perform this function in accordance with the trust document, the needs of the beneficiaries, and the prudent investor rule. The process outlined below contains some of these basic components:

THE INVESTMENT PROCESS

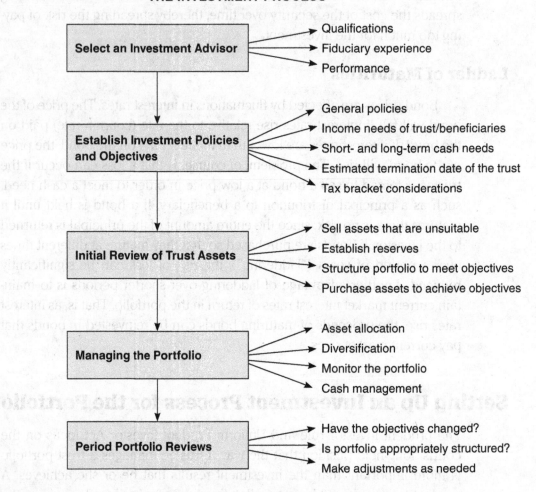

Select an Investment Advisor
- Qualifications
- Fiduciary experience
- Performance

Establish Investment Policies and Objectives
- General policies
- Income needs of trust/beneficiaries
- Short- and long-term cash needs
- Estimated termination date of the trust
- Tax bracket considerations

Initial Review of Trust Assets
- Sell assets that are unsuitable
- Establish reserves
- Structure portfolio to meet objectives
- Purchase assets to achieve objectives

Managing the Portfolio
- Asset allocation
- Diversification
- Monitor the portfolio
- Cash management

Period Portfolio Reviews
- Have the objectives changed?
- Is portfolio appropriately structured?
- Make adjustments as needed

ESSENTIAL

The investment process you establish and follow will always be more important than how the portfolio performs.

Selecting an Investment Manager

The management of a trust portfolio is not a part-time activity. A trustee must be able to respond to fast-moving events in unpredictable securities markets and changing economic conditions in managing the portfolio. This can be a full-time job. A prudent trustee would be wise to seek the assistance of a qualified investment professional. Commentators on the prudent investor rule have suggested that the rule encourages, and may even require, a trustee to seek professional expertise in managing the trust's portfolio. The Uniform Prudent Investor Act (Section 9), the new law, encourages trustees to delegate the investment responsibility to others by providing that:

"A trustee may delegate investment and management functions that a prudent trustee of comparable skills could properly delegate under the circumstances."

However, the Act goes on to say that:

"The trustee shall exercise reasonable care, skill, and caution in:

1. selecting an agent;
2. establishing the scope and terms of the delegation, consistent with the purposes and terms of the trust; and
3. periodically reviewing the agent's actions in order to monitor the agent's performance and compliance with the terms of the delegation."

This means the trustee must act prudently in deciding to delegate the investment function to an advisor, but at the same time is required to retain significant responsibility by supervising the professional he or she hires.

Establish Investment Policies and Objectives

Investment policies articulate the general framework under which the assets of the trust will be managed. The following should be among the items covered in the policy:

- Whether or not an investment advisor will be retained and, if one is hired, to what extent the advisor will be used. For example, will the advisor provide assistance as needed or will the investment responsibility be delegated to the advisor?
- What quality standards will be applied to investments in stocks?
- What will be the minimum ratings for bonds that are purchased for the portfolio and what will be the maximum maturity or duration?
- If mutual funds are used, will there be any restrictions regarding the use of "load" and "no-load" shares?
- What will be the maximum percentage of the portfolio invested in any one security?
- What general asset allocation weightings will be used?
- What will be the frequency of investment reviews for the trust?
- What benchmarks will be used to measure the portfolio's performance?

ESSENTIAL

Establishing investment policies and objectives will keep you and your advisor on the right track!

In addition, the trustee should develop general investment objectives for meeting the needs of the trust beneficiaries—both income beneficiaries and remaindermen. Before these objectives can be formulated, the trust document must be reviewed thoroughly. The terms of the trust may impose restrictions on investing trust assets or give directives that will affect how the funds are managed. For example, the trust may require the trustee to retain certain assets, restrict investments to specific kinds of securities, give preference to one or more beneficiaries, require that all of the income be paid to a beneficiary to maintain a specified standard of living, provide that certain amounts of principal be paid at specified times, and other provisions that the trustee may need to consider in making investment decisions. In addition to reviewing the trust document, there are other issues to consider in developing the investment objectives for the portfolio:

- The amount of income required to meet trust expenses and the needs of the beneficiaries
- The ages of the beneficiaries
- The income tax bracket of the trust and the beneficiaries
- The estimated termination date of the trust
- The short- and long-term needs for principal distributions
- The amount of unrealized capital gains
- The overall size of the trust, relative to the anticipated needs of the beneficiaries
- The nature of the other assets (other than securities) of the trust

ESSENTIAL

The investment objectives of the trust can by no means remain static. The nature of the trust and the needs of the beneficiaries will change over time, and the investment objectives must be adjusted to accommodate those changes.

When more income is needed, the portfolio objectives can be weighted toward fixed income investments to increase cash flow. If a total return strategy is used, the objectives must consider how much will be paid out to the beneficiaries each year. A trustee should consult with a qualified investment advisor in developing these guidelines.

Initial Review of Trust Assets

Within a reasonable time after accepting the trusteeship, the trustee should review the assets of the trust. If there are large concentrations in a single investment and the beneficiaries do not want the investment liquidated, the trustee must ascertain whether retention is authorized by the terms of the trust document or local law. If not, the holding must be diversified. Another purpose of the initial review is to begin restructuring the portfolio to meet the new investment objectives. This may involve selling some assets and purchasing others to achieve the desired asset allocation and positioning of the portfolio. Cash reserves need to be established for the trust to meet anticipated cash-flow shortages and principal distributions. The portfolio strategy may also call for keeping some cash available for future investment. At the time of the initial review, these cash needs should be identified and the funds raised and invested in a money market fund or other liquid short-term vehicle.

Managing the Portfolio

Managing a trust portfolio on a part-time basis and with limited investment knowledge is risky. Hiring an investment advisor substantially reduces the risk and allows the trustee to handle other trust matters more effectively. Establishing procedures for managing the assets of the trust and documenting investment decisions are good trust-management practices. Part of the ongoing managing process involves maintaining the general asset-allocation strategy for the portfolio. Fluctuations in the value of trust assets will affect asset allocation and the trustee may need to make adjustments to the portfolio to maintain the proper mix. Diversification of the portfolio can also be affected by changes in market values and yields. Changing circumstances within a given market or company can also affect diversification. Maintaining a well-diversified portfolio is important. As mentioned earlier, the portfolio should be diversified by asset type, industry, and company to minimize the risk of loss to the trust.

ESSENTIAL

The cash requirements of the trust and its beneficiaries can also change during the course of the year. This needs to be taken into account when managing the portfolio. As the need for cash arises, the funds should be raised as soon as is practical without loss to the portfolio, if possible.

Under the Uniform Prudent Investor Act, a trustee can delegate the investment responsibility for the trust to an agent (an investment advisor). However, the Act imposes a duty on the trustee in selecting the agent, establishing the terms of the delegation, and reviewing the agent's compliance with those terms. As part of the ongoing management of the trust, the trustee needs to communicate with and regularly oversee the activities of the agent, whether or not the trustee delegates this responsibility under the Act or hires someone to assist in the management of the portfolio.

Periodic Portfolio Reviews

Review of the trust portfolio should take place at least every twelve months and more frequently if needed. The review determines if changes in the circumstances of the beneficiaries necessitate a change in the investment objectives or basic portfolio structure. The need for more income, for instance, may require a realignment of the portfolio toward fixed income securities. Or the need for income may have diminished, in which case the trustee might consider a shift to equities. Changes in the securities markets are frequent, and portfolio reviews should take these events into account and, if necessary, appropriate adjustments in the portfolio should be made.

The review is also an opportunity for the trustee to measure and evaluate how the portfolio and the investment advisor (agent) have done relative to meeting the investment objectives. The policies and objectives should also be reviewed and adjustments made where appropriate. Although communication with beneficiaries should be frequent and ongoing anyway, the portfolio review is a good time to discuss objectives, performance, and other investment matters with them.

Checklist for Managing the Trust's Portfolio

- Select an investment advisor (agent) to assist in evaluating and managing the portfolio.
- Review the trust document for any provisions that place investment restrictions on the trustee.
- Ascertain what investment standards (i.e., "Prudent Investor Rule," "Uniform Prudent Investor Act," etc.) apply under local law, and familiarize yourself with the law.
- Review the portfolio immediately to determine if any of the securities are illegal, substandard, or unsuitable trust investments. Liquidate all inappropriate investments.
- Invest idle cash in a money market fund or other suitable short-term investment vehicle.

- Establish an investment policy and strategy for the trust based on: how much income will be required to cover trust expenses and meet the income requirements of trust beneficiaries; the short-, intermediate-, and long-term cash needs to cover anticipated principal distributions; the income tax brackets of the trust and the beneficiaries who receive income from the trust; and the known or estimated termination date of the trust.

- Diversify the portfolio by: types of securities (stocks, bonds, cash, real estate, mortgages, etc.); characteristics (income, growth, size of company, etc.); industry (durable goods, utilities, transportation, technology, finance, etc.); companies within industries; and bond maturities.

- Establish specific dates (not less than once a year) to review the portfolio. The review should cover: any changes regarding the needs of the beneficiaries, such as a requirement for more income or a principal distribution, which will necessitate an adjustment to the portfolio; the need to switch to taxable or nontaxable bonds based on changes in interest rates and/or the tax brackets of beneficiaries; a review of the investment policies to determine if they continue to be appropriate to the objectives of the trust or need to be modified; and a review of the investment advisor's performance, fees, and adherence to the terms of the contract.

CHAPTER 13

How to Manage Trust Real Estate Assets

There are two reasons why real estate is kept in a trust. The first reason is that a surviving spouse may continue to occupy the family residence, or some other property that is being maintained for use by the children. The second reason is that the settlor made investments in real estate and, as part of his or her estate plan, transferred the property into a revocable living trust. The terms of the trust and the type and nature of the real estate will determine how the trustee manages the property. The trustee's management of the residence is relatively simple; the surviving spouse occupies the home and usually assumes responsibility for routine maintenance. Investment real estate, on the other hand, can require a considerable commitment of time, especially if multiple commercial properties are owned by the trust.

ALERT

Regardless of what type of real estate is owned, the trustee must see to it that it is properly managed. Some of the responsibilities will include reviewing and making sure that the properties have adequate insurance coverage, addressing any environmental concerns, maintaining the properties by making repairs, paying property taxes and other expenses, and collecting rents.

Protecting Real Estate Assets

An important task for the trustee is to review the insurance on the property and be sure that the coverage is sufficient to protect the property and the trust. The policy should name the trustee as an additional insured and provide for replacement of the property at its current market value should a loss occur. It should also have adequate liability coverage in the event of a lawsuit that results from an accident on the property. It may be necessary to obtain a current appraisal in order to evaluate whether or not the coverage is adequate. Extended coverage for broader protection from wind, explosions, civil disturbances, aircraft, and other causes should be considered, if appropriate. The coverage should also include worker's compensation and rent insurance in addition to fire, liability, and casualty protection.

ALERT

Depending on the type of property, the trustee may also want to obtain coverage for environmental cleanup in case contamination is discovered in the future. A trustee would be wise to seek the advice of an insurance agent who specializes in this area of risk management.

Dealing with Environmental Issues

When environmentally contaminated property becomes an asset of a trust, the trustee may be responsible for the cleanup. A trustee can be held liable under the Comprehensive Environmental Response, Compensation, and Liability Act of 1980 (CERCLA) and the Superfund Amendments and

Reauthorization Act of 1986 (SARA) for any contamination that is discovered while the property is owned by the trust. In 1996, Congress changed the extent to which fiduciaries were held liable under CERCLA for environmental damages on property held in trust. Until the new law was enacted, trustees could have been held personally liable for cleanup costs associated with environmental damage if the assets of the trust could not cover those costs. However, the new law limits the liability for the cleanup to the value of the assets in the trust and does not hold the trustee responsible for any excess costs under the following conditions:

- The trustee cannot be both the trustee and the beneficiary of the trust.
- The trustee cannot receive benefits from the trust that exceed customary or reasonable compensation.
- The trustee cannot have caused or contributed to the contamination.
- The trust cannot be organized for the primary purpose of, or engaged in, a trade or business for profit.
- There must be a bona fide trustee and not one who acquires ownership or control with the objective of avoiding liability.

Even if liability is limited to trust assets, managing contaminated trust property may be more than a trustee wants to take on. Unintentionally, a trustee might cause or contribute to the contamination of the property, potentially exposing him or her to personal liability. Performing some due diligence before accepting the trusteeship is prudent. Corporate fiduciaries do an extensive evaluation before accepting a trustee appointment where property is contaminated or where there is a possibility of contamination. An individual trustee would be wise to do the same. The following can be used as a guide for a preliminary evaluation of the property or to review an environmental inspection report:

- *Identify potential problem properties.* These include such things as industrial and manufacturing sites, agricultural land, properties containing asbestos materials, and sites where electric transformers or large capacitors have been stored. A partial list of additional problem properties would include service stations, dry cleaners, junkyards, plating companies, air conditioning companies, laundromats, and so forth.

- *Make inspections of all sites where there might be problems.* It is also a good idea to evaluate adjacent properties which might have contaminated the trust property.
- *Evaluate the types of activities in which tenants are engaged.* Businesses that handle certain types of hazardous materials may be required by state law to prepare a business plan consisting of emergency plans and procedures, inventory of hazardous materials, and a training program for employees. Fiduciaries should also be wary of seemingly innocuous tenants, such as jewelry stores, that use highly toxic chemicals in the manufacturing process.
- *Examine the chain of title for prior owners who might have used toxic materials.* If hazardous materials are being used, examine company records to determine whether the tenant is properly storing, transporting, and disposing of those materials. It is also advisable to examine regulatory agency files. The EPA and local agencies maintain records of companies that request permits to use hazardous materials and those involved in cleanups.
- *Obtain an environmental audit.* The EPA states that an environmental audit should be designed to "verify compliance with environmental requirements; evaluate the effectiveness of environmental management systems already in place; or assess risks from regulated and unregulated materials and practices."
- *Obtain indemnification from the current operator, tenant, or subsequent purchaser.* Check existing insurance policies to determine if they provide environmental coverage.
- *Consider sale, distribution, or abandonment.* Unfortunately, it is not likely that any of these three alternatives will protect a trustee who knows, or has reason to know, of the existence of hazardous materials on the property and doesn't disclose it.

Seeking professional assistance from an environmental specialist is a good idea. A professional evaluation will help to assess what will be necessary to properly manage the property. Some trusts allow a problem property to be segregated by the trustee into its own separate trust so that it does not contaminate other trust assets and subject them to cleanup liabilities. The following is an example of such a provision:

"The trustee shall have the power to set aside as a separate trust, to be held and administered upon the same terms as those governing the remaining trust property, any interests in property, for any reason, including but not limited to a concern that such property could cause potential liability under any federal, state, or local environmental law."

Regardless of how the trust is structured, the trustee needs to perform a thorough evaluation of environmentally plagued property in order to properly manage it. The trustee should also seek competent legal counsel in dealing with these matters.

Basic Maintenance

Maintaining real property falls in the category of preserving and protecting trust assets. It includes seeing to it that all applicable property taxes and assessments are paid when due. If the property is a residence that is occupied by the surviving spouse, an exemption or other allowance that will result in a lower tax may be available. The trustee should make the proper request or application to take advantage of the property tax reduction and should also consider filing an appeal to the tax authorities if the trustee feels that the property tax is too high relative to its value.

As previously mentioned, maintenance also includes adequate insurance and making sure that the premiums are paid when due. The trustee can be held personally liable if a claim for damages to the property is rejected because the premiums had not been paid on time. A tickler system should be established to cover these and any other payments that have a critical due date. Failure to receive a bill from the insurance company or taxing authority may not be a defensible position for not making the payment on time.

ALERT

In addition to protecting the value of the property, making timely repairs will also reduce the trust's liability exposure.

Repairs are always necessary to maintain the property. Conduct an initial inspection to identify anything that needs repair. If the repairs are large enough, say over $500, the trustee should solicit bids for the work. The repair work needs to be clearly described to the contractor, and any limitations on the scope of the work outlined and agreed to in writing. The trustee should also inspect the completed work and, if unsatisfactory, see that corrections are made.

Major improvements, such as a new roof, additions, construction of a new building, or other permanent types of improvements, are considered investments in the property. The decision to expend such funds should be based on the cost of the improvement and expected returns in terms of additional rent or potential appreciation in the value of the property. In considering expenditures for these purposes, the trustee needs to consider how they will affect the interests of the beneficiaries. Ordinary repairs are charged against the income account of the trust and reduce the amount payable to the income beneficiaries. Major improvements are paid from principal, which affects the interests of the remaindermen.

Managing a Residence

The trust document will usually contain language to maintain the family residence for the benefit of the decedent's surviving spouse. The trust will typically own a fractional interest in the residence, usually one-half, with the surviving spouse owning the other half. A well-drafted trust will have a specific provision that makes it clear that the surviving spouse has use of the residence during his or her lifetime:

> *"Upon the settlor's death, if the settlor's spouse survives, the settlor requests, but does not direct, that the settlor's spouse be allowed the full, free, and undisturbed occupancy of the primary residence of the settlor and such spouse as that residence was prior to the settlor's death."*

Some trusts make no reference at all to the use of the residence by the surviving spouse. However, as long as the surviving spouse is a beneficiary of the trust, the trustee usually has the authority to allow the spouse to have continued use of the property. Unless otherwise directed by the terms of the trust, expenses for maintenance of the residence should be shared equally between the spouse and the decedent's trust, assuming each owns a one-half interest. If the surviving spouse is entitled to receive income and/or principal from the trust, the trustee could pay all of the maintenance expenses. The trustee will have very little day-to-day management responsibilities, since the surviving spouse will be occupying the residence and should be handling the routine maintenance. The trustee's primary duty is to preserve the property for those who will ultimately inherit it. This means assuring that timely repairs are made, taxes are paid, and proper insurance coverage is maintained.

QUESTION

Can the surviving spouse sell the property if half of it is owned by the decedent settlor's trust?

The answer is yes, since the surviving spouse owns the other half and the surviving spouse is given use and possession of the property. The trustee, of course, has a responsibility to the other trust beneficiaries and should not agree to a sale if the terms of the sale are clearly a "bad deal" for the surviving spouse and the decedent's trust.

Managing Investment Property

Real estate assets will either be improved or unimproved property. If the property is vacant land, the trustee has a duty to make the property productive unless the trust directs otherwise.

Improved property could be a single-family dwelling that is leased, a small apartment building, large condominium, or a commercial or industrial investment. If the property is subject to a long-term lease, the trustee may only need to collect the rent and see to it that the lessee abides by the terms of the lease. The management of larger properties will take considerably more time and effort. This usually necessitates hiring a property manager to handle the day-to-day management of the property. The selection process should be thorough, ending with the trustee being assured that the agent will be responsive and produce the best results for the trust.

The trustee can sell the land and invest the proceeds, lease it, or operate it to produce income. If there is only one beneficiary and he or she is entitled to the income from the trust, the trustee can make the property available for the beneficiary's use and would not necessarily be obligated to make the property income-producing. If the land is in a rural or depressed area, selling the land may be the only alternative.

The key to effective management and control of large properties through an agent is to have a compensation agreement between the trustee and the agent. In detail, the contract should outline the rights, duties, responsibilities, and obligations of both the trustee and agent. The agent is usually responsible for collecting the rents, making repairs within the limits set by the trustee, and maintaining accounting records, including individual tenant files. The trustee should make sure that the net rental income is remitted on a timely basis so it can be paid out to the income beneficiaries or invested. The agent's accounting records should be reviewed periodically for accuracy and, if necessary, audited annually.

Managing Property Located in Another State

Managing real estate that is located in another state requires special attention. Unless the trustee travels frequently to the state in which the property is located, he or she will have difficulty responsibly managing the property. A well-drafted trust will address this problem and specifically authorize the trustee to appoint a special trustee to be responsible for managing the property:

> *"If at any time any trust property is situated in a jurisdiction in which any trustee is unable or unwilling to act, a person or corporation may be appointed in an instrument signed by the trustee to act as special trustee with respect to that property in that jurisdiction; such special trustee and every successor trustee so appointed shall have all the title, powers, and discretion with respect to the property that is given to the*

special trustee by the trustee. The net income from the property in the other jurisdiction and any net proceeds of its sale shall be paid over to the trustee."

If the trust document does not permit delegation of the responsibility to a special trustee, consideration should be given to petitioning the court for reformation of the trust or to seek the court's authority to appoint a special trustee. Absent either of these options, the trustee should at the very least hire an agent in the state in which the property is located to manage the property. As with any other agent that is retained for the trust, the trustee should provide good oversight and accountability.

Checklist for Managing Real Estate

- Conduct an initial inspection of all properties and make needed repairs.
- Evaluate all properties for environmental hazards and take appropriate steps to prevent contamination. Refer to the checklists earlier in this chapter.
- Have an insurance agent review the policies on all properties and make sure the coverage is adequate.
- Establish reminders to pay insurance premiums, pay property taxes and other expenses, and conduct periodic inspections of the property (or properties).
- Evaluate unimproved property and develop a plan to make it productive.
- Hire a property manager, if necessary, and monitor his or her activities.
- Hire a special trustee or property manager to handle out-of-state property.

CHAPTER 14

Managing Businesses and Other Property Interests

As the population ages, the small businesses upon which the family wealth was built will pass through trusts and be managed by trustees. The responsibility for managing a decedent's closely held business in his or her trust has some unique characteristics. A closely held business interest may have been held by the settlor's revocable living trust prior to death as part of the estate plan, or it may have been owned by the decedent individually and became an asset of the trust through a pour-over will.

Business Interest

The business interest can take the form of a sole proprietorship, general partnership, limited partnership, subchapter S corporation, C corporation, or limited liability company (LLC). Each form has distinguishing characteristics. Generally, the proprietorship, partnership, subchapter S corporation, and limited liability company are pass-through entities for tax purposes. That is, the income is taxed directly to the holder of the interest. The C corporation is taxed differently; it pays a tax on its earned income. As earnings are paid out to the stockholders in the form of dividends, the stockholders again pay income tax on the dividends they receive. This double taxation of income is what distinguishes the C corporation from the other forms of business ownership.

ALERT

Businesses and other similar interests held in a trust require special attention by the trustee. First and foremost, the trustee needs to protect the interest and then determine whether it is a suitable investment for the trust. The interest should have a specific role in the trust's portfolio and meet the standards of prudence. Because these interests are not typical investments made by a trust, it will require careful evaluation and good judgment on the part of the trustee.

Should the Business Be Sold or Retained?

Unless the trust document, local law, or a court order authorizes or directs the trustee to retain the business interest, the trustee, generally, has a duty to dispose of it and invest the proceeds in investments suitable for the trust. Continuing the business for any purpose other than its sale may not be considered prudent under some state statutes. Selling a closely held business takes time; a trustee must keep the business going to facilitate an orderly liquidation. The business must be managed to preserve its value as a going concern and to avoid defaulting on any loans that the business has. Contracts need to be performed in order to maintain the value of the business and avoid litigation.

ALERT

When a decision is made to sell the business, the trustee may discover that there is a very limited market or no market at all.

Prior to death, the settlor may have entered into a buy-sell agreement, which would make the sale of the business relatively easy. A buy-sell agreement is an agreement between an individual owner and the other owners of the business that provides for the purchase of a decedent owner's interest in the business. The agreement usually establishes the purchase price and often allows for periodic price changes as the value of the business changes. The trustee under a buy-sell agreement has no choice but to sell the business in accordance with the terms of the agreement. Often life insurance is used to provide funds for the purchase. Some buy-sell agreements only give the buyer a first right of refusal. If the right is not exercised, the trustee must then take on the responsibility of selling the business.

The trustee has a duty to use reasonable care, skill, and prudence in selling the business. If challenged, the trustee must be able to demonstrate that the price for which the business was sold was fair and reasonable. Selling a business interest is not like selling a publicly traded stock whose value is easily ascertained. There is no index or reference book that can give the trustee a value or sales price. Valuing a closely held business is complex. To establish a value, a professional appraiser needs to be retained. Competent appraisers use a variety of methods to arrive at a value, such as comparing the business with similar enterprises. Other techniques include evaluating the capitalization of income, book value versus market value, common stock of the company, liquidation value versus the going concern value, historical rates of return, price earnings ratio, and factual or intrinsic value versus market value.

The valuation of a business for estate tax purposes, which may consider minority interest and lack of marketability discounts, is not necessarily the same value that should be used to establish a sales price. The trustee should hire a specialist for this purpose and develop a marketing plan for selling the business. It is also a good idea to hire someone to assist the trustee to negotiate the terms and sell the business. As part of the selling process, the trustee should identify potential buyers, such as the decedent's business partners, family members who may want to own the decedent's interest in the business, owners of similar businesses, competitors, and customers of the business.

If the closely held business is a corporation and is a major estate asset, the trustee may want to take advantage of Section 303 of the Internal Revenue Code to pay taxes and expenses. Section 303 allows the trustee to redeem shares of the company stock without the proceeds being treated as a taxable dividend. When certain conditions are met, the redemption is considered a stock sale and the proceeds will be treated as long-term capital gains. This is a good way to get cash out of the business with favored tax treatment, if there is a desire to keep control of the business, by limiting the number of shares that must be redeemed to provide cash for the payment of estate taxes, funeral costs, and administration expenses. To qualify for a Section 303 redemption, the value of the stock must represent more than 35% of the decedent's adjusted gross estate, and only those shares that are needed to cover the expenses can be redeemed.

Ongoing Management of the Business

The rationale for retaining and managing a closely held business interest should be restricted to a limited number of scenarios. A trustee typically does not have the expertise or is not equipped to manage a business, much less oversee its management by others. The decision making process will need to cover a number of basic issues.

Retention is appropriate if:

- The trust document specifically directs the trustee to retain the business interest without any liability to the trustee.
- The trust will terminate in a relatively short period of time and the beneficiaries have indicated a desire to retain the business.
- The business interest is profitable, fits within the overall strategy of the trust's investment portfolio, and its retention does not represent an unreasonable risk.

As mentioned earlier, if the trustee is to retain a closely held business interest, the trust document or local law must authorize it. Hopefully, the trust provision protects the trustee from any liability for retaining the business and not selling it. A typical provision might read as follows:

"To conduct business in partnership or in a joint venture with other persons, partnerships, or corporations; to continue and operate any business, ranch, or farm transferred to the trust by the settlor, whether during the settlor's lifetime or by will; to do any and all things deemed appropriate by the trustee, including the incorporation of the business, ranch, or farm and the investment of additional capital for such time as the trustee shall deem advisable, without liability for any loss resulting from the continuance or operation of the business, ranch, or farm, except for the trustee's own negligence; and to close out, liquidate, or sell the business, ranch, or farm at such time and upon such terms as the trustee deems advisable."

Unless the trust document specifically directs the trustee to retain the business, a decision to keep it should only be made after a thorough evaluation. The following are some of the issues that need to be considered before a decision is made:

- Are the current managers capable of carrying on the business?
- Will the ages of the managers and other owners have an effect on continuing the business?
- Does the trust have a controlling or minority interest?
- Is the return on investment reasonable?
- Do past and projected future earnings of the company make it a worthwhile investment?
- Will the returns meet the needs of current beneficiaries and provide value for the remaindermen?
- Are there any current or potential business liability issues? If so, are they manageable?
- Will the business interest represent a concentration in the portfolio?

If the closely held business is a limited partnership interest, the trustee has no authority or control over the activities of the enterprise. Also, liability is limited to the amount invested in the partnership. The success or failure of the business is in the hands of the general partner. However, the trustee should review the activities of the general partner to assure that decisions to withhold or distribute cash flow coincide with the business of the partnership. The trustee must assess the general partner's ability and the viability of the business in deciding whether to retain the limited partnership interest. On the other hand, if a trust holds a general partnership interest, the trustee will control management of the business. A general partner has unlimited liability and has a duty to manage the partnership in the best interests of the limited partners. The trustee also has a duty to manage the partnership in the best interest of the beneficiaries; he or she should make sure that these obligations are consistent with each other and not create a conflict of interest. A trustee should also consider converting the general partnership interest to a limited liability company (LLC) or an S corporation to limit the trust's liability.

ESSENTIAL

The trustee should exercise as much control over the business as possible in order to protect the trust's interest in the company.

If the closely held business interest is a corporation (S corporation or C corporation), the trustee needs to determine whether the trust holds a controlling or minority interest. Control does not necessarily mean owning more than 50% of the outstanding shares of the company's stock. Depending on who the other shareholders are, such as shareholders who are the beneficiaries of the trust, a smaller holding could give the trustee effective control over the business. The trustee needs to assess whether or not to serve as an officer or director of the company. This decision should be based on the need to maintain control over the business and have access to information versus the potential liability in being actively involved in the day-to-day running of the business. If the trustee decides to serve as a director or officer, he or she should not receive any fees or other compensation from the company. The trustee should also be sure that the company maintains adequate officers' and directors' liability insurance. If the trustee chooses not to serve as an officer or director, he or she should attend all stockholder meetings to facilitate informed decisions when voting on issues that affect the company.

At the very least, the trustee needs to continually monitor the activities of the business. This should include the frequent review of the company's financial reports. The trustee should regularly evaluate the company's profit and loss statements, balance sheet, sales reports, and other pertinent financial data. In addition, the trustee should review the minutes of the meetings of the board of directors and any committee meetings that are pertinent to the operation of the business. Periodic onsite inspections should also be made to observe the general operation of the business, working conditions, and the condition of the plant and equipment.

Qualifying a Subchapter S Corporation Held in Trust

The subchapter S corporate (S corporation) form avoids the double taxation associated with the C corporation. There is no corporate income tax. Instead, the income is "passed through" to the stockholder and is only taxed once. This is an important income tax benefit that the trustee needs to preserve. After the death of the settlor, when a trust owns S corporation stock, it must meet certain requirements in order to maintain its status. Whether the stock is held in the marital or credit shelter trust, the terms of the trust must provide that:

1. There be only one income beneficiary.
2. Principal distributions can only be made to the income beneficiary.
3. The income beneficiary's interest must terminate on the beneficiary's death or the termination of the trust, whichever is earlier.
4. If the trust terminates during the life of the income beneficiary, the principal must be distributed to the beneficiary.
5. The trust income must be required to be distributed to the beneficiary or actually distributed to the beneficiary.

The marital trust will usually meet these qualifications. However, the credit shelter trust may not. If the business will be kept and it is a growth asset, it should be put in the credit shelter trust. If the credit shelter trust, or any other type of trust, does not qualify, the IRS says that the S corporation status will not be terminated if:

1. The situation resulting in disqualification was inadvertent;
2. Corrective steps are taken within a reasonable period of time; and
3. The S corporation and each shareholder agree to retain the S corporation election status.

The trustee may have to amend the trust to bring it into compliance if, by the terms of the trust, the trustee is given the authority to do so. If the trust does not allow the trustee to amend the trust, the trustee should consider petitioning the court for reformation of the trust to avoid losing the S corporation status.

Intellectual and Other Property Interests

A trademark, patent, or copyright might be among the assets included in the trust. These intellectual property rights must be managed like any other trust asset, taking into account the present and future needs of the beneficiaries, the terms of the trust, and whether or not they should be retained. A trustee should understand the basic characteristics of each type, evaluate their suitability to the particular trust he or she is managing, and, if retained, maintain the asset in accordance with the rules that apply to that particular asset.

ALERT

Information on the rules for renewals, documentation, etc., can be found at *www.uspto.gov*.

A trademark is normally associated with a business and has an endless life as long as it is used and renewed. The trademark will have value if used in a business or product interest owned by the trust, and the trustee should make sure that it is renewed and maintained to support that asset. Copyrights owned by a trust may have significant value. The settlor may have authored a book or song that generates cash flow to the trust that may represent the majority of the trust's income. The trustee, in addition to understanding the terms of the royalty contract, should also be aware of the expiration of the copyright. Copyrights have a long life of seventy years by statute. However, it could have only a few years left when the trustee takes over. If it represents a significant portion of a beneficiary's income, the trustee will need to plan for replacing that income when the copyright expires.

Unlike trademarks and copyrights, patents have a shorter life span. Patents for utility and plant classes are for twenty years, while a design patent lasts for fourteen years. The trustee's responsibilities for patent assets are basically the same as for trademarks and copyrights. If the decedent was a celebrity, these assets could have significantly more value than when the decedent was living. In this situation, a trustee would require professional assistance from someone who specializes in this area.

The trust may own gas and oil royalties. These are depleting assets, and the trustee needs to carefully review each one to determine its viability as a trust investment. An assessment should be made of its estimated duration and, like other assets that have a limited life, the trustee should have a plan for replacing this source of income. If the royalty is determined to be too risky an investment for the trust, the trustee needs to assess its marketability and make arrangements for sale through a reputable broker. Oil and gas royalties are unique investments, and the trustee should retain a qualified oil and gas professional to perform an analysis and make recommendations.

These types of assets may have been productive for the settlor prior to death, but may not necessarily serve the purpose and intent of the trust. Unless the trust specifically directs the trustee to hold the asset for distribution to beneficiaries in the future, the trustee must evaluate each one and make a determination as to whether or not it is a suitable asset for the trust.

Checklist for Managing a Business and Other Interests

- Check to see if the trust specifically authorizes retention of the business or other property interest.
- Evaluate rationale for retention.
- Obtain a valuation from a qualified appraiser.

- Check to see if there is a buy-sell agreement.
- If the business is an S corporation, take the necessary steps to retain its status.
- Get appointed as a director and/or officer of the enterprise.
- Evaluate the suitability of all intellectual property.
- Have a qualified professional evaluate all oil or gas royalty interests.

CHAPTER 15

Distributing Income and Principal

Making discretionary payments from a trust is perhaps the most important duty that a trustee has. After all, it was the primary reason the trust was established in the first place—the settlor (creator) of the trust wanted someone (the trustee) to exercise good judgment in how the financial resources are used to benefit the beneficiaries of the trust. This chapter will describe the process of distributing income and/or principal to beneficiaries and how these decisions should be made.

Under What Circumstances Are Distributions Made from a Trust?

Deciding when and under what circumstances the income and principal will be distributed to the trust's beneficiaries is one of the fundamental responsibilities of a trustee. Many trusts are designed specifically to have the trustee assume the role of a parent, grandparent, or other person who was concerned with, or had responsibility for, protecting and maintaining the financial well-being of the beneficiaries. In assuming this responsibility, trustees are usually given very broad authority, and the courts generally will not interfere with the trustee's exercise of this discretion unless the trustee has been dishonest, arbitrary, capricious, acted in bad faith, made a mistake, or was extraordinarily imprudent or unreasonable. Needless to say, this responsibility must be performed with great care and diligence, and it is important for the trustee to understand the basic principles of discretionary decision-making.

ESSENTIAL

A trustee sometimes assumes the role of a parent in deciding how much and under what circumstances a beneficiary receives income and/or principal.

The instructions in a trust can be very specific, can require the trustee to exercise discretion, or both. Specific payment directives are fairly straightforward. For example, if the trust directs that a beneficiary is to receive $1,000 per month for life, the trustee merely pays the beneficiary this amount. Exercising discretion, on the other hand, requires the trustee to make subjective judgments in distributing income and principal to the trust beneficiaries. It is important that a trustee clearly distinguish between discretionary and non-discretionary provisions.

The use of the word "shall" in a trust document indicates that the trustee is *required* to take an action or make an income or principal distribution. The use of the word "may" implies that the trustee must *exercise discretion* in disbursing funds or taking an action. It is helpful to distinguish between the common types of dispositive provisions in a trust where these terms have relevance. For income tax purposes, the Internal Revenue Service classifies trusts into two general categories that distinguish discretionary from nondiscretionary trusts: simple trusts and complex trusts.

Simple Trust

A simple trust requires all of its income to be distributed to the income beneficiaries. There is no provision for the payment of principal or the terms of the trust specifically prohibit principal payments. The following is an example of dispositive language under a simple trust:

"From the date of the settlor's death until the termination of this trust, the trustee shall pay to the beneficiary all of the net income of the trust."

FACT

A simple trust does not require a trustee to exercise discretion.

Some trust documents will simply not include a provision for the distribution of principal. Others will specifically prohibit principal distributions.

Complex Trust

Complex trusts give the trustee discretion with regard to the payment of income, principal, or both. A trust may require income to be paid out but gives the trustee discretion to distribute principal. Such a provision may read as follows:

"From the date of the settlor's death until the termination of this trust, the trustee shall pay to or for the benefit of the beneficiaries herein named all of the net income of the trust. The trustee shall also pay to or for the benefit of the beneficiaries such portions of the principal for their health, education, maintenance, and support as the trustee shall determine in the trustee's sole discretion. Discretionary payments may be made to the beneficiaries in such amount, for such purposes, at such time, and in such manner as the trustee shall determine in the trustee's uncontrolled discretion, with or without considering other resources

available to them and without being required to keep the payments equal or proportionate."

FACT

In a complex trust the trustee uses his or her judgment as to what amounts are paid to beneficiaries.

Another category of complex trust gives the trustee discretionary authority to distribute both income and principal. The language used in this type of trust might read as follows:

"After the settlor's death the trustee may, at any time, and from time to time, pay to or apply for the benefit of any one, all, or none of the beneficiaries, so much of the income and so much of the principal of the trust as the trustee, in his or her sole discretion, shall deem advisable for the health, education, maintenance, and support of such beneficiary or beneficiaries. In making any distributions, the trustee shall have discretion to take into consideration all other funds available to such beneficiary, or beneficiaries, for such purposes."

These discretionary powers are referred to as *express powers* because they are written instructions to the trustee. If the trust document does not contain a specific written directive, the trustee must look to state law for express authority, if any. If neither the trust document nor local law give the trustee express discretionary authority, the trustee can assume that he or she has the implied power to exercise discretion based on the general terms, purposes, and intent of the trust. In this latter case, it is a good idea for the trustee to get court approval and obtain the consent of all of the beneficiaries.

Distribution Guidelines

There is an inherent conflict between the current and remainder beneficiaries of a trust. Current beneficiaries (i.e., those that are entitled to income and/or principal during the term of the trust) want the trustee to maximize distributions to them during the period they are eligible to receive benefits. Also, if there is more than one current beneficiary, there will be competition among them for the resources of the trust. The trustee, unless otherwise directed by the trust, does not have to make equal distributions among the beneficiaries.

The remaindermen, on the other hand, want to maximize their inheritance and therefore hope that the trustee does not make frequent and/or large principal distributions during the life of the trust. In managing these conflicting viewpoints, the trustee is duty-bound to be impartial. In making discretionary distributions, a trustee must evaluate the needs and particular circumstances of each beneficiary when deciding who gets what and how much. In most trusts, the current beneficiaries will usually be given preference over remaindermen. However, the trustee must keep in mind that he or she has a duty to protect the principal of the trust for the remaindermen to the extent that it is not used for the current beneficiaries. To assure that distributions are used for the intended purpose, payments for the benefit of a beneficiary should be made directly to the payee (university, landlord, doctor, etc.) rather than to the beneficiary.

ALERT

If payments are made to a beneficiary, receipts should be obtained to prove that the payment was used for the purpose for which the distribution was made.

Making discretionary payments from a trust is not an exact science. It is a process that includes following the terms of the trust, ascertaining the needs of the beneficiaries, using good judgment, and exercising prudence. The place to start, obviously, is to read the provisions of the trust. In addition to defining who the beneficiaries are and their interest in the trust, many trusts will express the settlor's intent. The settlor's intent, whether expressed or implied, is what ultimately determines how a trustee is to exercise his or her discretion. Some trust documents will express the settlor's desire to benefit current beneficiaries first and that the interests of remaindermen are secondary to that purpose. This tells the trustee that the trust is to be managed primarily for the current beneficiaries. The settlor may also express that the needs of the surviving spouse shall have preference over the needs of other current beneficiaries, such as children and grandchildren.

There are common words and phrases that are used in a trust document to describe the purposes for which discretionary distributions are to be made. These words are usually defined under local law and generally have the following meanings:

- *Health:* Routine medical services, mental health care, hospitalization, medications, medical devices and supplies, long-term nursing care, substance-abuse program services, rehabilitation, ancillary health care services, x-ray and laboratory services, premiums for health insurance, ambulance services, and outpatient aftercare services.

- *Education:* Includes preschool, primary, and secondary education and education at an accredited public or private college or university. Graduate-level education and professional, technical, or vocational school is generally not included unless specifically provided by the terms of the trust. Education expenses include tuition, books, room and board, incidental expenses, clothing, travel expenses to and from school, supplies, student fees, tutors, and other expenses in connection with the education program.

- *Maintenance and support:* Includes normal living expenses, such as housing, clothing, food, insurance premiums, and medical care, and may include the expenses of dependents. The level of support is usually dependent upon the standard of living enjoyed by the beneficiary during the settlor's lifetime and the financial resources of the trust.

- *Welfare:* Having to do with those things in life that have a relationship to one's physical well-being and comfort, and which are dependent upon the individual's financial resources. This term generally means providing for basic living requirements.

- *Emergency:* Having to do with a sudden or unexpected occurrence where the beneficiary's financial resources are insufficient to deal with the matter and require that prompt action be taken.

- *Standard of living:* This is the style in which a beneficiary lived immediately prior to the death of the settlor, including the type of home that the beneficiary lived in, the type of automobile driven, the number of employees hired for domestic and other tasks, the amount of travel enjoyed, club memberships, etc.

If the settlor's intent in the document so directs to maintain the standard of living of the beneficiary, other financial resources that are available to the beneficiary need not be considered. On the other hand, if the trust document directs that distributions are to be based on need, then the trustee must consider the beneficiaries' other financial resources in determining whether or not a need exists. As with any other trust provision, if there is any doubt as to the meaning of a particular directive or stipulation, the trustee should obtain an interpretation from the attorney who drafted the trust. The trust attorney will also have knowledge as to the settlor's intent.

Protective Provisions

Most trusts contain a clause that is designed to protect current beneficiaries and the interests of remaindermen. The so-called *spendthrift provision* is a common trust concept and is sometimes provided for under local law. Its purpose is to prevent a current beneficiary from encumbering, in any way, his or her interest in the trust. For example, a beneficiary's creditors may not be able to make a claim against the trust for amounts owed, although the trustee could distribute funds to the beneficiary to pay off debts if a distribution under the circumstances was appropriate. Some states may not recognize this protective provision in a trust for certain creditor claims, so the trustee should consult with the trust's attorney if a claim is presented. A typical spendthrift provision might read as follows:

> *"No beneficiary shall have any right to anticipate, transfer, or encumber any part of any interest in the trust estate, nor shall any part of the beneficiary's interest be liable for that beneficiary's debts or obligations (including alimony) or be subject to attachment, garnishment, execution, creditor's bill, or other legal or equitable process, provided that this Article shall neither prevent any beneficiary from exercising any power of appointment granted in this agreement or limit a marital deduction otherwise available to the settlor's estate."*

Some states may have exceptions to the spendthrift provision. The trustee should consult with the trust's attorney if a questionable claim is made.

Another protective provision is a clause that directs the trustee not to make distributions to a beneficiary that would disqualify that beneficiary from receiving government assistance. This provision is intended to allow efficient use of the trust assets for all beneficiaries by requiring a beneficiary to first take advantage of any financial assistance that may be available through government programs, such as Medicare, before requesting funds from the trust. This type of protective provision is fairly specific and straightforward:

> *"In the event that any beneficiary of any trust established hereunder is entitled to Medicare, Medicaid, or other governmental assistance (or would be if the existence of such trust were ignored) because of physical or mental infirmity (including but not limited to being a patient in a long-term health-related facility), then the trustee shall not, in such circumstances, make any discretionary distributions of principal or income to or for the benefit of such beneficiary, other than for the purpose of providing for such expenses incurred by the beneficiary which are not otherwise covered by such government assistance."*

In some states, a beneficiary may not qualify for public assistance regardless of this language. Again, the trustee should seek guidance from the trust's attorney if the question is raised.

The Process of Making Discretionary Distributions

In evaluating a beneficiary's request for a distribution from income or principal, the trustee should follow a systematic process. This will facilitate the trustee's duty of impartiality, and establish a consistent method for making discretionary distributions. The process should include a thorough evaluation of all the facts and circumstances surrounding the beneficiary's request. The first step is to have the beneficiary submit his or her request in writing. The request should include all of the pertinent information to support the request and assist the trustee in making a decision. A format similar to the one outlined below can assist both the beneficiary and the trustee with this part of the process:

Dear (*name of trustee*):

The following information is furnished in support of my request for a discretionary distribution from the (*name of trust*):

Birth date:

Dependents: (*Give full details of ages, relationship to you, etc.*)

Nature and amount of request: (*Give full details, dates, amounts, bills, etc.*)

The following assets are owned by me: (*Indicate if ownership is in your own name, joint with spouse, or others*)

	Approximate Value	Income Generated	Mortgage
Home			
Other Real Estate			
Stocks and Bonds			
Bank Accounts			
Other Assets	_____	_____	_____
TOTALS			

Income generated from other sources:

Description	Amount
TOTALS	_____

Other facts regarding either the reason for this request or my income and property that I believe will help you in considering my request:

I hereby certify the above statements to be true, correct, and complete to the best of my knowledge and belief.

_____(Signature)_____   _____(Date)_____

_____(Name of beneficiary)_____   _____(Telephone number)_____

If the beneficiary's income has to be considered as part of the decision, the trustee should also obtain copies of the beneficiary's tax returns for the last three years. The trustee can also gather all of this information by meeting with the beneficiary.

ALERT

The distribution process should be methodical. A trustee needs to collect and review enough information to make an informed and prudent decision.

Before a distribution is made, the trustee must thoroughly evaluate the request. The review should take into consideration the following:

- What is the purpose of the request?
- Is the purpose authorized under the terms of the trust?
- Has the beneficiary clearly outlined how the funds will be used?
- Is the amount requested too large relative to the size of the trust? If the amount will significantly impact the ability of the trust to carry out its purpose for the term of the trust, a smaller distribution or other alternative—such as making a loan to the beneficiary—should be considered. If the trust has many years left before it terminates, principal distributions should be kept to a reasonable level.
- Will the distribution accomplish the purpose and intent of the trust?
- Are there liquid funds available to cover the amount(s) needed? If not, a plan to raise the needed funds must be developed and implemented.
- How will the distribution impact the other beneficiaries?
- Will the payment result in a taxable distribution, subject to a generation-skipping tax? If so, additional funds may need to be distributed to cover the tax. To determine the total amount of the distribution (including the tax), divide the amount of the request by one minus the generation-skipping tax rate. Example:

Amount of request: $10,000

Tax rate: 55%

$$\frac{\$10,000}{(1-.55)} = \$22,222.22 \text{ (Amount needed)}$$

Documentation

Maintaining complete and thorough records is important to the discretionary distribution process and trust administration in general. If asked to defend a particular discretionary decision many years after it was made, a trustee will be hard pressed to remember the facts and circumstances of the distribution when records are incomplete or not kept at all. Requests should always be in writing and should contain sufficient information to allow the trustee to make an informed and rational decision and to maintain an accurate record of the transaction. These records should be maintained for the entire term of the trust. A format similar to the following can be used to document each discretionary distribution:

Date:

Distribution requested by:

Age:

Purpose of distribution: (Attach letter of request)

Amount requested:

Previous discretionary distributions to this beneficiary during this trust year:

$_____ (Income) $_____ (Principal) $_____ Total

Purpose:

Previous discretionary distributions to this beneficiary since inception:

$_____ (Income) $_____ (Principal) $_____ Total

Income payments currently distributable to this beneficiary from the trust:

$_____

Source of funds from the trust:

Reasons for denial/approval of this request:

Date distribution was made:

Amount: $_____

ALERT

You will not remember why you made a distribution ten years ago unless you keep accurate and complete records.

Making Loans to Beneficiaries

As an alternative to an income or principal distribution, the trustee can facilitate the beneficiary's request by making a loan. A loan should be considered if an outright distribution would materially affect the trust's ability to meet the future needs of all beneficiaries. The loan would provide funds to meet the beneficiary's current need and be returned to the trust for use at some future date when the loan is paid off. In some circumstances, loans can also be made where the purpose of the request does not exactly fit the terms of the trust. The interest rate and terms of the loan should be similar to what is available in the marketplace at the time the loan is made. Contact a financial institution for current rates and terms. In addition, the trustee should obtain a life insurance policy on the life of the beneficiary borrower for the amount of the loan. The trust should be the owner and beneficiary of the policy. This is to protect the trust in the event the beneficiary dies before the loan is paid off. The premiums should be paid by the trust.

ESSENTIAL

Making a loan instead of an outright distribution is a good way to assist beneficiaries of a trust with limited resources.

Checklist for Making Distributions

- Obtain an interpretation of the trust's distribution provisions from the trust's attorney.
- Establish a process for obtaining the following information from a beneficiary who is making a request: purpose of the request; amount; list of assets; sources and amount of income; other facts and information in support of the request; and receipts for distributions made directly to the payee (for a university, landlord, doctor, etc.).
- Establish a process for evaluating a request to include: whether or not the distribution is authorized under the terms of the trust; whether or not a need exists; the amount of the request relative to the size of the trust (will the distribution materially affect the ability of the trust to meet the future needs of the beneficiaries?); and whether sufficient funds are available to cover the distributions.
- Consider a loan as an alternative to making a distribution.

CHAPTER 16

Expenses, Accounting Records, and Termination of the Trust

A trustee will incur many expenses including the trustee's own fees during the administration of the trust. How these expenses are charged (i.e., to income or principal) are decisions the trustee will have to make throughout the term of the trust. Making the wrong choice could affect the value of a beneficiary's inheritance. Accounting records that report all of the financial transactions for the trust will also have to be kept. The trustee needs to understand the special accounting rules that apply to trusts in order to properly maintain these accountings.

The Trustee's Responsibilities for Keeping Accounting Records

Beneficiaries of a trust have the right to be kept reasonably informed about the administration of the trust and the trustee has a duty to so inform them. Trustees also have an obligation to provide beneficiaries with information on the beneficiary's interest in the trust as it relates to the trust's assets, liabilities, receipts, and disbursements. This takes the form of a trust accounting that should be provided to the beneficiaries at least annually, if not on a more frequent basis. Trust accounting reports should reflect the actions taken by the trustee and other activities relating to the administration of the trust. Trust documents will usually contain language giving the trustee this responsibility and guidance on dealing with accounting decisions. Such a provision might read as follows:

"To determine all matters of trust accounting in accordance with generally accepted principles of trust accounting as established by controlling law or customary practices . . ."

Most state laws require that the trustee provide an accounting to beneficiaries at least annually.

Even without specific language, under the general law of trusts and local statutes a trustee is given this responsibility. Describing the various transactions that occur during the administration of the trust in a manner that provides beneficiaries with a clear picture of trust activities takes careful thought and application.

Understanding the differences between income and principal charges is essential to administering the trust.

Trust accounting has some unique characteristics compared to the accounting records and reports associated with a corporation, partnership, or proprietorship. Receipts and disbursements in a trust are classified as either income or principal. This is the one characteristic that distinguishes trust accounting from any other type of recordkeeping. As discussed earlier, a trust has two classes of beneficiaries: the current beneficiaries and the remaindermen. The current beneficiaries may be entitled to all or a portion of the income and principal during the term of the trust. Or, one group of current beneficiaries may only be entitled to the income while another group is limited to principal distributions. The remaindermen will inherit the trust assets when the trust terminates, and this is one reason why two separate accounts are maintained (income account and principal account). The classification of receipts and disbursements between the income and principal accounts will have a direct impact on what each class of beneficiaries receives from the trust. Therefore, the trustee has a duty to be impartial when allocating receipts and disbursements between income and principal, taking into account the interests of current beneficiaries and remaindermen.

Transactions should be described in plain language, and the accountings should contain enough information concerning the administration of the trust to fully explain the trust's activities. Trust accountings are normally maintained on a cash basis and should include:

1. A listing of all property owned by the trust, with a description of each asset.
2. Income on hand at the beginning of the accounting period.
3. Income received during the accounting period, the date it was received, and a description of its source.
4. Income disbursed during the accounting period, the date of payment, to whom payment was made, and for what purpose.
5. Income on hand at the end of the accounting period.
6. Additions to principal during the accounting period, the dates received, and a description of the source.
7. Assets that were sold or charged off during the accounting period.
8. Investments made during the accounting period, a description of the investment, the date of acquisition, and cost of purchase.

9. Principal disbursements made during the accounting period, the date of the payment, to whom payment was made, and for what purpose.
10. The trust principal cash and trust assets on hand at the end of the accounting period.

Uniform Principal and Income Act

A trustee is required to follow the terms of the trust in allocating receipts and disbursements between income and principal. For example, the trust document may direct the trustee to credit capital gains distributions from mutual funds to income. These distributions would normally be allocated to principal but, because the trust directs otherwise, the allocation must follow the terms of the trust. Absent specific directions under the terms of a trust regarding how a particular accounting transaction is to be handled, the Uniform Principal and Income Act, which most states have adopted in one form or another, should be referred to for guidance. The Acts are default laws. That is, they will apply in the absence of contrary provisions in the trust document.

The Acts cover the majority of trust transactions and are referenced by accountants and other trust professionals for the majority of trust accounting questions. It should be pointed out that, unlike other entities such as corporations and partnerships, trust accounting rules will differ from state to state and the directives under trust documents will not always be consistent. The Uniform Principal and Income Act contains some common trust accounting definitions:

- *Income receipts* = Income consists of earnings from the use or investment of principal. It includes dividends, interest, rents, and other receipts received as a return on principal or the corpus of the trust.
- *Principal receipts* = Principal is the trust property itself and is accounted for separately from income. It includes the proceeds received from the sale of any trust assets, stock dividends, insurance proceeds, royalties from depletable resources, allowances for depreciation, principal payments received on a loan, and other receipts that will eventually be distributed to the remaindermen.

- *Income charges* = All expenses incurred in connection with the administration, management, or preservation of the trust property are income charges.
- *Principal charges* = Costs of investing and reinvesting principal, principal payments on debts and obligations of the trust, trustee fees attributable to principal as provided by law or the terms of the trust, expenses incurred in taking or defending any action to protect the trust property, extraordinary expenses in making capital improvements to principal assets, and taxes on capital gains or other receipts allocated to principal are all principal charges.

ALERT

Trust accounting rules can be complex, but understanding the basics and getting help when you need it will keep you on the right track.

The Revised Uniform Principal and Income Act (1962) classifies the more common types of transactions that occur in a trust between income and principal:

Income Receipts	Principal Receipts
Dividends	Sales proceeds
Interest	Stock dividends
Rents	Insurance proceeds
Royalties	Receipts from business and farming operations
	Depreciation
	Principal payments on notes
Income Charges	**Principal Charges**
Insurance premiums	Capital improvements
Interest on notes	Taxes on capital gains
Ordinary repairs	Expenses for sale of trust property
Half of trustee fees	Trustee fees not charged to income

Depreciation

In theory, if an asset such as a building is depreciating in value, the remainder beneficiaries will receive a smaller inheritance. If the building was rented or leased, the income beneficiaries would receive the benefit from the asset through distributions of income, theoretically at the expense of the remaindermen. To preserve the value of the building for the remaindermen, some trust documents require that the trustee transfer from income to principal a reasonable amount for depreciation. The amount should be based on the useful life of the depreciating asset and does not need to be held as a separate fund.

The 1962 Revised Uniform Principal and Income Act mandated the depreciation charge against income. The 1997 Revised Uniform Principal and Income Act eliminates this mandatory requirement, but allows the trustee to make the charge in the trustee's discretion. This is a judgment call that will depend on what impact a depreciation charge will have on the income beneficiaries. The 1931 Uniform Principal and Income Act does not have a provision for depreciation. Again, the trustee needs to determine what is required under the trust document and/or local law. The trustee should seek advice from a CPA or an attorney if this is an issue.

What Can a Trustee Charge for Services?

Although many individual trustees, for one reason or another, do not charge a fee for their services, by law all trustees are entitled to receive reasonable compensation for the services they perform and the responsibilities they assume. Being a trustee can require a considerable time commitment and, as discussed in previous chapters, could expose him or her to personal liability. As in any other job, a trustee should rightfully receive remuneration for services performed, and the courts have always recognized a trustee's right to just compensation. There may be a practical reason to charge a trustee's fee. If the trust is a terminating trust, and the trustee is also the sole remainder beneficiary, taking a fee may be a good way to minimize taxes. Trustees' fees are deductible by the trust for tax purposes, and if the tax rate on taxable trust income is higher than the income tax bracket of the trustee/ beneficiary, taking trustee fees has the effect of having these funds taxed at a lower rate.

ESSENTIAL

As trustee you are entitled to be paid for what you do and the responsibilities you assume. In determining compensation, a trustee must first look to the trust document. If the document does not contain a trustee compensation provision, the trustee must then refer to local statutes.

Provisions in the Trust Document

Some trust documents contain a specific fee schedule for the trustee's compensation. The fee can be a percentage of income, principal, or both. In some cases, the trustee's fee is a flat fee and in others, an hourly rate. Some trust documents provide that the trustees' fees will be what is allowed under local statutes. Most modern trust documents do not prescribe a specific fee schedule, but make reference to "reasonable compensation." The following is a typical compensation clause:

"The trustee shall be entitled to reasonable compensation for his or her services. Such compensation shall be commensurate with the services actually performed. The trustee shall also be entitled to reimbursement for expenses necessarily incurred in the administration of the trust estate."

This language puts the burden of determining compensation on the trustee. In deciding what to charge, a trustee should look to local law and what is traditionally charged for trustee services in the community. Like any other trust issue, the trustee can ultimately seek the court's approval of his or her fees. An alternative would be to negotiate a fee directly with the beneficiaries of the trust.

Statutory Fees

Most states have laws that prescribe the compensation a trustee is entitled to charge. Some have rates for corporate trustees and separate schedules for individual trustees. In some jurisdictions, the fees are based on a percentage of the principal value of the trust. In others, the fee is based on a percentage of income; some allow both principal and income charges. The theory behind having both an income and a principal fee is that it provides an incentive for the trustee to increase both income and principal, thereby benefiting the income beneficiaries and remaindermen. It also allows both income beneficiaries and remaindermen to share in the cost of administration.

Other states do not prescribe a formula, but instead require that the trustee's fees be reasonable. The court ultimately makes the determination as to what is reasonable and what is not if the question is raised by a beneficiary. If the trust document makes specific reference to the statutes, of course that is what the trustee is entitled to charge. If the trust document does not contain any reference to trustee compensation, the trustee can usually charge what is provided for under local law.

Extraordinary Fees

Most statutory and traditional fee schedules set by banks, trust companies, or other professional fiduciaries are designed to compensate the trustee for administration services normally performed in a trust. They are not intended to cover extraordinary services, which may include:

- Managing a closely held business
- Gathering information for and managing litigation involving the trust
- Managing, selling, or leasing real estate
- Serving as an officer or director of a company whose stock is owned by the trust
- Filing the decedent's final income tax returns
- Filing fiduciary income tax returns for the trust
- Filing the estate tax return

These are generally outside the scope of services that a trustee is normally expected to perform. Charges for these and similar services should be made separately.

What Is "Reasonable"?

Reasonable compensation has been determined largely by tradition and the courts. The case law on the subject has taken several factors into consideration, which are good guidelines for trustees in determining what to charge.

Size of the Trust

Trustees' fees should bear some relationship to the size of the trust. The fees should not impose such an economic cost to the trust as to prevent achieving its purpose or to put an unreasonable financial burden on the beneficiaries. As a guide, the trustee should compare his or her fee, as a percentage of the value of the trust, with the percentage fee charged by professional fiduciaries and investment managers. For example, if a trustee receives $5,000 a year for managing a trust worth $500,000, this represents a fee of 1% ($5,000 ÷ $500,000). This percentage is roughly what investment managers charge for their services.

Responsibilities Assumed

In accepting the duties and responsibilities for a trust, the trustee can be held personally liable for any loss that may occur as a result of his or her actions. The larger the trust, the greater the potential liability. Part of the trustee's fees should take into consideration the trustee's willingness to take on these responsibilities and assume the associated risks.

Problems and Difficulties in Managing the Trust

Not all trusts are the same. Some are more difficult to manage than others. For example, a trust that owns several businesses or commercial real estate interests, some of which are involved in litigation, will be far more difficult to manage than a simple trust invested in mutual funds and bank deposits. Trusts that have a greater degree of difficulty should entitle the trustee to above-average compensation.

Time and Service Required

The time that it takes to manage the trust and serve its beneficiaries is a key factor. Challenges to a trustee's fees will often be based on how much time it would take someone else to manage the same trust and what those charges would be. Keeping time records is a good idea, not only to defend against a beneficiary complaint, but also as a basis for adjusting the trustee's compensation, where appropriate.

Other Considerations

Other circumstances also need to be considered. A trustee may possess a special skill, such as tax planning, and bring this expertise to bear on the management of the trust. This special service may result in tax savings for the trust that, without the expertise of the trustee, might not otherwise be realized. In this case, the trustee should be entitled to higher compensation. A trustee should also receive additional fees for unusual accomplishments, such as the sale of a closely held business or the successful completion of a real estate development deal.

ESSENTIAL

It's easier to defend your fees if they are less than what others charge for the same services in your community, but you should receive compensation that is just.

After considering these factors, a comparison of what other trustees are charging in the community and what is allowed under local law should be made in determining what is reasonable. A particular jurisdiction will have a range of fees that are customarily charged by banks, trust companies, and in some cases, individual professionals who serve as trustees. This information is readily available through banks and trust companies, estate planning attorneys, CPAs, and other financial professionals. This data should form the basis upon which an individual trustee's charges are made. A safe bet would be to charge something less than what others charge in the community.

Statutory fees or even the fees charged by banks and trust companies may be too low for a given trust. In this case, the trustee should consider negotiating the fee directly with the beneficiaries of the trust. If the fees are charged against income and the current beneficiaries agree to the fee, there should not be a problem. However, the current beneficiaries cannot bind the remaindermen and if some, or all, of the negotiated fees are charged to principal, questions regarding the appropriateness of the fees could be raised by the remaindermen at the termination of the trust.

Many statutory fees provide a division of charges between income and principal. Typically, if local law allows both an income and principal fee, the income fee is charged against income and the principal fee is charged against the principal of the trust. In the case of a trustee's fee based solely on the value of the principal, half of the fee should be charged to income and the other half to principal. This is the most equitable way to handle the charges and is consistent with the way the courts have ruled on this issue where a split has been disputed. Also, many state statutes require a 50/50 split.

QUESTION

Where an individual is named both the executor and the trustee, is the fiduciary entitled to executor and trustee fees on the same property?
While there are exceptions among the various states, the general rule is that a separate fee is paid to an executor for receiving and paying over to the trustee the assets of the estate. The trustee is entitled to a fee on those same assets for taking possession of and managing them in the trust. So the answer is yes.

Co-Trustees

The compensation of co-trustees is usually dictated by the terms of the trust document. Again, if there is no provision, the trustees must look to local law. Every state is different. In some states, each trustee is entitled to the full allowable trustee fees. In others only one fee is chargeable to the trust, and the co-trustees must share that fee as they agree between themselves. If there is no agreement, the court must decide how the fees are to be split. In the case of a bank or trust company serving as a co-trustee with an individual, the institution will normally insist on being paid the full fee.

However, in some cases they will negotiate a fee split with the individual co-trustee. Fee-splitting arrangements should always be in writing.

Preparing and Maintaining Trust Accountings

Trust accounting should provide useful information to the beneficiaries and other interested persons regarding the transactions that take place during the accounting period. Beneficiaries should be able to clearly understand the transactions that affect their interests in the trust. There is no one accounting format that is used for all trusts. States that require accountings to be filed with the court may prescribe a specific format. However, all trust accountings should incorporate the basic principles of accounting and the separation of income from principal.

Again, the trustee's objective should be to provide the beneficiaries with a clear picture of the trustee's management of the trust. At least initially, a trustee would be well-advised to seek assistance from a qualified CPA or other professional who is familiar with trust accounting rules to set up and maintain the accounting records for the trust.

Accounting Rules for Terminating Trusts

When a trust terminates at the death of the settlor, accounting for the administration during the period from the settlor's date of death through the final distribution of the trust assets is similar to accounting for a probate estate. A trustee must account for property (other than cash) that is specifically and separately bequeathed to a beneficiary from other trust property. All income attributable to the specific bequest property must be accounted for separately, and all expenses attributable to the bequest must be deducted from that income. The property's income includes all income accrued prior to and after the settlor's death. This income, less expenses, follows the property and is distributable to the beneficiary.

Accounting Rules for Terminating Income Interests

Under the 1931 and 1962 Uniform Principal and Income Acts, an income beneficiary or her estate is entitled to income (other than dividends) accrued but not received at the time her income interest ended. For example, if a beneficiary's income interest ends on June 30 as a result of that beneficiary's death, and a six-month interest check on a bond is received on July 15, the beneficiary's estate is entitled to the interest earned from the last interest payment through June 30. However, some trust documents eliminate this right to accrued income and makes accounting for the income a lot simpler:

> *"Upon the death of any income beneficiary, the interest and estate of such beneficiary in all income of the trust estate then undistributed shall terminate, regardless of when the same shall have accrued, and all such income shall be paid and distributed as though it had accrued immediately after the death of such beneficiary."*

Making the wrong accounting decision can be costly, as errors typically are not discovered during the period of administration. Accounting errors are often identified at the time the trust terminates, which can be many years after the error was made. For example, a remainder beneficiary may learn that an expense was charged against principal sometime during the term of the trust when it should have been charged to income. As a result, the remainder beneficiary received less than he or she would have received had the error not been made. Also, it may be difficult, if not impossible, to collect the amount of the erroneous charge from the income beneficiaries, who should have incurred the expense in the first place. Statutory interest or lost opportunity costs could be assessed against the trustee to reimburse the trust and make the remainder beneficiary whole. This is why it is important to maintain accurate trust accounting records.

A qualified accountant is the logical advisor to assist the trustee in addressing fiduciary accounting issues and maintaining accounting records for the trust. At the very least, a trustee should seek professional help in the initial stages of establishing the accounting records. Again, in dealing with accounting matters, the trustee and his or her accountant should first refer to the trust document regarding an accounting question, and then to the Uniform Principal and Income Act, for guidance.

Trust Accounting Checklist

- Review the provisions in the trust that pertain to trust accounting matters.
- Review the Uniform Principal and Income Act under local law.
- Check to see if the trust requires a transfer from income to principal for depreciation.
- Retain a qualified accountant to establish the accounting records for the trust and, if necessary, to maintain them.
- Establish a tickler to provide regular accounting reports (at least annually) to all beneficiaries.

When Does a Trust Terminate?

As a general rule, a continuing trust must terminate at some point in time unless it is a charitable trust, in which case it can continue in perpetuity. Many states have something called a *rule against perpetuities* in their statutes, which says that a trust cannot extend beyond a period measured by "lives in being plus twenty-one years." This period begins at the settlor's date of death, or when the trust becomes irrevocable, and extends for the lifetime of the youngest beneficiary who is alive at the point the trust became irrevocable, plus twenty-one years after the death of that beneficiary. This rule was developed as a matter of public policy to assure that the property placed in trust eventually passes from one generation to another and back into the public domain.

ALERT

Some common events that trigger a trust's termination include the death of a surviving spouse, the death of a beneficiary, or a beneficiary's attainment of a certain age. Another condition that may terminate a trust is if the market value of the trust assets falls below a specified dollar amount or level where it is no longer economical to maintain it. This amount is usually specified in the trust.

Upon termination, a trustee is required to close up the affairs of the trust within a reasonable period. A trustee will not be relieved of his or her responsibilities until all assets have been distributed or the court has formally discharged the trustee. During the termination process, the trustee is required to protect the trust property, pay final expenses, and distribute the assets to the remaindermen. A trustee will be held accountable for any unreasonable delay in this process.

ESSENTIAL

If a beneficiary refuses to approve your accountings and release you from liability, you can submit them to the probate court and have the court provide you with a release.

As a general rule, the trustee's responsibilities with respect to the administration of the trust terminate upon final distribution of the assets to the remaindermen. If the termination of the trust is subject to a court proceeding, the court will provide the trustee with a formal discharge of duties. Getting the beneficiaries to approve your trust accountings may be a way to avoid a court proceeding and thus reduce termination costs. If you submit your trust accountings to the probate court, a master will be appointed to audit the accountings and, of course, will charge a fee. If a beneficiary refuses to sign an approval of the accounting and the receipt and release, the trustee has the option of having the accounts approved by the court at the trust's expense.

Terminating a Marital Trust

As discussed earlier, in order to qualify for the marital deduction, an estate trust and a power of appointment trust must meet certain requirements. In the case of an estate trust, upon the death of the surviving spouse, all of the accrued income and principal must be paid to the surviving spouse's estate. The trustee needs to contact the executor of the surviving spouse's estate and obtain instructions for delivery of the trust assets to the estate. If the marital trust is a power of appointment trust, the trust must give the surviving spouse a testamentary power of appointment. A general testamentary power of appointment clause usually gives the trustee fairly specific directions as to how the assets are to be distributed if the surviving spouse exercises the power of appointment. The following is an example of such a provision:

> "Upon termination, the trust estate then remaining, including the accrued but undistributed income and particularly the income for the period between the last income distribution date and the death of the settlor's spouse, shall be paid to or held for the benefit of such person or persons, or corporation or corporations, or the estate of the settlor's spouse, in such amounts and proportions and for such estates and interests, and outright or upon such terms, trusts, conditions, and limitations as the settlor's spouse shall appoint by will by specific reference to this power of appointment."

The trustee must obviously obtain a copy of the surviving spouse's will in order to determine who the remainder beneficiaries of the trust are. If the surviving spouse does not exercise all, or a portion of, the power of appointment, the marital trust will usually say that the assets not appointed shall be added to the credit shelter trust (the bypass trust, family trust, residuary trust, "B" trust, etc.).

Since all marital trusts are subject to federal estate tax in the surviving spouse's estate, the trustee should coordinate the valuation of the marital trust assets with the surviving spouse's executor. The trust may also provide that it pay its proportionate share of the estate tax, due on the marital trust assets, to the executor.

Should You Distribute in Cash or in Kind?

Most trust documents give a trustee the power to make final distribution of the trust assets in cash or in kind (i.e., distribution of the assets themselves):

> "To make distribution in kind, in money, or partly in each, without requiring pro rata distribution of specific assets at fair market value as determined by the trustee on the effective date distribution."

If this or similar language is not contained in the trust, many states give the trustee this authority under local law. The reason for giving the trustee this authority is because it is not always possible to split some assets among several beneficiaries. For example, a $5,000 corporate bond could not be split evenly among six beneficiaries because the minimum denomination for a bond is $1,000. With the authority to distribute cash, the trustee can sell the bond and split the cash proceeds six ways. As an alternative, the bond, or other asset, could be given to one beneficiary and another asset given to the other beneficiaries.

FACT

You are not required to liquidate everything and distribute cash unless directed to do so under the trust.

Any differences in the value of these assets can be equalized with cash. However, the trustee should first obtain the consent of the beneficiaries to do this. Another issue has to do with creating a taxable transaction. If a beneficiary is entitled to receive a dollar, or pecuniary, amount under the trust and the trustee satisfies the bequest by making a distribution in kind, the trust will be treated as having sold the property to the beneficiary and will realize a capital gain, or loss. Pecuniary bequests should be satisfied with cash assets to avoid this problem. Assets should be sold only if directed by the terms of the trust, the sale is absolutely necessary to protect the value of an asset, all beneficiaries direct that an asset be sold, or an asset cannot be split among multiple beneficiaries. If there is only one remainder beneficiary, the trustee must distribute in kind. The Restatement (Second) of Trusts, Section 345, provides that:

> *"If upon termination of the trust there is a single beneficiary who is entitled to the trust property, it is the duty of the trustee to convey the property to him, rather than to sell it and to pay him the proceeds, unless it is otherwise provided by the terms of the trust."*

If sale of the assets is contemplated, the trustee should seek the approval of the beneficiary first. In a 1992 case, a bank trustee was surcharged by the court for not getting the approval of the beneficiary before liquidating the trust assets.

How to Deliver the Property to the Beneficiaries

Once the assets have been reregistered, delivery of the assets should be made in person for those beneficiaries who live close to the trustee. Where personal delivery of the assets is not possible, the name and address of a bank through which distribution can be made should be obtained from the beneficiary. The idea is to have a responsible entity deliver the assets and assure that the proper signature is obtained on the receipt from the beneficiary. If a beneficiary is a protected person (i.e., a minor or someone who is disabled), his or her share needs to be distributed to the beneficiary's legal representative. If the legal representative is unknown, the trustee must see to it that the share is protected for the benefit of that beneficiary. A well-drafted trust document will give the trustee guidance in this regard. Even if not specifically included in the trust document, the following outlines some of the options with respect to the disposition of protected property (property distributable to a protected person):

"The trustee may distribute any protected property to or for the benefit of such beneficiary (1) directly to the beneficiary; (2) on behalf of the beneficiary for the beneficiary's exclusive benefit; (3) to any account in a bank or savings institution either in the name of such beneficiary or in a form reserving title, management, and custody of such account in a suitable person for the use of such beneficiary; (4) to an individual or corporation as custodian for a minor under the Uniform Transfers to Minors Act or Uniform Gifts to Minors Act or for an adult under a Uniform Custodial Trust Act; (5) in any form of annuity; (6) in all other ways provided by laws dealing with gifts or distributions to or for minors or persons under disability; and (7) to any suitable person with whom the beneficiary resides or who has the care or control of the beneficiary, without obligation to see to the further application of such distribution, and the receipt for distributions by any such persons shall fully discharge the trustee."

ESSENTIAL

> Depending on the nature of the trust (difficult assets, difficult beneficiaries, existing or pending litigation), if the beneficiaries of the trust refuse to give the trustee a release and discharge, again, the trustee can seek court approval of its accounts to protect himself or herself from future claims.

Checklist for Termination and Distribution

- Identify who the remainder beneficiaries are. Considerable time may have lapsed since the settlor's death, and some beneficiaries may not have outlived the termination of the trust. The dispositive provisions of the trust must be carefully reviewed to determine proper succession (per stirpes, per capita, per capita at each generation, etc.).
- Notify the beneficiaries that the trust has terminated and describe the specific provisions that relate to their inheritance. Also, outline the steps that will be taken and an approximate time frame for closing the trust.
- If termination is due to death, obtain a certified copy of the death certificate. If termination was due to attainment of an age, obtain a birth certificate.
- Obtain reissue instructions from all beneficiaries, including how assets are to be titled, current addresses, Social Security numbers, and the name and address of a local bank through which delivery can be made if assets cannot be delivered personally.
- Obtain current values for all securities, real estate, and other assets that will be distributed to the beneficiaries.
- Prepare a distribution schedule that includes the tax cost basis for each asset.
- Check the trust document for language regarding the accrual of income. If the document is silent and local law does not otherwise preclude the requirement to accrue income, accrue all undistributed income from the last income distribution to the beneficiary to the date of termination and pay this amount to the beneficiary or his/her estate.
- Have the attorney for the trust prepare new deeds for all real estate assets.

- Arrange for the preparation and filing of the final fiduciary income tax return(s). Reserve sufficient funds to cover the preparation fee and any taxes that may be due.
- Reregister all securities in accordance with the beneficiary's instructions and the distribution schedule.
- Prepare the final accounting for the period from the termination date of the trust through and including all transactions prior to making final distribution of the assets to the beneficiaries. Deliver the accounting to the beneficiaries and file with the court, if required.
- Obtain an approval of the final accounting, receipt for the assets delivered, and a release of liability from all beneficiaries. Sample approval and release:

I, the undersigned, being a beneficiary of the (name of trust), for the purpose of receiving distribution without a court order:

    I. Acknowledge that I have examined the account of the trustee for the period from (beginning date) to and including (ending date) and approve the same, which approval shall have the same effect as if the account had been approved by the court;

    II. Acknowledge receipt of income and principal distributable to me under the terms of this trust consisting of: (itemize all assets, including cash, that are being distributed); Agree to indemnify, hold harmless, and release and discharge the trustee from any liability in connection with the above trust or its administration;

In witness whereof I have executed this instrument this _____ day of _____, 20___, with the intention of being legally bound.

_____

- Prepare a supplemental final accounting from the end date of the final accounting through and including the final distribution of the cash balance. Provide this to the beneficiaries and file with the court, if required.

CHAPTER 17

Managing Other Types of Irrevocable Trusts

The discussion, thus far, has centered primarily on the management of the marital and credit shelter type trusts. The same duties, responsibilities, and principles of trust administration also apply to other types of irrevocable trusts. Some types of irrevocable trusts have unique rules that apply to their administration. These requirements are primarily tax related and will either be described under the terms of the trust or under the Internal Revenue Code.

Children's Gift Trusts

These are trusts established by a parent to make gifts to a child and qualify for the annual gift tax exclusion. The trustee controls when and under what circumstances the child receives the funds. Children's gift trusts, which are described under Sections 2503(b) and 2503(c) of the Internal Revenue Code, have the following administration characteristics:

- The trust must terminate when the child reaches age twenty-one and the trustee must distribute all of the income and principal to the child at that time.
- In a 2503(c) type of trust, distributions can be made in the discretion of the trustee. However, in the 2503(b) type of trust, income *must* be distributed to the beneficiary.
- Distributions from the trust are taxed at the parent's marginal tax rate until the child attains the age of fourteen. This is referred to as the *kiddie tax.* After the child reaches age fourteen, the tax is paid at the child's individual income tax rate.

ALERT

During the period of administration a trustee must follow the IRS rules that apply to that particular trust in order to preserve its tax status.

It is important that the trustee obtain a copy of the beneficiary's birth certificate, and make a record of the key dates.

Irrevocable Life Insurance Trusts

The purpose of an irrevocable life insurance trust is to remove the ownership of life insurance from the settlor and avoid taxation of the face amount of the policy at the settlor's death. When the trust is created, the settlor will either transfer an existing insurance policy to the trust or have the trustee purchase a new policy on the settlor's life. The settlor deposits funds to the trust periodically to cover the payment of premiums and any administration costs. In administering this type of trust, the trustee needs to be aware of certain requirements:

- If an insurance policy is transferred or added to the trust, the settlor must survive three years in order to avoid having the proceeds taxed in the settlor's estate. If the settlor dies within three years, the trustee must so notify the settlor's executor and provide the executor with Form 712, which is provided by the insurance company and reports the amount of the insurance and interest paid on the policy.
- As deposits are made to the trust to cover premiums and administration costs, the trustee must notify the beneficiaries that they have the right—referred to as *Crummey power*—to withdraw those funds. This right lapses after a period of time stated in the trust document. The Crummey power is required to qualify the deposit for the annual gift tax exclusion. Failure of the trustee to give proper notice will subject the deposits to gift taxes.
- The trustee should periodically review the policies with an insurance agent to assure that they are performing as expected and that the insurance company is viable. If a problem exists, the trustee is required to take appropriate action to safeguard the interests of the beneficiaries.
- Often the irrevocable life insurance trust is established to provide cash to pay estate taxes. To the extent that this cash is used directly to pay the estate tax, that amount will be included in the decedent's taxable estate. A well-drafted trust will allow the trustee to purchase assets from the estate to provide the needed cash, thereby avoiding this problem. The trustee needs to coordinate the purchase of assets with the executor.

ALERT

The Crummey power is named after the plaintiff in a famous case, Crummey v. Commissioner (9th Circuit, 1968), in which the court found that deposits to a trust that contained this power would be considered present interest gifts and thereby qualify for the annual gift tax exclusion.

GRITs, GRATs, and GRUTs

The grantor-retained income trust, or GRIT, grantor-retained annuity trust, or GRAT, and grantor-retained unitrust, or GRUT, serve primarily to shelter future appreciation of the property transferred to the trust from federal estate tax. As previously mentioned, Congress has significantly curtailed the advantages of these devices in recent years. However, they still have application in some circumstances, and many of these trusts that were established in earlier years still exist. A trustee's responsibilities in managing these types of trusts include:

- In the case of a GRIT, paying all of the net income of the trust to the grantor. In the case of a GRAT, this calls for computing the fixed annuity amount required by the trust and paying the grantor each year. In the case of a GRUT, determining the amount of the payout each year, based on the percentage stated in the trust document and the fair market value of the trust assets at the beginning of each tax year.
- For GRATs and GRUTs, this calls for managing the trust's portfolio to efficiently produce the returns necessary to meet the payout requirement in the trust document.
- If the grantor dies before the end of the stated term of the trust, the trust assets will be taxed in the grantor's estate and the trustee must value the assets as of the grantor's date of death for federal estate tax purposes.
- If the grantor survives the term of the trust, the trust must be terminated and the assets distributed to the named remainder beneficiaries.

Charitable Trusts

Charitable remainder trusts are one of the last tax-advantaged trust arrangements that have remained virtually untouched by Congress. For those individuals who have a charitable intent, the charitable remainder trust offers significant advantages, including an income tax deduction based on the amount transferred to the trust, an estate tax deduction, avoidance of capital gains taxes if the property in the trust is sold, and the retention of an income stream for life. There are several types of charitable remainder trusts.

The most common are the charitable remainder annuity trust, or CRAT, and the charitable remainder unitrust, or CRUT. The CRAT pays a fixed annuity to the grantor and/or the grantor's spouse or other beneficiary for life. The CRUT pays an amount based on a stated percentage of the trust assets to the grantor and/or the grantor's spouse or other beneficiary for life. Another type of charitable trust is the Charitable Lead Trust, or CLT. It pays a specific dollar amount or fixed percentage of the value of the trust to a charity each year for a specified term. At the end of the term, the trust property is either distributed to or retained in trust for the benefit of noncharitable beneficiaries (children, grandchildren, etc.). The purpose of the CLT is to remove the income from the grantor, having the same effect as a charitable income tax deduction, and also to make a gift to the remainder beneficiaries.

ESSENTIAL

Charitable trust rules need to be followed to the letter to avoid jeopardizing the trust's charitable status. Charitable remainder trusts, in particular, are subject to many rules that the trustee must follow in order to maintain the trust's tax advantaged status.

Some of the administrative duties that apply to a charitable remainder trust include:

- In the case of a CRAT, computing the fixed annuity amount and paying it to the grantor each year. For a CRUT, determining the amount of the payout each year, based on the percentage stated in the trust document and the fair market value of the trust assets at the beginning of each tax year.
- Managing the investments efficiently to meet the payout requirement of the trust. If the trust allows the use of principal to supplement income, and the payout percentage is high, a total return strategy should be used to manage the portfolio. With a high payout percentage such as 9% or 10%, the portfolio should be weighted toward equities (stocks) in order to achieve the return needed to meet the payout requirement.
- Some trusts provide that only the net income can be distributed. These trusts are referred to as *net income trusts* or NIMCRUTS. If the payout requirement is 9% and the current income (dividends, interest,

rents, etc.) is only 4%, that is all that can be paid out. These types of trusts usually have a "make up" provision that will require the trustee to maintain records of the years in which there is a shortfall. If the net income in future years exceeds the stated percentage payout, the trustee can pay the excess to make up for the shortfalls in prior years.

- The trustee must adhere to some specific rules that apply to these trusts under the Internal Revenue Code. Under these rules the trustee: shall not engage in any act of self-dealing, as defined in Section 4941(d) of the Internal Revenue Service Code (Code); shall not make any taxable expenditure as defined in Section 4945(d) of the Code; shall not make any investments that jeopardize the charitable purpose of the trust, within the meaning of Section 4943 of the Code; is prohibited from incurring unrelated business taxable income within the meaning of Section 512 of the Code; is prohibited from incurring debt-financed income within the meaning of Section 514 of the Code.

Other Types of Trusts

Other types of irrevocable trusts are established for a variety of purposes. Again, the important thing to remember is that the standards of conduct and principles of trust administration discussed in this book apply to all irrevocable trusts. It is important that the trustee understand the basic purpose and intent of these trusts in order to manage them properly:

- *Qualified Personal Residence Trust (QPRT)*—A QPRT is a trust that holds the grantor's residence for a specified period of years while allowing the grantor to retain the right to use the property. If the grantor dies before the term ends, the property will be included in the grantor's estate. However, if the grantor survives the term, it will be excluded from the grantor's estate because title will have passed at that point, typically to the settlor's children. The trust can provide for the payment of fair market rent to allow the grantor to continue to live in the house beyond the term of the trust. The trust document must prohibit the trustee from selling or transferring the property to the grantor or the grantor's spouse.

- *Special Needs Trust*—A special needs trust is designed to put funds aside for a beneficiary without those funds disqualifying the beneficiary from receiving public assistance. The trust provides that the trustee is to use his or her discretion in making distributions to the beneficiary and only to supplement the funds available through public assistance programs, such as Medicaid.

- *Wealth Replacement Trust*—A wealth replacement trust is nothing more than a separate irrevocable life insurance trust, or ILIT, whose purpose is to replace the inheritance that was lost as a result of property transferred to a charitable remainder trust (CRT). A life insurance policy equal to the value of the property transferred to the CRT is purchased in the wealth replacement trust. It is subject to the same rules that apply to an ILIT, and should be managed accordingly.

- *Spendthrift Trust*—Although most family or credit shelter trusts contain a spendthrift provision, a separate irrevocable trust is sometimes created specifically to protect a beneficiary from his creditors and divorce. The spendthrift trust precludes the beneficiary from having access to principal, either by prohibiting principal distributions or by giving the trustee sole discretion to make payments from principal. This restriction prevents the creditors of the beneficiary from reaching the trust assets. The trustee must evaluate every principal distribution and be assured that the funds are being used for the purpose for which they were disbursed.

As is the case with almost any arrangement that attempts to avoid taxes and creditor claims, some will stay within the spirit of the law and others will try to push the limits. The Internal Revenue Service has recently given notice that they consider the following trust arrangements abusive:

- *The Business Trust*—The owner of a business transfers the business to a trust in exchange for units or certificates of beneficial interest. The business trust makes payments to the trust unit holders or to other trusts created by the owner that purport to reduce the taxable income of the business trust to the point where little or no tax is due from the business trust. Most states do not recognize business trusts.

- *Equipment or Service Trust*—An equipment trust is formed to hold equipment that is rented or leased to the business trust, often at inflated rates. The service trust is formed to provide services to the business trust, often for inflated fees.
- *Family Residence Trust*—The owner (grantor) of the family residence transfers the residence, including its furnishings, to a trust, which is leased back to the grantor. The trustee takes depreciation and other expenses to reduce or eliminate the taxable income from lease rent. The trust claims the exchange results in a stepped-up basis for the property, and the owner reports no gain.
- *Charitable Trust*—The owner transfers assets to a purported charitable trust and claims either that the payments to the trust are deductible or that payments made by the trust are deductible charitable contributions. However, in fact, the payments are principally for the personal educational, living, or recreational expenses of the owner or the owner's family.
- *Final Trust*—In some multitrust arrangements, the U.S. owner of one or more abusive trusts establishes a trust that holds trust units of the owner's other trusts and is the final distributee of the income. A final trust often is formed in a foreign country that will impose little or no tax on the trust.

For obvious reasons, it would be prudent for an individual not to serve as a trustee for any of these types of trusts. The IRS has advised that taxpayers and/or the promoters of these trust arrangements may be subject to civil and/or criminal penalties.

Checklist

- Identify the specific rules that apply to the trust you are managing.
- Read the trust document and identify any special provisions that apply to the administration of the trust.
- Identify, by consulting with the attorney for the trust or other qualified professional, any special legal requirements that apply to the administration of the trust.
- Develop an investment strategy that meets the specific current payout requirements of the trust and protects the interests of remaindermen.

CHAPTER 18

Do You Need Help?

Executors and trustees face many difficult and time-consuming tasks while administering an estate or trust. It is incredibly difficult to deal with some of the more complex issues without professional help. Individual fiduciaries are responsible for their actions, and in some situations may be held personally liable for not getting professional help when they lack the necessary expertise to properly perform the task. Don't be afraid to ask for help. Becoming a trustee or executor is a big commitment, but you don't have to go through it alone!

Deciding If and When You Need Assistance

When and where to get help will, of course, depend on the particular issue that needs to be addressed. If the matter is one of legal interpretation or consequence, an attorney who specializes in that area of law should be consulted. If the question is procedural or authoritative in nature, such as whether or not the executor or trustee can hire agents to assist in the administration of the estate or trust, the answer can usually be found in the will or trust or by referencing local statutes.

ALERT

Most modern will and trust documents authorize hiring agents. The reason is obvious. It is highly unlikely that an individual executor or trustee will possess all of the skills and expertise necessary to handle all aspects of administration in an estate or trust.

Some individuals may feel that the reason they were selected was to save money. They may also think that they would betray this intent by hiring agents and incurring the additional expense. Just the opposite is true. While minimizing expenses is always an objective, the testator or settlor also expects the individual to perform the job correctly to protect the interests of beneficiaries. The expectation is that the individual will use the resources of the estate or trust to carry out this objective. The laws are also written with this in mind. Hiring consultants to assist and advise the executor or trustee is proper and an appropriate administration expense chargeable to income. In fact, some statutes make specific reference to the charging of agents' fees to the estate or trust.

What Services Can Accountants Provide?

Accountants should be used for their expertise in the fields of accounting and taxation. Because of the high level of accounting and tax expertise required, only certified public accountants (CPAs) should be retained. A CPA can provide assistance with tax returns, tax elections, trust accounting reports, court accountings, inventories, business valuations, and addressing a variety of tax, fiduciary accounting, and planning issues. In addition, a CPA can assist the executor or trustee in developing and analyzing budgets, auditing business and commercial real estate interests, and helping resolve management problems that may exist with a closely held business.

However, accountants should not be the final answer to a particular tax or accounting question. Accountants are prohibited from engaging in the unauthorized practice of law. A tax attorney should be retained if a particular tax or accounting question requires a legal opinion with regard to interpretation or application of the tax law. Most accountants will refer a client to an attorney when this situation occurs. Accountants can also be relied upon to make objective recommendations. CPAs do not receive compensation for recommending a particular investment or insurance product or referring a client to another professional. Accountants work closely with other professionals in the community and are a good source for referrals to stockbrokers, insurance agents, attorneys, and other professionals.

What Services Can Attorneys Provide?

An attorney is usually required when an executor or trustee interacts with the courts. This is typically the case in a formal probate proceeding. Attorneys can give advice on a broad range of legal and nonlegal matters. These include guidance with regard to probate proceedings, interpretation of contracts and other legal documents, guidance on the effects of local law on the administration of estates and trusts, dealing with creditor rights issues, interpreting the legal rights of heirs, and other issues that require interpretation and application of the law.

The attorney who prepared the will or trust is the logical choice to represent the estate or trust in court, as he or she should be familiar with the decedent's estate plan, family, and financial affairs. However, the attorney who prepared the original will and/or trust may not have an interest in representing the estate or trust or may not have sufficient experience in the area of administration. The executor or trustee is responsible for hiring the attorney and it is therefore important to retain someone who will devote the time and who has experience with estate and trust administration. The fiduciary should also make sure that expensive attorney time is not used for tasks that can be accomplished at a lower cost by someone else.

What Services Can Banks or Trust Companies Provide?

Banks and trust companies are in the business of providing fiduciary services, including serving as an executor and trustee or acting as an agent to assist the fiduciary with administration. Banks and trust companies bill themselves as "one-stop" shops because typically, they have all of the facilities to administer estates and trusts in-house. Using a bank or trust company to serve as an executor or trustee can be expensive, particularly for smaller accounts. However, if the bank or trust company provides services as an agent of the executor or trustee, the cost might be lower depending on the particular services that are needed.

One of the advantages of using a bank or trust company is that they do not get sick or go on vacation and therefore provide continuity in the administration of the estate or trust. Individuals are human and must devote time to their own business and family affairs. Banks and trust companies can also be useful in mitigating conflicts between the executor or trustee and other family members. For example, if the individual executor or trustee is also a beneficiary, he or she could be viewed by other family members as not being totally objective with regard to the management decisions that are made. Banks and trust companies are usually not well equipped to manage a closely held family business. A family member or other individual who is familiar with the business can better handle this type of asset. If the estate or trust is complex, using a corporate fiduciary may be a way of reducing liability exposure. Banks and trust companies do this for a living and are also covered by insurance for any errors they make.

What Services Can Investment Firms and Financial Planners Provide?

Most investment firms provide individual portfolio management services in addition to their retail brokerage activities (i.e., recommending stocks and bonds for purchase or sale). The large investment firms now own one or more trust companies through which fiduciary services are also offered. However, they are new at this business and the services may be limited and only available in the state where the trust company is located. Some firms deliver limited fiduciary services through their local offices, using the account executive (broker) as a liaison between the trustee client and the trust officer who works out of the nearest trust company office.

Investment firms are capable of managing a trust's securities portfolio, but are not usually equipped to handle the management of other assets, such as real estate. Management of the portfolio is either handled by portfolio managers within the firm or outside money managers hired by the company. Management fees can run anywhere between 1% to 3% of the portfolio's value annually.

A financial planner's primary function is to help individuals develop and implement a comprehensive personal financial plan. Financial planning includes budgeting and cash flow analyses, long-term savings, retirement planning, investments, tax planning, estate planning, and risk (insurance) management. Financial planners can assist an executor or trustee with any of these component needs if the planner has experience in dealing with these issues in a fiduciary context. Financial planners usually have an orientation toward investments and insurance, since they may be compensated through the use of these products. A financial planner may also have a strong background in estate planning and can be helpful to an executor or trustee in making decisions that affect a beneficiary's estate plan. Some planners emphasize tax planning and may have expertise in fiduciary taxation.

What Services Can Insurance Agents and Realtors Provide?

An insurance agent should be consulted when evaluating the insurance coverage for estate and trust assets. Agents should be engaged to investigate the physical condition of estate or trust property and recommend any changes necessary to reduce hazards and protect fiduciary assets. The coverage should include protection from fire, theft, loss of use, liability, and other risk exposures. If additional coverage is needed, the executor or trustee should be advised as to the most economical way to obtain the needed coverage. The fiduciary should use the insurance agent who handled the decedent's policies prior to death. However, the executor or trustee can use any agent or firm as long as it does not create a conflict of interest.

A real estate agent should be retained if the estate or trust holds real estate that needs to be sold. Hiring an agent that has expertise in the area in which the property is located is the prudent choice. The realtor should also specialize in the particular type of property (residential, commercial, or industrial) that is being sold. Before making a selection, the executor or trustee should discuss the sale with three different realtors and list the property with the realtor that has the highest level of experience and success in marketing the particular type of property that is being sold.

Some real estate firms can also provide property management services for income-producing residential and commercial properties, including marketing and advertising, collection of rents, physical care of the premises, procuring supplies and equipment, making repairs, hiring employees, and maintaining accounting records. Although a realtor may be familiar with the principles of valuing real estate, most do not provide formal appraisal services. However, they are a good source for referrals. Most are very familiar with the quality and price ranges of experienced appraisers and can recommend one that is best suited to the particular property that needs to be valued.

How to Select Professional Advisors

Who should you hire to assist with the administration? Does he or she have the necessary skills and expertise? Will you pay too much? The number and variety of financial experts out there is mind-boggling. Anyone can call him- or herself a financial planner or advisor, and there are many to choose from. There are a variety of certified professionals out there, including certified public accountants (CPAs), chartered financial analysts (CFAs), certified financial planners (CFPs), chartered life underwriters (CLUs), chartered financial consultants (ChFcs), certified trust and financial advisors (CTFAs), and many, many others. To add to the confusion, there is no one agency that regulates all financial advisors or uniform standards that apply to all groups. Fees that financial advisors charge vary widely, and some will not accept a client whose assets fall below a minimum dollar amount. Deciding on who to hire can be a perplexing experience, but it does not have to be.

Ask the Right Questions

Doing your homework and asking some basic questions will greatly improve your chances of hiring the right person. Some basic questions to ask when selecting an advisor include:

- What relevant education and/or credentials does the advisor have in his or her field?
- Do the credentials require continuing education to maintain the designation? If so, how many hours are required?
- What professional organizations does the advisor belong to and how active is he or she in those organizations?
- How long has the advisor been practicing?
- Ask the advisor for references, including a list of his or her clients. Talk to other professionals.
- Ask your banker about the advisor's reputation in the community.
- Discuss the prospect with friends, relatives, etc. who may have some knowledge about the advisor.
- Are you compatible with the advisor's personality and business philosophy?
- Check with the appropriate government regulatory agency as to whether any complaints have been registered against the advisor.
- Ask for a list of other professionals with whom the advisor maintains a close working relationship.
- Ask the advisor if he or she will be working directly with you or if an associate will be the primary contact.
- Find out how the advisor will be compensated. Will you be advised before extraordinary services are performed and before charges for these services are made?
- Ask the advisor how much errors and omissions insurance he or she carries.
- Discuss the procedures and methods that the advisor will use to assist you.

The selection should be based on the particular service that is needed and additional information pertaining to the advisor's particular area of expertise should be obtained before you make the final selection.

In carrying out the responsibilities imposed on an executor or trustee as set forth in the governing document and/or local law, a fiduciary must select advisors wisely. While technical competence is important, so too is the advisor's business philosophy regarding the management of the estate or trust. The advisor's attitudes should be agreeable and compatible with your own. The needed services should be clearly explained to the agent and outlined in a written agreement signed by both the agent and the executor or trustee. Professional advisors should not be used for routine work that you can perform yourself.

You should keep good records of the services each agent provides. The records can be used as a reference in the event a question arises regarding the services that were performed. Remember that the executor or trustee is expected to exercise care, skill, and caution in managing the estate or trust. In carrying out this responsibility, he or she must exercise a reasonable degree of prudence in selecting the agent. Once an agent has been hired, the executor or trustee must employ oversight and supervision of the agent's activities to assure that the services contracted for are delivered satisfactorily and that the integrity and interests of the beneficiaries are preserved.

Checklist for Hiring an Accountant

- Is the individual a certified public accountant (CPA)?
- Is the CPA licensed to practice in the state in which the estate or trust is located?
- Does the CPA have experience in handling fiduciary matters (preparation of estate tax returns, fiduciary income tax returns, fiduciary accountings, etc.)?

- What percentage of the CPA's practice is devoted to fiduciary services?
- Is the CPA a member of the American Institute of Certified Public Accountants (the AICPA), which subjects its members to a code of professional ethics?
- Will other individuals within the firm be performing any of the work? If so, what is their level of experience, and will the CPA closely supervise them?
- What will be the charges for the work performed?

Checklist for Hiring an Attorney

- How long has the attorney practiced in his or her given field?
- What percentage of his or her time is spent handling the type of estate or trust matter that the fiduciary needs assistance with?
- Is the attorney amenable to consulting with the fiduciary's other advisors, such as the CPA, banker, insurance agent, etc.?
- Is there a charge for an initial consultation?
- What is the attorney's hourly rate?
- Will the attorney consult with you when the charges are likely to exceed the initial estimate and before you are billed for the services?
- Will providing the needed services affect the attorney's malpractice insurance coverage? In other words, are the services excluded under the policy?
- Will others who are compensated at a lower rate perform clerical services, and will the fees reflect that lower rate?

Checklist for Hiring a Bank or Trust Company

- How large is the operation? What is the value of assets under administration and management?
- How long has the institution been in the fiduciary services business?
- What are the charges? Is there a minimum? Obtain fee schedules.
- What is the size and structure of the investment department?
- What investment style is used to manage fiduciary portfolios?

- What is their investment performance record? Obtain results from the last year and the past three, five, and ten years.
- Obtain a sample of accounting reports. What is the quality? How frequently are reports provided?
- What is the rate of personnel turnover?
- What is the average experience (number of years) of investment officers, trust officers, management personnel, and others who are directly involved in handling fiduciary accounts?
- What credentials are trust and investment officers required to hold?
- Who (trust officer, committee, manager, etc.) will make the decisions concerning the services that will be provided?
- Obtain annual reports, booklets, and other materials describing the institution and the services provided.
- Interview trust officers and supervisory personnel.
- Obtain the name and title of the manager of the trust department.
- How much of the operation is outsourced to other companies, and what effect will that have on the services provided?

Checklist for Hiring a Financial Planner

- What credentials (CFP, ChFc, CPA, etc.) and licenses does the planner hold?
- What experience does the planner have in advising clients on fiduciary matters?
- How long has the planner been in business?
- How is the planner compensated? Is it fee for service, commissions for selling products, or both?
- What kind of investment track record does the planner have?
- Who are the other professionals that the planner works with and what is their level of experience?
- What percentage of the planner's practice is devoted to assisting executors and trustees?
- How familiar is the planner with the rules and regulations that affect executors and trustees?
- How many estate and trustee clients does the planner have?

Checklist for Hiring an Investment Firm

- Is the investment firm familiar with the Uniform Prudent Investor Act?
- Will an advisor hired by the investment firm manage the portfolio?
- What is the manager's performance record? Obtain performance numbers for the past year and for the last three, five, and ten years.
- How many fiduciary accounts does the investment firm handle?
- What is the investment philosophy and strategy of the firm?
- What is the rate of personnel turnover?
- Is diversification to reduce risk part of the investment firm's style?
- How often will the account manager contact the executor or trustee to review the portfolio and investment results?
- Can the agency agreement be terminated at any time? If so, is there an exit or termination charge?
- Interview the manager who will handle the account to ascertain whether or not the manager's personality is compatible with yours.

Checklist for Hiring an Insurance Agent

- What credentials and licenses does the agent hold?
- How long has the agent been in business?
- Is the agent a broker who uses insurance products from various companies, or does he or she sell one company's products only?
- What type of insurance does the agent specialize in?
- Will the insurance agent service the policy after it is sold?
- How often will the agent review the coverage?
- Will the agent keep the executor or trustee current with the estate's or trust's loss exposures and informed about changes in insurance laws, forms, and rates?
- Has the agent handled insurance cases for estates and trusts before?
- How many estate and trust clients does the agent serve?
- What is the reputation of the insurance companies the agent represents? How do Best, Standard and Poor's, Duff and Phelps, and other rating services rate them?

Checklist for Hiring a Realtor or Property Manager

- What credentials and licenses does the agent hold?
- How long has the realtor or property manager been in business?
- Is the prospective agent familiar with the area in which the property is located?
- Is the prospective agent licensed to perform the services required?
- Does the property manager have experienced personnel to handle collections, repairs, supplies, insurance, accounting, etc.?
- How many properties does the agent handle at any one time?
- What are the charges?
- What is the frequency of accounting reports? Are they audited?
- If a sale is involved, how will the property be marketed?
- Can the sales contract be canceled after six months if the property has not been sold?
- How frequently will rental income be disbursed?
- Before rental income is paid out, will the funds be invested in a money market account?
- What threshold disbursement amount will require the authority of the executor or trustee before the agent makes payment?

APPENDIX A

Estate Administration Checklist

Estate of _____

Date of death _____

BENEFICIARIES

Name	Relationship

Date of will _____

Date of trust _____

	Estimated Completion or Due Date	Date Completed
Obtain original will		
Obtain copy of trust		
Arrange funeral		
Select attorney		
Arrange for:		
Special administration		
Family allowance		
Elective share		
Gather information:		
Obtain names, addresses, and phone numbers of all beneficiaries		
Obtain birthdates for all minors		
Obtain birthdates of individuals whose inheritance is contingent on attainment of a certain age		
Obtain names and addresses of witnesses to will		
Prepare inventory of probate assets		
Prepare inventory of nonprobate assets		
Obtain list of insurance policies		
Prepare list of known debts		
Obtain copies of deeds, leases, contracts, etc.		

	Estimated Completion or Due Date	Date Completed
Obtain copies of 401(k), profit-sharing, IRA, and other employee benefit plan documents		
Obtain copies of income, gift, or other tax returns filed by the decedent		
Retain advisors (if needed):		
Accountant		
Investment advisor		
Realtor		
Insurance agent		
Bank		
Other		
Review will and trust with family		
Assemble and protect assets:		
Secure residence		
Safeguard personal items		
Store automobile		
Change mailing address		
Reregister bank and other accounts		
Insure real estate and other property		
Evaluate securities and other financial assets		
Arrange for the management of the decedent's business		
Estimate cash requirements		
Raise needed cash		
Pay claims		
File tax returns:		
Decedent's final income tax returns		
Fiduciary income tax returns		
Federal estate tax return		
State inheritance tax return		
Exercise tax elections		
Prepare accountings:		
Annual		
Final		
Pay administration expenses:		
Attorney's fees		
Executor's fees		
Appraiser fees		
Advisor fees		

	Estimated Completion or Due Date	Date Completed
Debts		
Taxes		
Other		
File Form 5495, Request for Discharge from Personal Liability		
Final distribution of assets		
Obtain receipts and release from beneficiaries		
Obtain discharge from court		

APPENDIX B

Trust Administration Checklist

Name of trust: _____

Date of trust: _____

CURRENT BENEFICIARIES:

Name	Address	Telephone Number

Remaindermen:

Name _____

_____

_____

_____

_____

_____

Terminating or continuing trust? _____
(If terminating trust, refer to Estate Administration Checklist)

Probate: Yes _____ No_____

Personal representative:

Name: _____

Address: _____

_____

Telephone number: _____

Fax number: _____

	Estimated Completion or Due Date	Date Completed
Obtain pertinent documents:		
Trust document and all amendments		
Copy of will		
Deeds		
Leases		
Insurance policies		
Contracts		
List of trust assets		
Death certificate		
Copy of pension, profit-sharing, IRA plan documents		
Copy of income & gift tax returns		
Other		
Gather information:		
Names, addresses, phone numbers, dates of birth, and tax brackets of all current beneficiaries		
List of remaindermen		
Obtain bank and brokerage account statements		
Trust accounting reports, if any		
Family tree		
Copy of federal estate tax return (From 706)		
Initial Set-Up Steps:		
Prepare inventory		
List debts and encumbrances		
Obtain an appraisal/valuation of all trust property as of settlor's date of death or inception date of trust		
Take possession/control of all trust assets		
Apply for Employer Identification Number (EIN)		
Reregister all bank and brokerage accounts and other assets into the name of the trustee		
Collect life insurance proceeds		
Collect employee benefits payable to trusts		
Notify all payors to mail future payments to trustee		
If specific bequest is income-producing		
Property, separate into segregated account		
Review terms of the trust with beneficiaries		
Accrue income to date of death, if applicable		

	Estimated Completion or Due Date	Date Completed
Retain advisors:		
Attorney		
Accountant		
Investment advisor		
Realtor		
Insurance agent		
Trust company, bank		
Other		
Initial administration steps:		
Determine income needs of the beneficiaries		
Exercise tax elections		
File final tax returns (estate and decedent's final return)		
File Form 5495, Request for Discharge from Personal Liability		
Perform initial review of trust investments		
Estimate initial cash requirements (estate taxes, specific bequests, debts, final expenses, etc.)		
Raise needed cash		
Fund marital, credit shelter, and generation-skipping trusts, if applicable		
Distribute/pay specific bequests		
Review the terms of the trust and clarify provisions that are ambiguous or misleading		
Review the Uniform Principal and Income Act		
Review the Prudent Investor Act		
Develop an investment policy and strategy		
Obtain fee-sharing agreement from co-trustee(s)		
Ongoing administration:		
Principal distributions? Yes _____ No _____		
Income distributions:		
Discretionary? _____ Nondiscretionary? _____		
Frequency of investment reviews:		
Quarterly _____ Semiannual _____ Annual _____		
Frequency of accounting reports:		
Monthly _____ Quarterly _____ Annual _____		
Event that triggers termination of the trust:		
Termination date of trust:		

APPENDIX C

Glossary

Accumulated Income
A portion of the income in a trust that is retained for future payment to a beneficiary or for another future use.

Adjusted Gross Estate (AGE)
The aggregate of a decedent's property (gross estate) less allowable funeral expenses, administration expenses, debts, taxes, and losses.

Affidavit
A specific statement that is sworn before a notary public.

Alternate Valuation Date
A date six months from the decedent's date of death that is used for valuing estate assets as an alternative to using the date-of-death value for determining the federal estate tax.

Ancillary Administration
Subordinate or auxiliary and in addition to the principal settlement or administration of an estate or trust. Usually outside the jurisdiction of the state in which the principal estate or trust is being managed.

Annuity
A series of payments at regular intervals for a number of years or over a lifetime.

Appraisal
The valuation of property.

Appreciation
The increase in value of property.

Assignment
The legal conveyance of the title to property from one person or entity (i.e., estate, trust, etc.) to another person or entity.

Basis
The purchase cost of an asset, less depreciation on depreciable property.

Beneficiary
An individual or organization that receives a benefit from a trust, estate, life insurance policy, pension plan, or other contract or agreement that designates who is to receive the property upon death.

Bequest
A gift of property under a will.

Bond
An obligation, usually of a corporation, government, or municipality, whereby the entity agrees to pay interest and repay the amount borrowed upon certain conditions.

Book Value
The value at which a corporation or other entity carries its assets on financial statements.

Capital Gain
The difference between what was paid for an asset (income tax basis) and what it is sold for.

Cash Value
The amount of cash that is available upon the surrender of an insurance policy.

Charitable Lead Trust
A trust arrangement that requires a stream of payments to a charitable beneficiary for a specified period, with the remainder distributable to noncharitable beneficiaries.

Charitable Remainder Trust
A trust where the income is paid to an individual over time, usually the lifetime of the beneficiary, with the remainder paid to a charitable organization.

Claim
The application for the amount due from a decedent's estate and the amount due under an insurance policy.

Codicil
A formal amendment to a will.

Common Law
The legal system in existence in English-speaking countries. A term that refers to its general principles as contrasted with specific statutes.

Community Property
Property acquired during marriage in which a husband and wife have an undivided one-half interest by virtue of their marriage.

Conservator
A person or corporate fiduciary that is appointed by a court to care for the property of a protected person (i.e., minor or incompetent).

Construction
A court procedure that seeks interpretation of a will or trust.

Contingent Remainder
A future interest in property, usually through a trust, that is dependent on a stated condition, such as the death of a present beneficiary.

Corporate Fiduciary
A bank or trust company that is authorized to perform fiduciary services in its capacity as personal representative, trustee, or guardian.

Corpus
The principal or capital of an estate or trust.

Credit Shelter Trust
A trust that is funded with the Unified Credit Exemption Equivalent amount. The purpose of the trust is to avoid taxation of this amount and any appreciation upon the death of the surviving spouse.

Crummey Power
A provision in a trust that allows a beneficiary to have direct access to deposits made to an irrevocable trust, which allows the deposits to qualify for the annual gift tax exclusion.

Current Beneficiaries
Beneficiaries that are entitled to the income and/or principal of a trust during its term and prior to the termination of the trust.

Current Yield
The annual income from an investment divided by its current market value.

Custody Account
An account that has as its purpose the holding, safeguarding, and accounting of the property that is deposited into it.

Decedent
A deceased person.

Deed of Trust
A document conveying property to a trustee. Usually, but not necessarily, real property.

Depreciation
The decrease in value of property.

Descendant
An individual who is descended in direct line from another.

Devise
A bequest of real property by a will.

Devisee
A person who receives real property by will.

Direct Skip
An outright transfer of property to a skip person during one's lifetime or at death.

Disclaimer
Intentionally refusing to accept property for the purpose of avoiding estate, gift, and generation-skipping transfer taxes.

Discretionary Trust

A trust whose provisions give the trustee the authority to pay income or principal to or for the benefit of the beneficiaries as the trustee sees fit.

Distributable Net Income (DNI)

The amounts paid, credited, or required to be distributed from an estate or trust that is includable in the beneficiary's gross income for tax purposes.

Diversification

The process of investing a trust portfolio in different types of securities and industries and among other asset classes for the purpose of spreading risk.

Dividend

A distribution of cash or stock by a corporation to its shareholders.

Document

Anything that is printed or written that serves as proof of something, such as a will, trust, deed, etc.

Donee

A person or entity that receives a gift.

Donor

A person who makes a gift. Also, a person who creates a trust and transfers property to it.

EIN

A number, called an Employer Identification Number, which is required by the Internal Revenue Service for identifying estate and trust taxpayers.

Election

Making the choice between an alternative right, such as tax and funding elections, for an estate or trust.

Elective Share

A statutory right given to a surviving spouse to elect to receive a specified amount of the deceased spouse's estate instead of what has been provided under his or her will.

Equities

A reference to the stock holdings in an investment portfolio.

Estate

The property of a decedent.

Estate Tax

A tax imposed on the value of property upon the death of the owner.

Exculpatory Provision

A clause in a will or trust that relieves the fiduciary from liability.

Executor

An individual (male), bank, or trust company appointed by a court to settle a decedent's estate. Also referred to as a personal representative.

Executrix

A female individual appointed to settle a decedent's estate.

Exemption Equivalent

The amount whose gift or estate tax is equal to the Unified Credit and which can be given away during one's lifetime and at death without any transfer tax.

Face Amount

The amount stated on an insurance policy that will be paid upon the death of the person whose life is insured.

Fair Market Value

The price at which property would change hands between a willing buyer and a willing seller.

Fiduciary

A person, bank, or trust company that holds property for the benefit of someone else, such as an executor of an estate, a guardian for a protected person, or a trustee of a trust.

Fiduciary Accounting

Financial records that reflect the value of assets and all transactions that affect the administration of an estate or trust and the interests of the beneficiaries.

Fiduciary Accounting Income (FAI)

The amount of net income (i.e., income less expenses charged against income) that is distributable to beneficiaries as distinguished from income that is taxable to the beneficiaries.

Future Interest

The right to possession or use of property that has been postponed until some future event.

Generation-Skipping Tax

A tax imposed on transfers of property to persons at least two generations below the transferor.

Gift Tax

A tax imposed on transfers of property by gift during one's lifetime.

Gift Tax Exclusion

The amount that is not subject to a gift tax.

Governing Document

The will, trust, or other document that controls the activities of the personal representative, guardian, or trustee.

Grantee

The person who is given property or granted property rights by means of a trust or other document.

Grantor

The person who transfers property or property rights to another person, or one who creates a trust.

Grantor Trust

A trust that is considered owned by its creator, the grantor, under the Internal Revenue Code, which subjects the grantor to taxation of all of the trust's income and capital gains.

Gross Estate

The fair market value of all property in which a decedent had an interest at date of death and which is required to be included in his or her estate for federal estate tax purposes.

Guardian Ad Litem

A person, bank, or trust company appointed by a court to represent a minor or incompetent person with regard to a court proceeding.

Heir at Law

A person legally entitled to receive the property of a decedent who died without leaving a valid will.

Holographic Will

A will written entirely in a person's handwriting.

Incapacity

The condition of a person who is incapable of managing his or her affairs due to physical or mental impairment.

Incidence of Ownership

Having sufficient rights in an insurance policy that makes the proceeds subject to estate tax.

Income

The earnings from property in an estate or trust, such as dividends, interest, rent, etc., as distinguished from the principal or corpus.

Income Beneficiary

A beneficiary who is entitled to receive the income from a trust.

Individual Retirement Account (IRA)

An account, set up by an individual, that allows deductible contributions and tax deferral on earnings until funds are withdrawn.

Inheritance Tax

A tax imposed by some states on the right to receive property at death as distinguished from the federal estate tax, which is a tax imposed on the value of one's property at death.

In Kind
Distribution of the property itself (i.e., stocks, bonds, real estate, etc.) as contrasted to a distribution of cash.

Instrument
A formal or legal document.

Insured
The person who is covered by an insurance policy.

Intangible Property
Property, such as stocks, bonds, or notes, that represents an ownership interest.

Inter Vivos
Transactions conducted while someone is living, such as an inter vivos gift, and the creation of an inter vivos trust.

Intestate
Dying without leaving a valid will.

Inventory
List of assets in an estate or trust that describes the property and their values.

Irrevocable Trust
A trust that, by its terms, cannot be revoked.

Issue
All descendants from a common ancestor (i.e., children, grandchildren, etc.).

Joint Tenancy (with rights of survivorship)
The holding of property between two or more persons. Upon the death of one tenant, the surviving tenant(s) will become the owner(s) of the property by operation of law.

Judicial Accounting
An estate or trust accounting that is required to be submitted to a court for review.

Jurisdiction
The place or area of authority to hear and determine legal matters by a court.

Legacy
A gift made by will.

Legal Title
Title to property that is enforceable by the courts.

Legatee
A person who receives a bequest under a will.

Letters of Administration
A document issued by a court giving authority to an administrator the court appoints to settle an estate.

Letters Testamentary
A document issued by a court appointing an executor (personal representative) who has been nominated under a will and giving that person the authority to settle the estate.

Lien
An encumbrance on property to secure a monetary obligation.

Life Estate
The right to use or enjoy the income from property for someone's lifetime.

Life Insurance Trust
An irrevocable trust that owns life insurance. The proceeds from the policy that are paid to the trust are not subject to estate taxes.

Lineal Descendant
A person in the direct line of descent, such as a child or grandchild.

Living Trust
A trust that is established during the creator's lifetime.

Living Will

A document that states the wishes of a person regarding the removal of life support procedures and other matters in the event of a terminal illness.

Lump-Sum Distribution

Distribution in one payment as opposed to equal installments. Special tax treatment applies to distributions of this type from a retirement plan.

Marital Deduction

A gift and estate tax deduction for property passing to a spouse.

Marital Trust

A separate trust created under a revocable living trust at the settlor's death that qualifies for the marital deduction.

Minor

A person that is under legal age.

Municipal Bond

A bond issued by a public authority, such as a county, city, or state, the interest from which is exempt from federal income tax.

Net Income

The gross income received by an estate or trust less the expenses that are chargeable against the income.

Nominatio

The naming of a person, bank, or trust company to serve as an executor under a will or trustee of a trust.

Non–Skip Person

Any person who is not a skip person. See Skip Person.

Notice to Creditors

A notice published in a newspaper by an executor or trustee notifying the creditors of a decedent when and where to make their claims.

Partnership

An association of two or more people in a business enterprise that is established by a partnership agreement. Each partner has joint and several (individual) liability under this type of arrangement as contrasted with a corporation.

Par Value

Face value or nominal value.

Pecuniary Legacy

A gift of money under a will.

Per Capita

Distribution of property from an estate or trust in equal shares among all named beneficiaries—share and share alike.

Personal Property

Everything that is not real property.

Personal Representative

An individual, bank, or trust company appointed by a court to settle an estate. Also called an executor.

Per Stirpes

Inheritance by right of representation in each generation. A distributee takes the share that a deceased ancestor would receive if living.

Petition

A formal request to a court for instructions, remedy, or relief on a particular matter.

Pour-Over Will

A will that names a revocable living trust as beneficiary. Its purpose is to transfer (pour over) probate assets into the trust.

Power of Appointment

A right given to an individual to distribute property that he or she does not own. The exercise of this right is usually done through a will.

Power of Attorney

A written document that legally authorizes someone to act for another.

Precatory Words

Words or phrases in a will or trust expressing a desire that something be done, but not directing that it be done.

Principal

The property of an estate or trust as distinguished from its income. Also referred to as corpus.

Probate

The court-supervised procedure to prove a decedent's last will and testament and to settle his estate with respect to the property he owns in his name.

Profit-Sharing Plan

An employee benefit plan, the contributions to which are based on the profits of the company. The vested balance in the plan is payable to the participant upon retirement, to her beneficiaries, or to her estate upon death.

Protected Person

A person who, by reason of minority, incompetence, or other incapacity, is under the protection of the court.

Qualified Domestic Trust (QDOT)

A trust established for a non–U.S. citizen surviving spouse that qualifies for the marital deduction.

Qualified Terminable Interest Property (QTIP) Trust

A trust that qualifies for the marital deduction and also allows the grantor to decide on the ultimate disposition of the trust property upon the death of the surviving spouse.

Real Property

Land, buildings, and all that is permanently attached to the land as distinguished from personal property.

Remainder Interest

The interest that passes to a beneficiary upon the expiration of a period of time in which another beneficiary was entitled to the benefits from the property. In the case of a trust, what remains at the termination of the trust.

Remaindermen

The beneficiaries that are entitled to a remainder interest.

Renunciation

When an individual, bank, or trust company declines to accept the nomination to serve as personal representative or trustee.

Residue

What's left in an estate or trust after payment of all debts and expenses.

Revocable Living Trust

A trust established by a trust agreement in which the settlor (creator) retains the right to amend or revoke the trust.

Rule Against Perpetuities

A common-law rule that prohibits a trust from lasting longer than a period of time that is measured by lives (i.e., beneficiaries) in being at the time the trust became irrevocable, plus twenty-one years.

Second to Die Life Insurance

An insurance policy that is based on joint lives, typically a husband and wife. The face value is payable at the death of the surviving insured individual.

Settlor

The person who creates a trust during his or her lifetime. Also referred to as the trustor, grantor, and donor.

Skip Person

A person who receives property, either by outright gift or as a beneficiary, who is at least two generations below that of the transferor. This is a term defined under the Internal Revenue Code under its generation-skipping tax provisions.

Special Administrator

A person, bank, or trust company appointed by a court to handle an estate until a permanent personal representative or administrator is appointed. Usually used in situations where some immediate action needs to be taken.

Special Use Valuation

A provision in the Internal Revenue Code that allows a personal representative to elect to value real property used for farming or other business use at its current use value instead of its highest and best use for estate tax purposes.

Spendthrift Provision

A provision in a trust that prohibits a beneficiary from transferring his interest in a trust. It also prevents a beneficiary's creditor from making a claim against his interest in the trust.

Stock

A certificate evidencing ownership in a corporation.

Stock Power

A form, similar to a limited power of attorney, which is signed by the owner of stock that authorizes someone to transfer the stock.

Succession

A person becoming entitled to property under a decedent's will or by operation of law.

Successor Trustee

A trustee that follows, and assumes the responsibilities of, a prior trustee as provided for in a trust document.

Tangible Personal Property

Property that can be touched, such as jewelry, furniture, automobiles, etc., as distinguished from intangible property.

Taxable Estate

The adjusted gross estate less the marital deduction and/or charitable deduction.

Tenancy in Common

An undivided ownership interest in property, which upon death will pass to the decedent owner's heirs and not to the other owner(s).

Tenancy by the Entirety

Joint ownership between a husband and wife. Upon the death of one, the survivor becomes the sole owner of the property by operation of law.

Testamentary Capacity

The mental capacity to make a valid will.

Testamentary Trust

A provision under a will that establishes a trust.

Total Return

A measure of investment performance that combines capital appreciation or depreciation and the income from the investment.

Trust

A legal arrangement where the creator of the trust— the settlor or testator in the case of a testamentary trust—transfers property to a trust and names a trustee to manage the property for the benefit of the trust's beneficiaries.

Trust Accounting

The accounting record of a trust account's activity in which income transactions are distinguished from principal transactions.

Trust Agreement

A written document outlining the terms of a trust arrangement.

Trust Company

A corporation authorized to provide fiduciary services as personal representative, administrator, trustee, or guardian.

Trust Department

A department of a bank that provides fiduciary services. See Trust Company.

Trust Document

A will, under which a trust is created, or a trust agreement.

Trustee

An individual, bank, or trust company that has title to trust property and is charged with managing that property in accordance with the terms of a trust for the benefit of the trust's beneficiaries.

Trust Estate

All of the property belonging to a trust.

Trust Instrument

See Trust Document.

Trust Officer

An employee of a bank trust department or trust company who has the responsibility of supervising the administration of an estate or trust account.

Trust Property

See Trust Estate.

Trustor

A person who creates a trust. Also referred to as the settlor, donor, or grantor.

Undue Influence

The influence that someone exercises over someone else to the extent that a person does something, such as signing a will, against his or her free will.

Unfunded Insurance Trust

A revocable living trust that has no assets. Its purpose is to receive the proceeds from life insurance policies upon the death of the settlor who is the insured. Unlike the irrevocable insurance trust, the insurance proceeds are subject to federal estate tax.

Unified Credit

A specified dollar credit amount that is applied against federal gift and estate taxes.

Unitrust

A trust, usually a charitable remainder trust, which provides a stream of income to a beneficiary, based on a percentage of the value of trust assets each year.

Variable Annuity

An annuity whose income payout fluctuates in relation to the underlying securities in the contract. Variable annuities are often used as investments. Tax on the investment's earnings is deferred until payments are made to the annuitant.

Vested Interest

A fixed interest in property whose possession and enjoyment may be postponed to a future date or event.

Vested Remainder

A fixed interest in a remainder interest. See Remainder Interest.

Wasting Trust

A trust whose assets are continually being consumed and will eventually be used up.

Widow's Allowance

A widow's right to access a specified amount of personal property, set by statute, to meet her immediate needs after her husband's death.

Will

A legal document in which a person directs the disposition of his or her property at death.

Will Contest

A legal process by which an individual attempts to prevent the probate of a will or the disposition of the estate property in accordance with its terms.

Yield

The annualized rate of return on an investment expressed as a percentage of the amount invested.

Index